W9-AUO-775

LOOKING GOOD IN PRINT

A Guide to Basic Design
for Desktop Publishing

Roger C. Parker

VENTANA PRESS

LOOKING GOOD IN PRINT:
A Guide to Basic Design for Desktop Publishing, Second Edition
Copyright © 1990 by Roger C. Parker

All rights reserved. This book may not be duplicated in any way without the expressed written consent of the publisher, except in the form of brief excerpts or quotations for the purposes of review. The information contained may not be duplicated in other books, databases or any other medium without written consent of the publisher or author. Making copies of this book, or any portion for any purpose other than your own, is a violation of United States copyright laws.

Library of Congress Cataloging-in-Publication Data
Parker, Roger C.
   Looking good in print : a guide to basic design for desktop publishing / Roger C. Parker, —2nd ed.
      p.   cm.
   Includes bibliographical references and index.
   ISBN 0-940087-32-4
   1. Desktop publishing—Style manuals. 2. Printing, Practical—Layout—Data processing. I. Title
Z286.D47P35 1990
686.2'2544—dc20   90-39959
                                                   CIP

Cover design and graphics by Suzanne Anderson-Carey, Berkeley, CA
Book design by Karen Wysocki, Ventana Press, Chapel Hill, NC
Illustrations for Second Edition by Charlotte Kirchgessner and Susan Worsley of Chapel Hill, NC
Presentation graphics and makeovers for Second Edition by Southern Media Design and Production, Inc.
   Chapel Hill, NC
Desktop publishing production by Laser Image Corporate Publishing, Durham, NC
Linotronic output by Azalea Typography, Durham, NC
Editorial Staff: Marion Laird, Terry Patrickis, Jeff Qualls, Elizabeth Shoemaker, Carol Shumate

Second Edition, Sixth Printing
Printed in the United States of America
Ventana Press, Inc.
P.O. Box 2468
Chapel Hill, NC 27515
919/942-0220
FAX 919/942-1140

Limits of Liability and Disclaimer of Warranty

The author and publisher of this book have used their best efforts in preparing the book. These efforts include the development, research and testing of the theories and programs to determine their effectiveness. The author and publisher make no warranty of any kind, expressed or implied, with regard to the instructions and suggestions contained in this book.

ACKNOWLEDGMENTS

The author and publisher wish to express appreciation to the following contributors who assisted in the production of this book:

Carolyn Bakamis

Charlotte Kirchgessner

Holly Russell

Teresa Smith

Southern Media Design and Production, Inc.

Mary Votta

Susan Worsley

ABOUT THE AUTHOR

Roger C. Parker is author of *Newsletters from the Desktop, Desktop Publishing with WordPerfect* and *The Makeover Book: 101 Design Solutions for Desktop Publishing*, all published by Ventana Press. He has conducted numerous seminars and workshops on desktop publishing design. He is president of The Write Word, Inc., an advertising and marketing consulting firm based in Dover, NH.

The author may be reached at

The Write Word
466 Central Ave., Suite 3
Dover, NH 03820
603/742-9673

TRADEMARKS

Trademarked names appear throughout this book. Rather than list the names and entities that own the trademarks or insert a trademark symbol with each mention of the trademarked name, the publisher states that it is using the names only for editorial purposes and to the benefit of the trademark owner with no intention of infringing upon that trademark.

TABLE OF CONTENTS

SECTION TWO: **Makeovers: Putting Your Knowledge to Work**

SECTION THREE: **Getting Down to Business**

INTRODUCTION

Until recently, graphic design was the exclusive domain of art directors and design professionals whose livelihoods depended upon creating professional, effective graphic images.

Desktop publishing has changed all that.

By eliminating the tedious instruments of design (T squares, rubber cement, etc.), desktop publishing has brought graphic design into the office and home. However, for many people using desktop publishing, graphic design is a mystery.

Most people have an inherent sense of good design.

Looking Good in Print is a design book for computer users with little or no design background who want to make the most of their desktop publishing investment. This design resource guide outlines the skills necessary to create attractive, effective printed materials, such as newsletters, advertisements, brochures, manuals and other documents.

Regardless of your level of experience, you already may have more design skills than you suspect. In fact, you probably have an inherent, but as yet undeveloped, sense of good design—often referred to as taste!

Consider, for example, what your experiences as a reader and consumer reveal concerning the fundamentals of design:

- You subscribe to one newspaper or magazine rather than another of similar content.

As a reader, you've gained insights into the fundamentals of good design.

- You dislike reading your community group's newsletter but force yourself in order to find needed information.
- While watching television, you pay attention to some commercials but use the remote control to avoid watching others.

In such instances, your inherent sense of design helps you screen for effective messages.

This book teaches you how to consciously analyze your preferences and translate them into effective, good-looking printed materials.

Effective Graphic Design—Luxury or Necessity?

Which is more important—the content of your message or the way it looks?

The question is obviously rhetorical. Effective print communications depend on appearance as well as content.

From the simplest wall drawings of cave dwellers to the illuminated manuscripts of the Renaissance to yesterday's newspaper, history is rich with examples of the important role appearance has played in written communications. Johann Gutenberg's introduction of the printing press to Europe more than 500 years ago, and the subsequent design of decorative typefaces, was a decisive turning point in mass production of good-looking print communications.

Today, effective graphic design is more important than ever.

The advent of the computer was another; and because of it people are bombarded with print communications. Today, effective graphic design is more important than ever. Magazines and newspapers are crowded with ads. Mailboxes are stuffed with catalogs, newsletters and other direct-mail solicitations.

Consequently, your message has a lot of competition, increasing the need for a compelling graphic presentation.

In addition, because of the increasing complexity of products and services (coupled with recent changes in sales techniques), buying decisions are often based on information gleaned from brochures, proposals and other print communications rather than on direct hands-on, pre-purchase experience or person-to-person contact.

Buying decisions are often influenced by print communications.

Effective Graphic Design Helps You Succeed

First impressions last. Effective graphic design favorably predisposes people to accept your product, service or point of view. Often buying decisions are based on emotional and intuitive feelings, which are highly influenced by the print communications that describe the product or service.

If your print communications fail to create a favorable first impression, the buying cycle may be short-circuited.

Because you never get a second chance to make a first impression, design is all-important to the success of your message.

Who Should Read *Looking Good in Print*?

Looking Good in Print is a design guide, not for Madison Avenue art directors but for individuals discovering the challenges and joys of desktop publishing, including

- Retailers, entrepreneurs and other professionals who are producing their own printed materials.
- Managers who need to motivate personnel.
- Writers producing their own finished material.
- Educators who need to communicate on a large scale.

In short, anyone who wants to improve the appearance and effectiveness of his or her desktop-published projects—whether they are printed on a relatively inexpensive laser printer or a high-resolution Linotronic—will find *Looking Good in Print* a lasting reference tool.

How to Use This Book

Looking Good in Print is organized into three sections.

Discover the challenges and joys of desktop publishing.

- Section One, "The Elements of Design," outlines the common graphics tools available in desktop publishing, the underlying principles of design and techniques for putting them into effect.
- Section Two, "Putting Your Knowledge to Work," features makeovers that demonstrate how the communicating power of a variety of different projects can be enhanced by simply rearranging the design elements in more effective ways.
- In the final section, "Getting Down to Business," you will learn to apply the basic tools of graphic design to specific projects you're likely to undertake as you begin to put your desktop publishing hardware and software to work in the real world.

People new to desktop publishing should read the book from beginning to end, with particular emphasis on Section One.

Intermediate and advanced users can probably skip Section One, but will gain valuable insights from reading the remaining two sections.

For those who want further material on the subject, an extensive and carefully researched bibliography contains outstanding ancillary reading material on graphic design, typography, printing, production and related subjects.

How Well Should You Know Desktop Publishing?

This book assumes you're already comfortable with your desktop publishing hardware and software. It assumes your computer and printer are up and running, and that you've gone through the tutorials included with your software and are familiar with its basic commands.

While it's not a substitute for your software's documentation, *Looking Good in Print* will help you get the most from your program.

You may find that techniques you once found intimidating—say, runarounds or drop shadows—are less formidable if you know when and how to use them.

Please note that throughout this book, the terms *publication* and *document* are used to refer to any desktop publishing project regardless of size or content: it may be as small as a business card or as large as a book!

Good design is neither hardware nor software dependent.

Hardware/Software Requirements

Looking Good in Print is a generic guide, independent of any particular hardware or software. In other words, this book will be a valuable resource, regardless of whether you use an Apple Macintosh or a PC, a dedicated page layout program like PageMaker or Ventura Publisher, a state-of-the-art word processing program like WordPerfect 5.1 or Microsoft Word for Windows, or any of the other fine software programs available. The elements of good design are constant, and are achievable in any system.

All combinations of hardware and software are as capable of producing excellent results as they are mediocre results. The difference lies not so much in your system as in your willingness to develop your inherent talents and abilities and to learn new ones.

About the Design of This Book

When producing *Looking Good in Print*, I was tempted to hire one of the nation's top graphic designers to create an award-winning statement on contemporary design.

I resisted for several reasons. The main reason is that a design showcase would defeat the basic premise of *Looking Good in Print*—that high-quality results are attainable by anyone who wants to learn the basics of good design. Second, today's design trends often are tomorrow's rejects.

Desktop publishing provides an exciting freedom of expression.

A third reason is that I wanted the book to speak not just to those desktop publishers who are advancing the frontiers of design but also to newcomers to the field—those discovering for the first time the exhilarating freedom of expression that desktop publishing provides.

Consequently, the examples featured throughout this book were produced in a simple, unembellished style. As your design and desktop publishing skills grow, you undoubtedly will produce far more elegant materials than those found in this book. In the meantime, I hope *Looking Good in Print* will serve as a valuable stepping stone.

Let's get started.

Roger C. Parker
Dover, NH

SECTION ONE

The Elements of Graphic Design

1 | BEGINNING OBSERVATIONS

Part of the challenge of graphic design is that it has no "universal rules." Everything is relative; it can't be reduced to a set of "if. . . then. . ." statements. Tools and techniques that you use effectively in one situation won't necessarily work in another.

For example, framing an advertisement in a generous amount of white space may draw a lot of attention to the message and look striking. On the other hand, a large border of white space on a newsletter page may make the text look like an afterthought and create a very sparse, uninviting look.

Design techniques used effectively in one situation may not work in another.

Or consider typeface choices. A combination of Palatino for text and Helvetica for headlines may look great for an instruction manual, but too bland for a flyer announcing a jazz concert in the park.

If design were governed by a set of universal rules, computer programs would replace graphic artists—and every advertisement, book, brochure, newsletter and poster would look the same. The resulting uniformity would rob the world of the diversity and visual excitement that add so much to magazines, newspapers and even our daily mail!

Good design stems from a thorough knowledge of the building blocks of graphic design and specifying them appropriately, based on the format and function of an individual project.

Successful design also evolves from a mindset:

- A willingness to experiment.
- Confidence in your perceptions.
- Recognition that effective design is a process, not an event.
- Devotion to detail.

Part of the challenge of graphic design is that it has no universal rules.

Because good design is often transparent, understanding the fundamentals of design—those building blocks that transform a scribbled note into a professional, attractive print communication—will give you the tools you need to use your desktop publishing system to full advantage.

First, let's examine some general principles and preliminary steps that will give you solid footing in designing your projects.

PLANNING

The design process is simply an extension of the organizing process that began as you developed the concept for your project.

To the extent that you can define your project's purpose and can prioritize the different parts of your message, you can create effective, good-looking print communications.

Effective design is often transparent.

If, however, you're unclear about the purpose and undecided about the sequence and relative importance of the information you want to communicate, you're in dangerous waters. You're forced to operate subjectively rather than objectively.

Let's say you're designing a layout for a newsletter article that includes a series of photographs. Unless you've thought through the role of the photographs in the article, you won't know how to position them. You'll be forced to be strictly subjective: "I think this photograph looks good here," etc.

But if you know how they relate to the story and each other, you can easily decide on the proper order and size for them.

In a sense, desktop publishing and the tools of graphic design are an extension of your communication skills. They make it easier for you to give visual organization and emphasis to your message.

However, they cannot compensate for a lack of initial planning or organization, which is why the success of your project hinges on this initial stage.

Before starting a project, ask yourself these questions:

The more you define a project's purpose, the better you'll do.

- Who is the intended audience?
- What is the basic message you're trying to communicate?
- In what format will readers encounter your message?
  Book
  Newspaper
  Magazine
  Brochure
  Mailer
  Slide presentation
- What similar messages have your readers encountered from other sources or competitors?
- How does this publication relate to your other publications?

The more you define your project's purpose and environment, the stronger your design will be.

EXPERIMENT

Turn off your computer and start to experiment.

Let's dispel the myth that design solutions appear like magic in a burst of creative energy or like a light bulb illuminating over the head of a cartoon character. Successful graphic design usually emerges from trial and error. Solutions are the result of a willingness to try various design options until one looks right.

Although desktop publishing lets you produce graphics on your computer, it's often best to loosely sketch initial ideas and trial layouts with pencil and paper.

Try out ideas. When you finish one sketch, begin another. Let speed become a stimulant.

Effective design emerges from trial and error.

You'll find your ideas flow much faster—and you'll arrive at a design solution much quicker—if you sketch out alternative ways of arranging text and graphics by hand.

Don't bother with detail for now. Think big: use thin lines for text, thick lines or block lettering for headlines, and "happy faces" for art or photographs.

SEEK INSPIRATION

Train yourself to constantly analyze the work of others.

Sensitize yourself to examples of good and bad design. If a direct-mail piece you like appears in your mailbox, examine it and determine why it appeals to you. If you see an advertisement in the newspaper that's all wrong, dissect it and identify why it doesn't work.

Maintain a Clip File

Most experienced graphic artists maintain "inspiration" files containing samples they like.

When you get stuck on a project, spend a few moments reviewing your favorite designs on file. Chances are, they may serve as a catalyst for your design decisions.

Look Beyond Desktop Publishing

It's easy to become so involved with desktop publishing hardware and software features you forget that they're simply tools—that your real challenge is creating the overall design.

To focus on design without the technological trappings, skim professional design publications that showcase elegant, excellent design examples (see the Bibliography).

Analyze good design and keep a file of it for inspiration.

Join a local advertising group, art directors club or communications forum. You may have more in common with advertising and public relations people than you think: you share a common goal of informing, motivating and persuading others. You're likely to return from these meetings with a fresh perspective on your communication and design efforts.

RELEVANCE

Every graphic element should relate to its particular communications function and unique environment.

Just as in music, there's nothing right or wrong about notes such as Middle C or B-flat, there are no "good" or "bad" typefaces or type sizes—only appropriate or inappropriate ones.

A newsletter of serious opinion, for example, requires a totally different design than a gardening newsletter with lots of pictures and short articles.

There are no "good" or "bad" typefaces, only appropriate and inappropriate ones.

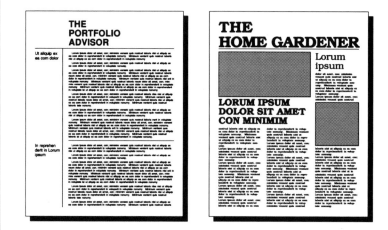

An image-building magazine ad requires a different design approach than a product- and price-oriented newspaper ad.

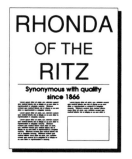

A letterhead for a prestigious law firm should be easily distinguishable from a letterhead for a rock music promoter.

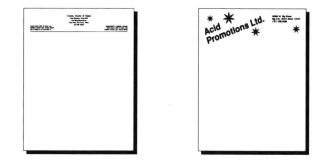

Think of design as a means of communication rather than decoration.

Graphic design must be relevant. Each design should be judged on its ability to help the reader quickly and easily understand your message.

Form must always follow function. Think of graphic design as a means of communication rather than mere decoration.

And a word of caution: Don't let enthusiasm for the capabilities of your desktop publishing system get in the way of clear communication.

Clarity, organization and simplicity are as critical to design as they are to writing.

Always strive for cohesiveness between appearance and content. Important ideas, for example, should be made visually more prominent than secondary ideas or supporting facts and figures.

YEAR-END SALE
ENDS DECEMBER 31

This should come as good news to those who have been intimidated by graphic design, thinking of it as an art practiced only by the gifted or the trained. If you use the appropriate tools, you should be able to produce effective, good-looking publications.

PROPORTION

The size of all graphic elements should be determined by their relative importance and environment.

Because there are no absolutes in graphic design, success is determined by how well each piece of the puzzle relates to the pieces around it.

For example, proper headline size is determined partly by its importance and partly by the amount of space that separates it from adjacent borders, text and artwork. A large headline in a small space looks "cramped."

Good design depends on how well each piece of the puzzle fits with the pieces around it.

Likewise, a small headline in a large space looks "lost."

NOBODY IS PAYING

ATTENTION TO ME

Lorum ipsum dolor sit amet, con; minimim venami quis nostrud laboris nisi ut aliquip ex ea com dolor in reprehenderit in voluptate nonumy. Minimiami quis nostruiami quis nostrum veniami quisd laboris nisi ut aliquip ex ea com dolor in reprehenderit in voluptate nonumy. Minimiami quis nostruiami quis nostruum   veniami quis nostrud d laboris nisi ut aliquip ex ea com dolor in reprehenderit in voluptate nonumy. Minimiami quis nostruiami quis nostrum veniami quis nostrud d laboris nisi ut aliquip ex ea com dolor in reprehenderit in voluptate nonumy. Minimiami quis nostruiami quis nostruum veniami quis nostrud nostrud laboris nisi ut

The proper thickness of lines—called rules—should be determined by the size of the type and the surrounding white space.

Rules that are too thick can interfere with reading.

I Feel I'm Being Overwhelmed

Rules that are too thin can lack effectiveness.

WAR DECLARED

Good design provides a road map guiding readers from point to point.

Likewise, type size and the distance between lines should properly relate to the column widths that organize the type.

As you'll see later, wide columns are generally preferable for large type. And narrow columns are appropriate for small type.

DIRECTION

Effective graphic design guides the reader through your publication.

Readers should encounter a logical sequence of events as they encounter and read your advertisement or publication. Graphic design should provide a road map that guides your readers from point to point.

The design of that map should follow the readers' natural tendency to read an advertisement or publication from upper left to lower right.

A big challenge is to reconcile the need for both variety and consistency.

CONSISTENCY

Consistency leads to an integrated style.

Style reflects the way you handle elements that come up again and again. Part of a document's style is decided from the beginning. The rest emerges as the document develops visually.

Consistency is a matter of detail. It involves using restraint in choosing typefaces and type sizes, and using the same spacing throughout your document.

One of your biggest challenges as a desktop designer is to reconcile the continuing conflict between consistency and variety. Your goal is to create documents that are consistent within themselves, without being boring. Boredom occurs when predictability and symmetry dominate a document.

Thus, your publications should be consistent within themselves and with your organization's other print communications, yet they should be visually distinct. If you use one-inch margins in the first chapter of a book, you should use one-inch margins in all chapters.

Page-to-page consistency can be provided in any of the following ways:

- Consistent top, bottom and side margins.
- Consistent typeface, type size and spacing specifications for text, headlines, subheads and captions.
- Uniform paragraph indents and spaces between columns and around photographs.
- Repeating graphic elements, such as vertical lines, columns or borders, on each page.

Predictability and symmetry result in visual boredom.

For example, you can create an "artificial horizon" by repeating a strong line or graphic on each page in your publication.

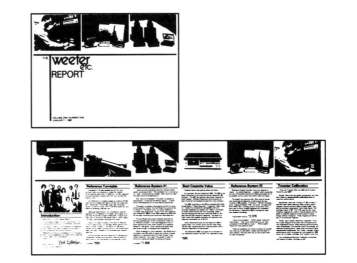

CONTRAST

Contrast provides dynamic interest.

Contrast gives "color" to your publication by balancing the space devoted to text, artwork and white space. When analyzing an attractive publication, compare "dark" areas—such as large, bold headlines, dark photographs or blocks of text—and notice how they're offset by lighter areas with little type.

High-impact publications tend to have a lot of contrast. Each page or two-page spread has definite "light" and "dark" areas, with lots of white space and illustrations.

Lively, attractive documents tend to have a lot of contrast.

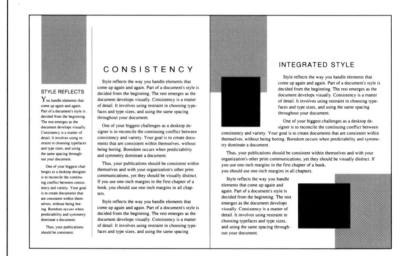

You can create publications low in contrast, where all pages and parts of pages are a uniform shade of "gray." Formal reports, policy statements and press releases often have low contrast.

Also, a dominant visual helps guide the reader's eye movement through the pages of your publication, in addition to communicating relative importance and adding contrast.

For example, consider a page with four equal-sized photo-graphs. The reader is disconcerted: "Which photo should I look at first?" It's not clear which photograph is most important. It's also visually boring. Hence, the message is weakened.

A dominant visual communicates relative importance.

When one photo is larger than others, the page is less symmetrical and more interesting.

When one photograph is larger, it enhances interest and sends the reader a nonverbal message about the relative importance of the photographs. And it makes the page less symmetrical and therefore more balanced.

Contrast enhances the communicating power of your publication.

Contrast can be observed by turning the publication upside down. Viewed from that perspective, your eyes aren't misled by the tendency to read individual words. Instead, you concentrate on the overall "color" of the publication.

Contrasting sizes can create visual tension, which can keep the reader interested. For example, you might have a headline set in a large size above a subhead set in the same typeface at a much smaller size.

Effective graphic design is based on balancing contrast and consistency. Your designs must be dynamic enough to keep the reader interested, yet consistent enough so that your advertisement or publication emerges with a strong identity.

THE TOTAL PICTURE

Think of graphic design as the visual equivalent of a jigsaw puzzle.

Your job is to assemble a total picture from a series of individual parts. No piece of the puzzle should be isolated from the others. The various parts must fit together harmoniously.

The "total picture" includes consideration of the environment in which your advertisement or publication will be distributed.

Designers assemble a total picture from individual parts.

For example, when designing a newspaper advertisement, consider how it will look when surrounded by news items and other advertisements.

When planning a newsletter or direct-mail piece, imagine how it will look when it arrives in the recipient's mailbox. When designing a magazine cover, consider how it will look surrounded by other magazines on the newsstand. When creating product literature, visualize how it will appear when displayed in a brochure rack.

Inside a publication, the most important part of the total picture is the two-page spread. When designing multipage publications, such as newsletters, brochures or books, work on two-page spreads instead of individual pages.

If you make the mistake of concentrating on each page as though it were a self-contained entity, you might end up creating two pages that look good individually, but don't work side by side.

This left-hand page is visually attractive and self-contained.

Design two-page spreads instead of individual pages.

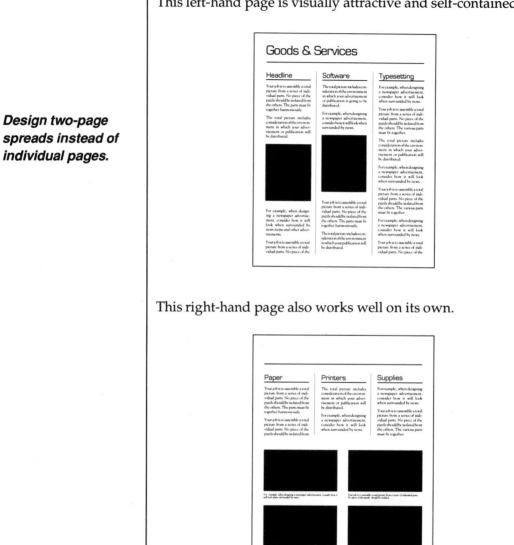

This right-hand page also works well on its own.

When viewed side by side, however, they "fight" each other and present a disorganized, difficult-to-read image.

Readers seldom encounter just one page, but see facing pages together.

Remember that readers seldom encounter individual pages, but see left- and right-hand pages together.

RESTRAINT

Strive for simplicity in design.

Restraint is the hardest design principle to apply in a consistent manner.

Restraint is probably the most difficult design principle to apply in a consistent manner. That's because desktop publishing presents you with tremendous design power—power which just a few years ago was limited to those who had years of training and tens of thousands of dollars worth of equipment.

With so much power at your fingertips, it's easy to forget that straightforwardness is a virtue and that graphic design should be invisible to the reader.

Consider the degree to which good design enhances your message.

Restraint is exemplified by sticking to a few carefully chosen typefaces, styles and sizes.

In making design decisions, consider the degree to which design enhances the basic message you want to communicate.

Remember that emphasis can be effective only within a stable framework. Like the boy who cried "Wolf!" too often, excessive emphasis weakens your publication to the point where it loses all impact.

DETAIL

Success in desktop publishing is based on attention to detail.

Design is detail. And the smallest offending details can sabotage the appearance of an otherwise-attractive project.

Extra spaces after periods, for example, can create annoying rivers of white space in a text block that can be distracting and cause a reader's eye to drag diagonally through a column.

Even the smallest offending detail can sabotage a project's design.

> sit amet, consectetuer adipiscing elit, sed diam nonummy nibh. Euismod tincidunt ut laoreet dolore magna aliquam erat volutpat. Ut wisi enim ad minim veniam, quis nostrud exerci tation. Ullamcorper suscipit lobortis nisl ut aliquip ex ea commodo consequat.

Headlines and subheads placed at the bottoms of columns or pages set the readers up for disappointment, when the promised topic doesn't appear until the start of the next column or page.

Success Depends on Attention to Detail

Design is detail. The smallest offending details can sabotage the appearance of an otherwise-attractive project. Extra spaces after periods, for example, can create annoying rivers of white space in a text block that can be distracting and cause a reader's eye to drag diagonally through a column.

Headlines and subheads placed at the bottoms of columns or pages set the readers up for disappointment, when the promised topic does not appear until the start of the next column or page.

Text placed in boxes should be surrounded by margins. Otherwise, it may bump into the borders of the boxes.

Editorial tasks such as proofreading require a lot of attention to detail. For example, correctly spelled, misused words sneak by spell-checking programs, which can't differentiate spelling from usage.

Headlines and subheads placed at the bottoms of columns or pages set the readers up for disappointment, when the promised topic does not appear until the start of the next column or page.

Extra space after periods, for example, can create annoying rivers of white space in a text block that can be distracting.

Do's and Don'ts

Editorial tasks such as proofreading require a lot of attention to detail.

Text placed in boxes should be indented on both sides. Otherwise, it may bump into the borders of the boxes.

Proofreading demands a lot of attention to detail.

Editorial tasks such as proofreading also require a lot of attention to detail. For example, correctly spelled, misused words sneak by spell-checking programs, which can't differentiate spelling from usage.

The inns and outs of hotel/motel management opportunities.

Be careful not to let these and other errors go unnoticed until the presses are running.

EXAMINING PROOFS

Analyze reduced-size copies of your pages.

Most desktop publishing programs let you print out "thumbnail" proofs or a number of pages at a reduced size on a single sheet of paper.

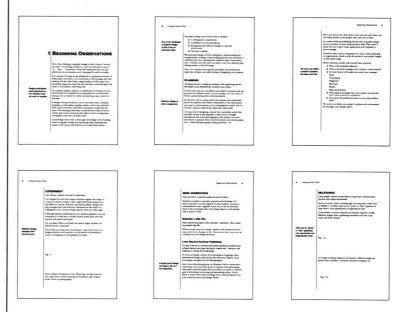

"Thumbnail" proofs reveal where design has been sacrificed for expediency.

These programs typically organize facing pages next to each other, so you can see how spreads will look.

"Thumbnail" proofs let you see where good design has been sacrificed for expediency. Too much symmetry or too much contrast also becomes obvious.

Many desktop presentation programs that let you create slides and overhead transparencies offer a "handouts" feature. This lets you print the visuals for six or more slides or overheads in a reduced size on one page so that each audience member can take one along to use for future reference.

MOVING ON

These qualities—practicing restraint, achieving a balance between consistency and contrast, and paying attention to detail—will ensure the effectiveness and attractiveness of your designs.

Now let's get down to the actual page makeup by exploring important organizational tools you'll use in creating your desktop-published projects.

2 | TOOLS OF ORGANIZATION

Effective graphic design is based on organization. It guides readers' eyes from one point to another in a document and alerts them to what's of primary importance and what is supplemental. It helps readers locate information quickly.

By applying various organizing tools, the two primary page elements, *graphics* and *type*, are given form, and the function of the document itself is defined.

Graphic organizers are at the heart of effective page design.

In short, these "graphic organizers" are at the heart of page design and can be created by using your desktop publishing program's drawing tools.

PAGE ORGANIZERS

Fundamental to the overall page layout are page organizing tools. Different desktop publishing programs offer different ways of implementing those tools.

Grids

Grids establish the overall structure of a page by specifying the placement of text, display type and artwork.

Grids consist of nonprinted lines that show up on your computer screen but not on the finished publication. Grids determine the number of columns, margin size, placement of headlines, subheads, pull-quotes and other page ingredients.

They're valuable for a number of reasons, including setting page-to-page or project-to-project consistency, as well as helping you avoid reinventing the wheel each time you create another ad or newsletter issue.

In other words, layout can be determined once and reused with slight variations.

Desktop publishing programs differ in their ability to create grids. Some programs provide you with ready-made grids that you can modify.

Many programs use a series of horizontal and vertical lines that define columns and page margins.

Grids set up page-to-page and project-to-project consistency.

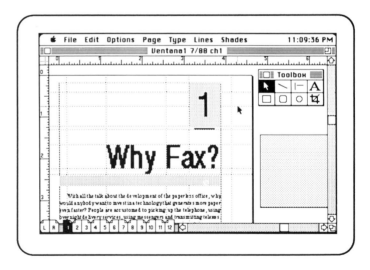

Other page-layout programs are based on setting text into boxes, or frames.

By creating grids, layout can be determined once and reused later.

Word processing programs define column placement and margins mathematically so that text appears in columns, even though the column boundaries aren't visible on-screen.

One way or another, all programs let you establish formats that are automatically maintained from page to page or throughout a series of documents.

Columns

The most fundamental part of a grid, columns organize text and visuals on a page.

Text and visuals rarely extend in an unbroken line from the left side of the page to the right. They're usually arranged in one or more *columns*, or vertical blocks. For most documents, column formats range from single-column to seven-column page layout.

Column width affects readability.

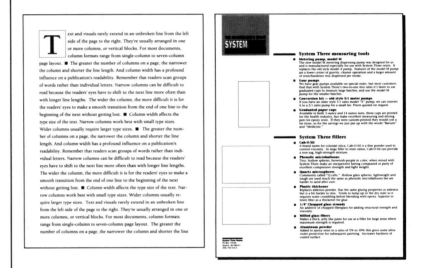

The greater the number of columns on a page, the narrower the column and the shorter the line length. And column width has a profound influence on a publication's readability. Remember that readers scan groups of words rather than individual letters. Narrow columns can be difficult to read because the readers' eyes have to shift to the next line more often than with longer line lengths.

The wider the column, the more difficult it is for the readers' eyes to make a smooth transition from the end of one line to the beginning of the next without getting lost.

8 point text placed on a 24 pica column is very difficult to read. 8 point text placed on a 24 pica column is very difficult to read.8 point text placed on a 24 pica column is very difficult to read.8 point text placed on a 24 pica column is very difficult to read. 8 point text placed on a 24 pica column is very difficult to read. 8 point text placed on a 24 pica column is very difficult to read.8 point text placed on a 24 pica column is very difficult to read.8 point text placed on a 24 pica column is very difficult to read.

Readers tend to scan groups of words rather than individual letters.

Column width affects the type size of the text. Narrow columns work best with small type sizes.

But 8 point text in a 12 pica column is read-able. But 8 point text in a 12 pica column is readable. But 8 point text in a 12 pica column is readable. But 8 point text in a 12 pica column is readable. But 8 point text in a 12

Wider columns usually require larger type sizes.

12 point type looks good when placed in 24 pica columns. 12 point type looks good when placed in 24 pica columns. 12 point type looks good when placed in 24 pica columns. 12 point type looks good when placed in 24 pica columns.

Not all columns on a page have to be the same width. Good-looking publications can be created by varying column widths based on an established multicolumn grid.

For example, the five-column grid lends itself to a variety of arrangements.

Attractive documents can be created by varying the widths of columns.

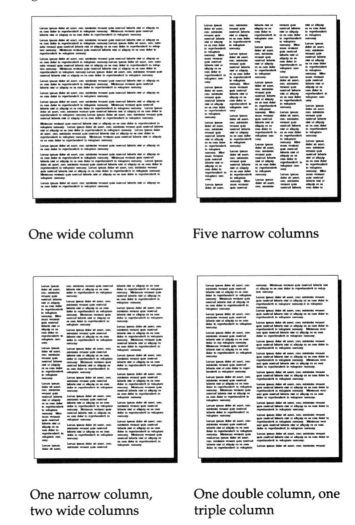

One wide column   Five narrow columns

One narrow column,   One double column, one
two wide columns   triple column

In a five-column format, subheads and illustrations can be laid out side by side in a narrow column adjacent to one or two wide columns of text.

The distance between columns also affects the "color" of a publication.

Variations on the above are permissible within a document, but should always conform with the overall column scheme. A two-column photo, "A," on a five-column grid looks good when its edges are aligned with column guides.

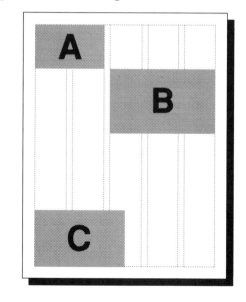

Likewise, a three-column photograph, "B," on a five-column grid works well when the edges of the photograph are lined up with the column guides.

Closely spaced columns "darken" a document.

But, a two-and-a-half-column photograph, "C," on a five-column grid creates unsightly "half-columns" of white space or short columns of type.

Just as establishing the number of columns influences the "color" of a publication, so does the distance between columns.

Closely spaced columns "darken" a document and often make it more difficult to read—the reader's eye tends to jump the gap between columns.

Extra space between columns "lightens," or opens up, a page and clearly separates one column from another.

The width of a gutter depends upon a project's binding method.

Gutters

In designing multipage documents, pay particular attention to the gutter, or inner space of facing pages.

Gutter size depends primarily on the type of binding you plan to use. For example, perfect binding used in this and most books will reduce the size of the inner margin. It's usually a safe bet to leave a traditional gutter margin of a half-inch to accommodate this type of binding.

T ext and visuals rarely extend in an unbroken line from the left side of the page to the right. They're usually arranged in one or more columns, or vertical blocks. For most documents, column formats range from single-column to seven-column page layout. ■ The greater the number of columns on a page, the narrower the column and shorter the line length. And column width has a profound influence on a publication's readability. Remember that readers scan groups of words rather than individual letters. Narrow columns can be difficult to read because the readers' eyes have to shift to the next line more often than with longer line lengths. The wider the column, the more difficult it is for the readers' eyes to make a smooth transition from the end of one line to the beginning of the next without getting lost. ■ Column width affects the type size of the text. Narrow columns work best with small type sizes. Wider columns usually require larger type sizes. The greater the number of columns on a page, the narrower the column and shorter the line length. And column width has a profound influence on a publication's readability. Remember that readers scan groups of words rather than individual letters. Narrow columns can be difficult to read because the readers' eyes have to shift to the next line more often than with longer line lengths. ■ The wider the column, the more difficult it is for the readers' eyes to make a smooth transition from the end of one line to the beginning of the next without getting lost. ■ Column width affects the type size of the text. Narrow columns work best with small type sizes. Wider columns usually require larger type sizes. Text and visuals rarely extend in an unbroken line from the left side of the page to the right. They're usually arranged in one or more columns, or vertical blocks. For most documents, column formats range from single-column to seven-column page layout. The greater the number of columns on a page, the narrower the column and shorter the line length. And column

F or most documents, column formats range from single-column to seven-column page layout. The greater the number of columns on a page, the narrower the column and shorter the line length. And column width has a profound influence on a publication's readability. Remember that readers scan groups of words rather than individual letters. ■ Narrow columns can be difficult to read because the readers' eyes have to shift to the next line more often than with longer line lengths. The wider the column, the more difficult it is for the readers' eyes to make a smooth transition from the end of one line to the beginning of the next without getting lost. Column width affects the type size of the text. Narrow columns work best with small type sizes. Wider columns usually require larger type sizes. ■ The greater the number of columns on a page, the narrower the column and shorter the line length. And column width has a profound influence on a publication's readability. Remember that readers scan groups of words rather than individual letters. Narrow columns can be difficult to read because the readers' eyes have to shift to the next line more often than with longer line lengths. The wider the column, the more difficult it is for the readers' eyes to make a smooth transition from the end of one line to the beginning of the next without getting lost. Column width affects the type size of the text. ■ Narrow columns work best with small type sizes. Wider columns usually require larger type sizes. Text and visuals rarely extend in an unbroken line from the left side of the page to the right. They're usually arranged in one or more columns, or vertical blocks. For most documents, column formats range from single-column to seven-column page layout. The greater the number of columns on a page, the narrower the column and shorter the line length. ■ And column width has a profound influence on a publication's readability. Remember that readers scan groups of words rather than individual letters. Narrow

|← X →|

For ring binding, reserve a 5/8- to 3/4-inch gutter. Most plastic spiral bindings don't require such wide gutters, but it's best to choose a particular binding first and design your gutter width around it.

Margins

Margins determine the space between columns and/or the borders and edge of a page.

Effective design allows "breathing room" between the live area and the physical boundaries of a page, referred to as trim size.

The larger the margin, the "lighter" the publication.

The larger the margin, the "lighter" the publication. Thinner margins result in "darker" publications.

TEXT ORGANIZERS

Text organizers include headlines, subheads, captions and more.

Often referred to as display type, these organizing tools highlight your message and help readers understand it quickly and easily.

Headlines

Use headlines to invite readers to become involved in your advertisement or articles in your publication.

The most basic text-organizing tool, headlines help readers decide whether to read a document. They should be as short and concise as possible so they can be quickly read and understood.

To be effective, headlines should be clearly differentiated from text, which can be done in two ways.

Effective headlines are clearly differentiated from text.

In addition to setting them in a large type size, you can add emphasis to headlines and give contrast to your page by setting them in a different typeface than the one used for the text.

For example, headlines set in sans-serif type are often used with text set in a serif typeface—a popular technique for documents such as advertisements, books, brochures and newsletters.

Alternately, you can emphasize headlines by setting them in the text typeface, but in a larger size and/or heavier weight.

Headlines should be designed for impact and readability.

The greater the difference between headline and text, the easier it is for readers to identify and read your headline.

Even though headlines should be designed for impact, make them as readable as possible. This can be accomplished in several ways.

In general, avoid long headlines set in uppercase type.

Headlines set in all uppercase type occupy more space. More important, they slow readers down because they're difficult to read. Limit uppercase headlines to several words.

Long headlines can look too complex and wordy.

The most readable type scheme for headlines is to use uppercase for the first letter of each word (other than articles and short prepositions). However, try to limit headlines to three lines. Long headlines of four or more lines can look too wordy and complex to read at a glance.

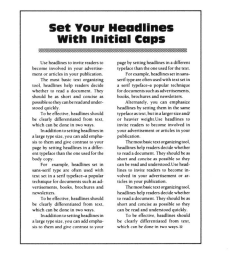

Also, avoid centering headlines that contain more than two lines. Long, centered headlines slow readers down because they have to search for the beginning of each line.

Centering long headlines forces readers to search for the beginning of each line.

Flush-left headlines, on the other hand, let readers move directly down to the first words of the following paragraph.

Kickers

Lead into your headline with a kicker, a short summary phrase.

Kickers can introduce the headline by relating it to other articles or existing information. Kickers also can categorize an article.

Subheads

Subheads clue readers into the content organization within an article.

Subheads break text into manageable segments, improve the appearance of a page and enhance readership by providing a transition between headlines and text. They also provide visual contrast and identify the subject of the text. They let readers quickly locate information.

Compare these two examples.

In the left-hand example, you're faced with a long expanse of type. Because the page is so "dark" and you don't have a clue to its contents, reading it is a chore.

Subheads can provide a transition between headlines and text.

Left-hand example

Subheads clue readers into the content organization within an article. Subheads break text into manageable segments, improve the appearance of a page and enhance readership by providing a transition between headlines and text. They also provide visual contrast and identify the subject of the text. They let readers locate information.

Subheads can be set apart from text by using various techniques. For example, they can be placed inside or next to the text. Subheads should always be closely associated with the text they introduce. There should be more space above the subhead than below it to link it with the text.

Like headlines, subheads tend to stand out when set in a larger type size than the text and in a typeface that contrasts with the text. Subheads can be set centered, flush-left or flush-right.

As with other organizing tools, uniformity is important. Subheads should be treated consistently.

Don't Make Reading A Chore

Subheads clue readers into the content organization within an article. Subheads break text into manageable segments, improve the appearance of a page and enhance readership by providing a transition between headlines and text. They also provide visual contrast and identify the subject of the text. They let readers locate information.

Subheads can be set apart from text by using various techniques. For example, they can be placed inside or next to the text. Subheads should always be closely associated with the text they introduce. There should be more space above the subhead than below it to link it with the text. Like headlines, subheads tend to stand out when set in a larger type size than the text and in a typeface that contrasts with the text. Subheads can be set centered, flush-left or flush-right.

As with other organizing tools, uniformity is important. Subheads should be treated consistently. Subheads clue readers into the content organization within an article. Subheads break text into manageable segments, improve the appearance of a page and enhance readership by providing a transition between headlines and text. They also provide visual contrast and identify the subject of the text. They let readers locate information. Subheads can be set apart from text by using various techniques. placed inside the text. Subheads should always be closely associated with the text they introduce. There should be more space above the subhead than below it to link it with the text.

Right-hand example

Don't Make Reading a Chore

Open up Your Pages

Subheads clue readers into the content organization within an article. Subheads break text into manageable segments, improve the appearance of a page and enhance readership by providing a transition between headlines and text. They also provide visual contrast and identify the subject of the text. They let readers locate information.

Subheads can be set apart from text by using various techniques. For example, they can be placed inside or next to the text. Subheads should always be closely associated with the text they introduce. There should be more space above the subhead than below it to link it with the text.

Like headlines, subheads tend to stand out

when set in a larger type size than the text and in a typeface that contrasts with the text. Subheads can be set centered, flush-left or flush-right. Subheads clue readers into the content organization within an article. Subheads can be placed inside text.

Add Subheads Frequently

Subheads can be set apart from text by using various techniques. For example, they can be placed inside or next to the text. Subheads should always be closely associated with the text they introduce. There should be more space above the subhead than below it to link it with the text. Subheads should contrast with text. Subheads should be closely associated with the text they introduce.

Use Various Subhead Techniques

Subheads can be set centered, flush-left or flush-right.

As with other organizing tools, uniformity is important, subheads should be treated consistently throughout your document.

Subheads clue readers into the content organization within an article. Subheads break text into manageable segments, improve the appearance of a page and enhance readership by providing a transition between headlines and text. They also provide visual contrast and identify the subject of the text. They let readers locate information.

Subheads can be set apart from text by using various techniques.

The right-hand example is more inviting because the page is more "open" and you can easily decide whether the text relates to your interests.

Subheads can be set apart from text by using various techniques.

For example, they can be placed inside or next to the text.

Subheads should be visually linked with the text they introduce.

Don't Make Reading a Chore

Open up Your Pages

Subheads clue readers into the content organization within an article. Subheads break text into manageable segments, improve the appearance of a page and enhance readership by providing a transition between headlines and text. They also provide visual contrast and identify the subject of the text. They let readers quickly locate information.

Subheads can be set apart from text by using various techniques. For example, they can be placed inside or next to the text. Subheads should always be closely associated with the text they introduce. There should be more

space above the subhead to link it with the text.

Subheads clue readers into the content organization within an article.

Add Subheads Frequently

Subheads should always be closely associated with the text They introduce. There should be more space above the subhead than below it to link it with the text. Subheads should always be closely associated with the text Subheads can be set apart from text by using various techniques. For example, they can be placed inside or next to the text. Subheads should be closely associated with the text they introduce.

Use Various Subhead Techniques

Subheads can be set centered, flush-left or flush-right. As with other organizing tools, uniformity is important. subheads should be treated consistently.

Subheads clue readers into the content organization within an article. Subheads break text into manageable segments, improve the appearance of a page and enhance readership by providing a transition between headlines and text. They also provide visual contrast and identify the subject of the text. Subheads can be set apart from text by using various techniques.

Don't Make Reading a Chore

Open up Your Pages

Subheads clue readers into the content organization within an article. Subheads break text into manageable segments, improve the appearance of a page and enhance readership by providing a transition between headlines and text. They also provide visual contrast and identify the subject of the text.

Add Subheads Frequently

They let readers locate information. Subheads can be set apart from text by using various techniques. For example, they can be placed inside or next to the text. Subheads should always be closely associated with the text they introduce. There should be more space above the subhead than below it to link it with the text.

Like headlines, subheads tend to stand out when set in a larger type size than the text and in a typeface that contrasts with the text. Subheads break text into manageable segments, improve the appearance of a page and enhance readership by providing a transition between headlines and text.

Use Various Subhead Techniques

They also provide visual contrast and identify the subject of the text. They let readers quickly locate information. Subheads can be set apart from text by using various techniques. For example, they can be placed inside or next to the text. Subheads should be closely associated with the text they introduce. There should be more space above the subhead than below it to link it with the text. Subheads should contrast with the body copy.

Subheads should always be closely associated with the text they introduce. There should be more space above the subhead than below it to link it with the text.

Subheads clue readers into the content organization within an article. Subheads break text into manageable segments, improve the appearance of a page and enhance readership by providing a transition between headlines and text.

Subhead Linked to Text Mystery

Subheads can be set apart from text by using various techniques. For example, they can be placed inside or next to the text. Subheads should always be closely

Subheads clue readers into the content organization within an article. Subheads break text into manageable segments, improve the appearance of a page and enhance readership by providing a transition between headlines and text.

Subhead Linked to Text Mystery

Subheads can be set apart from text by using various techniques. For example, they can be placed inside or next to the text. Subheads should always be closely

Incorrect   Correct

Like headlines, subheads tend to stand out when set in a larger type size and a different typeface than the text.

Subheads clue readers into the content organization within an article. Subheads break text into manageable segments, improve the appearance of a page and enhance readership by providing a transition between headlines and text.

Missing Contrast Is Suspected

Subheads can be set apart from text by using various techniques. For example, they can be placed inside or next to the text. Subheads should always be closely associated with the text they introduce. There should contrast between the sub-

Subheads clue readers into the content organization within an article. Subheads break text into manageable segments, improve the appearance of a page and enhance readership by providing a transition between headlines and text.

Correct Contrast Has Been Located

Subheads can be set apart from text by using various techniques. For example, they can be placed inside or next to the text. Subheads should always be closely associated with the text they introduce.

Subheads tend to stand out when set in a different type than the text.

Subheads can be set centered, flush-left or flush-right.

Subheads clue readers into the content organization within an article. Subheads break text into manageable segments, improve the appearance of a page and enhance readership by providing a transition between headlines and text.

Subheads Offer Great Variety

Subheads can be set apart from text by using various techniques. For example, they can be placed inside or next to the text.

Subheads clue readers into the content organization within an article. Subheads break text into manageable segments, improve the appearance of a page and enhance readership by providing a transition between headlines and text.

Subheads Offer Great Variety

Subheads can be set apart from text by using various techniques. For example, they can be placed inside or next to the text. Subheads should always be closely associ-

Subheads clue readers into the content organization within an article. Subheads break text into manageable segments, improve the appearance of a page and enhance readership by providing a transition between headlines and text.

Subheads Offer Great Variety

Subheads can be set apart from text by using various techniques. For example, they can be placed inside or next to the text. Subheads should always be closely associ-

Subheads can be emphasized by horizontal rules above or below the words.

> Subheads clue readers into the content organization within an article. Subheads break text into manageable segments, improve the appearance of a page and enhance readership by providing a transition between headlines and text.
>
> ### THE RULES OF SUBHEADS
>
> Subheads can be set apart from text by using various techniques. For example, they can be placed inside or next to the text. Subheads should always be closely associ-

As with other organizing tools, uniformity is important. Subheads should be treated consistently throughout your document.

Captions

Use captions to tie photographs and illustrations into the rest of your publication.

Studies show that headlines and captions are more likely to be read than any other part of a publication. Accordingly, use captions to summarize important points.

Captions can be placed in a variety of ways.

Captions can be placed next to the artwork they describe or they can be placed above the artwork.

Next to headlines, captions are the most widely read part of a publication.

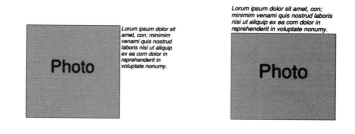

Most often, captions are placed below the artwork.

Lorum ipsum dolor sit amet, con; minimim venami quis nostrud laboris nisi ut aliquip ex ea com dolor in reprehenderit in voluptate nonumy.

Use captions to summarize important points.

Another alternative is to place the caption inside the artwork (see page 175).

When set above or below the artwork, captions can be centered, or aligned with the left- or right-hand edge of the visual.

Caption width should be in a pleasing proportion to the width of the photograph or illustration, and to surrounding white space and text.

This caption is too long.

This caption is too short.

But this caption is just right.

Regardless of their position or alignment, captions should be treated the same way throughout a publication. Thus, if you align captions with the left-hand edge of photographs on Page 5, align them the same way on Page 20.

Headers and Footers

Information at the top or bottom of each page in a newsletter, book or training manual can be used to reinforce the publication's identity as well as serve as a road map to help readers locate specific information.

Header information at the top of a page can include publication, section and chapter titles, chapter number and page number.

Headers serve as road maps that help readers quickly locate information.

Alternately, this space can be used to summarize the content of each page, helping readers quickly locate information. Can you imagine how hard it would be to locate a specific word in a dictionary without the aid of headers?

Footers can include the same information as the header but at the bottom of a page.

Jumplines

Use jumplines to inform readers when articles are continued from one page to another.

By continuing articles on inside pages, you can offer readers a wider variety of editorial material on the front page of your publication. As the number of articles included on Page 1 increases, so does the likelihood you'll interest the reader.

Continuing articles on other pages also allows for more flexibility in laying out a long story that won't fit on a page. The jumpline eliminates any confusion readers may have about where to read next.

Jumplines eliminate confusion about where to read next.

Publishing **POTPOURRI**

Volume 22   Fall 1992

Bits of Type for Everyone

Use jumplines to inform readers when articles are continued from one page to another. By continuing articles on inside pages, you can offer readers a wider variety of editorial material on the front page of your publication. As the number of articles included on Page 1 increases, so does the likelihood you'll interest the reader.

Continuing articles on other pages also allows for more flexibility in laying out a long story that won't fit on a page. The jumpline eliminates any confusion readers may have about where to read next.

Establish the identity of you publication with a distinctive nameplate.

Continued on page 3

Hundreds of Design Solutions

Use jumplines to inform readers when articles are continued from one page to another. By continuing articles on inside pages, you can offer readers a wider variety of editorial material on the front page of your publication. As the number of articles included on Page 1 increases,

so does the likelihood you'll interest the reader.

Establish the identity of you publication with a distinctive nameplate. A nameplate is a distinctive type treatment of your publications's title. Establish the identity of you publication with a distinctive

Continued on Page 5

Nameplates and Logos

Establish the identity of your publication with a distinctive nameplate.

A nameplate is a distinctive type treatment of your publication's title. As the first item on the first page, it should be prominent enough to immediately establish a lasting visual identity and should remain the same from issue to issue.

OCTOBER 1989

A NEWSLETTER FOR PARENTS & KIDS

kidscope

A logo reflects the nature and philosophy of a business.

Although large and recognizable at a glance, a nameplate should not overshadow the headlines on a page.

Use your firm's logo as a "signature" on your document.

A logo is a graphic symbol that relates to your firm's type of business.

EMPLOYEE BENEFIT PLANS
3644 Golden Years Drive•Malibu CA 92777
213 555-3333

It also can reflect your firm's philosophy.

Often, the letter-spacing has been specially modified to create a distinct effect called *logo type*.

Sometimes the letters touch or overlap.

A logo should not be so large it over-whelms the page.

In other cases, portions of the letters are omitted or exaggerated.

Logos should be large enough to be easily identified, yet they shouldn't overwhelm or detract from surrounding copy.

Logos are particularly important in magazine and newspaper advertisements. They not only provide immediate visual identi-fication and ad-to-ad consistency, but they also give the ad a strong finish.

MOVING ON

By now you have an understanding of some of the organizing tools that form the foundation of a well-designed document. In the next two chapters, you'll learn how to manipulate text and graphics to further enhance the communicating power of your printed materials.

3 | THE ARCHITECTURE OF TYPE

Typography—the design of the characters that make up text and display type (headlines, subheads, captions, etc.) and the way they're configured on the page—influences the appearance of your print communications more than any other single visual element.

The typeface you choose can help, or hinder, your readers' ability to understand your message.

However, many other factors must be considered in choosing type: column alignment, column width and spacing. When these decisions are made, you then can go on to determine type family, size, style and weight.

The type you choose can help or hinder readability.

In addition, your desktop publishing system may give you such options as rotating or distorting type, as well as wrapping type around visuals and composing it to fit the available space.

Just as establishing a grid for your document is the first step in creating a page layout, choosing an alignment scheme is often the initial step in developing the typographic treatment.

ALIGNMENT

Lines of type can be set justified (flush-left/flush-right); flush-left with a ragged-right margin; flush-right with a ragged-left margin; or centered.

The option you choose influences the "color" and tone of your publication, as well as the cost.

Readability studies tend to favor flush-left/ragged-right alignment, meaning the first letters of each line are lined up with each other, but the lines themselves are of irregular length. The irregular line endings create a ragged margin of white space, which gives publications a lighter look. In addition, the even word spacing enables readers to easily recognize word groups.

Flush-left/ragged-right type gives a publication an informal, contemporary, "open" feeling. The space between each word is the same. Flush-left/ragged-right lines generally end where words end. Only long words that fall at the end of lines are hyphenated.

Flush-left/ragged-right alignment provides an "open," informal feeling.

"This country, with its institutions, belongs to the people who inhabit it. Whenever they shall grow weary of the existing government, they can exercise their constitutional right of amending it, or their constitutional right to dismember or overthrow it."

Abraham Lincoln

Justified type produces lines of equal length. Type is aligned on both left and right margins. Word spacing is adjusted automatically to create the even line endings.

Because of the uniform line length, justified columns lack the white space created with ragged alignment, and thus tend to "darken" a publication. In addition, justified type is sometimes considered more difficult to read because more words are hyphenated and large gaps can appear between words.

Nevertheless, many magazines, newspapers and books use justified type because the word density is higher. As a result, less space is needed to communicate the same amount of information, which can reduce the number of pages required and result in cost-savings.

Justified columns of type can "darken" a page.

> "This country, with its institutions, belongs to the people who inhabit it. Whenever they shall grow weary of the existing government, they can exercise their constitutional right of amending it, or their constitutional right to dismember or overthrow it."
>
> *Abraham Lincoln*

For display type, centering is another alignment scheme that's particularly useful for short headlines that span more than one column of type.

Centering lends a formal tone to a document and is frequently used for wedding invitations and official announcements.

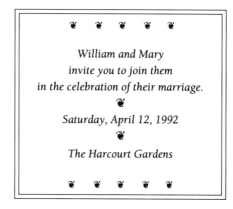

William and Mary
invite you to join them
in the celebration of their marriage.

Saturday, April 12, 1992

The Harcourt Gardens

However, avoid centering long blocks of type, even for a three- or four-line headline. Because readers have to search for the beginning of each line, centered type is more difficult to read.

Centering lends a formal tone to a document.

> **Offshore Production Cost Increases for Consumer Electronics and Cars Tied to Rising Standards of Living Around the World**

Type also can be set flush-right/ragged-left.

But, like centered type, flush-right alignment forces the reader to slow down to find the beginning of the next line, and therefore should be used with discretion.

> **Reading flush-right copy takes more time because your eyes have to search for the beginning of each line.**

Setting short headlines flush-right is a way to lock them to adjacent photographs or to text-heavy columns on a facing page of a spread.

KERNING, TRACKING AND LETTER SPACING

Kerning is the adjustment of space between selected pairs of letters.

Certain pairs of letters sometimes appear to be separated by too much space. This effect is particularly apparent in a headline with an uppercase T next to a lowercase o, or an uppercase W next to a lowercase a, etc.

Adjusting space between letters often improves readablity.

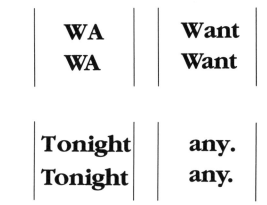

Kerning reduces the space between individual pairs of letters to improve readability.

Kerning can also be used to add space between certain letter pairs. This is often done to improve legibility when setting white type against a black background.

Tracking automatically governs the amount of space placed between each character throughout a block of text.

By tightening tracking, you increase the density of your text, fitting more words into the same amount of space. This tends to "darken" a publication. Conversely, loose tracking lightens a page.

You, of course, want to avoid leading so spacious that readers get lost when their eyes leave the end of one line and try to find the beginning of the next line. Leading should be in proportion to line length. In general, use narrow leading for short lines if type. Increase	You, of course, want to avoid leading so spacious that readers get lost when their eyes leave the end of one line and try to find the beginning of the next line. Leading should be in proportion to line length. In general, use

Most desktop publishing systems have a default tracking that can be adjusted.

Letter-spacing can be used for special effects.

Letter-spacing can transform a word into a graphic element.

Stretching a word across the top of a column or page can transform that word into a graphic element. Letter-spacing is often used to create department headings, identifying standard recurring features in periodicals.

WORD SPACING

The amount of space between words affects word density and the readability of a publication.

When word spacing is tight, more words can be included on each line. In certain situations, that can reduce the number of hyphenated—or split—words.

Usually, if you've set reasonable parameters for justification in your program, the very worst offenders in hyphenation will be lines with bad breaks, caused by long	**Usually, if you've set reasonable parameters for justification in your program, the very worst offenders in hyphenation will be lines with bad breaks, caused by long single-syllable words or**

Word spacing and tracking are often adjusted simultaneously.

However, word spacing should be adjusted with care. If you reduce word spacing too much, the text becomes difficult to read and the publication becomes "dark."

Tracking and word spacing are often adjusted simultaneously. One common technique, especially with high-x-height typefaces (see page 71), is to slightly reduce letter spacing and increase word spacing.

When experimenting with tracking and word spacing, be sure to review proofs before deadline time to ensure you've achieved the right balance.

PARAGRAPH SPACING

Extra space between paragraphs enhances readability.

Adding space between paragraphs makes each paragraph appear more like a self-contained unit. It also adds an openness to a publication by breaking up the "grayness" of large expanses of text.

Increasing paragraph spacing can add an openness to a page.

To increase paragraph spacing, always use your desktop publishing program's paragraph-spacing command, rather than using two carriage returns, which can result in far too much space between paragraphs.

The paragraph-spacing command lets you add just enough white space between paragraphs to add interest without creating a page filled with distracting parallel bands of white space.

Extra space between paragraphs enhances readability. Adding additional space between paragraphs makes each paragraph appear more like a self-contained unit. It also adds an openess to a publication by breaking up the "grayness" of large expanses of text.

To increase spacing, between paragraphs, always use your desktop publishing program's paragraph-spacing command, rather than using two carriage returns, which can result in too much space between paragraphs.

The paragraph-spacing command lets you add just enough white space between paragraphs to add interest without creating a page filled with distracting parallel bands of white space.

Extra space between paragraphs enhances readability. Adding additional space between paragraphs makes each paragraph appear more like a self-contained unit. It also adds an openess to a publication by breaking up the "grayness" of large expanses of text.

To increase spacing, between paragraphs, always use your desktop publishing program's paragraph-spacing command, rather than using two carriage returns, which can result in too much space between paragraphs.

The paragraph-spacing command lets you add just enough white space between paragraphs to add interest without creating a page filled with distracting parallel bands of white space.

TABS AND INDENTS

Use tabs and indents to emphasize paragraph divisions and set off extended quotations and lists.

Tabs can be used in conjunction with extra space between paragraphs to further "open up" a publication. Most paragraph tabs are set at two to five spaces from the left-hand margin.

Indention can be used to draw attention to quotations.

Prison Reforms Mean Added Taxes to Finance New Facilities

Lorum ipsum dolor sit amet, con; minimim venami quis nostrud laboris nisi ut aliquip ex ea com dolor in reprehenderit in voluptate nonumy.

Lorum ipsum dolor sit amet, con; minimim venami quis nostrud laboris nisi ut aliquipiquip ex ea com dolor in reprehenderit in voluptate nonumy. Minimum veniami ex ea com dolor in reprehenderit in voluptate nonumy.

Lorum ipsum dolor sit amet, con; minimim venami quis nostrud laboris nisi ut aliquip ex ea com dolor in reprehenderit in voluptate nonumy. Minimum veniami quis nostrud laboris nisi ut aliquip ex ea com dolor in reprehenderit in voluptate nonumy.

Lorum ipsum dolor sit amet, con; minimim venami quis nostrud

Indents can be used to call attention to quotations in a publication by moving a text block in from the left- and right-hand margins. Indents also can set a list off from the body copy.

> Bills to Pay
> 1. IRS
> 2. Home Mortgage
> 3. Car Payment
> 4. Utilities
> 5. Medical Insurance
> 6. Hobby Shop

LINE SPACING

The spacing between lines affects overall legibility.

Adjust leading between lines of type—to improve the appearance and readability of your publication.

Leading is the space above and below a line of type. It's a critical factor in determining legibility. Leading, like type size, is measured in points (72 points equal one inch).

The default, or automatic, line spacing, found on most desktop publishing systems is approximately 20 percent greater than the type size being used. Thus, the default leading for 10-point type is 12 points.

Headlines often improve in appearance and readability when leading is reduced between lines. Tighter leading integrates the words into a distinct visual unit instead of a series of seemingly unrelated lines.

default

adjusted

On the other hand, extra leading often improves the appearance of text. It opens up the page, making it less "gray."

Extra leading is usually called for when sans-serif typefaces (see page 62) are used for text.

default   adjusted

You, of course, want to avoid leading so generous that readers get lost when their eyes leave the end of one line and try to find the beginning of the next line.

Leading should be proportionate to line length. In general, use minimal leading for short lines of type. Increase leading as line length increases.

Leading also can be used as a design tool for special effects. You may sometimes want to tighten leading so much that descenders (letter stems such as g and p that drop below the invisible line text rests on) from one line of type touch the ascenders (rising stems of letters such as b and d) from the line below. That lets you create special effects, particularly in designing logos and nameplates.

Extra leading can make a page look less "gray."

Symbolic
Connections, Inc.

One of the advantages of using uppercase letters for headlines is that you can substantially reduce leading, since capitals lack descenders.

Highway Robbery on the Rise	HIGHWAY ROBBERY ON THE RISE

TYPEFACE

Choose a typeface that "speaks" to your readers in the tone most appropriate to your publication.

Typeface refers to the design of letters, numbers and other characters. Thousands are available, each representing its designer's unique approach to clarity and expressiveness.

Each typeface influences the tone of a publication. For example, some are authoritative:

Recall Demanded

Typefaces set the tone of a document and "speak" to the reader.

Others are friendly:

Sunny Weekend

Others look expensive:

Your Dream House

Still others have a classy look:

Wine Tasting

Typeface design generally falls into two broad categories: serif and sans-serif.

Serif Type

Serif typefaces are commonly used for text.

Serif type is categorized by small strokes at the ends of each letterform. These strokes, called serifs, serve both decorative and functional purposes. Besides adding visual character to the letters, they guide the reader's eye movement from letter to letter, helping the reader see your message in terms of words and sentences instead of as individual letters.

Typefaces with rounded serifs tend to be friendly:

Yard Work Made Easy

Serifs help guide readers from letter to letter.

Typefaces with squared serifs look official or architectural:

Grant Money Awarded

Times Roman, one of the most frequently used serif typefaces, is a resident font in most laser printers. Other frequently used serif typefaces include

New Century Schoolbook

Bookman   Souvenir   Palatino

Sans-Serif Type

Sans-serif type is ideal for display type—headlines, subheads, pull-quotes, captions, etc.

Sans-serif type is just what the name says: type without serifs.

Serifs Reported Missing

The simplicity and elegance of many sans-serif typefaces make them ideal for large headlines and other display treatments. Serif type, on the other hand, works well in smaller sizes, particularly for a text face, and can look busy and cluttered when set in large sizes for display purposes. (For this reason, you rarely encounter serif type on road signs.)

In small doses, sans-serif type adds impact to a document.

However, while sans-serif type in small doses can add impact to a document, it's often difficult to read in long blocks of text. Serifs help the reader recognize the shapes of the letters. Take away the serifs and there's less letter-to-letter differentiation.

Sans-serif typefaces look best when surrounded by plenty of white space, as in headlines or widely spaced lines of text.

Sans-serif type looks best when surrounded by white space.

Helvetica, the best-known sans-serif typeface, is built into most laser printers.

Other popular sans-serif typefaces include

normal, **bold,** *italics* and ***bold italics.***

Frutiger and Stone Sans are two relatively new sans-serif typefaces that can safely be used for text (if leading is increased), because they contain enough letter-to-letter differences to enhance legibility. Both can add a contemporary look to your publication.

This is Frutiger.
This is Stone Sans.

Decorative and Script Fonts

Choose decorative or script typefaces for situations in which type is more ornamental than informative.

Decorative and script fonts can work well for some advertisements, invitations, menus and posters. These fonts are also ideal for creating logos and other applications in which style and emotional response are more important than the reader's ability to easily decipher each letter.

Script fonts can offer a tone of elegance or informality.

This is Hobo.

This is Revue.

THIS IS STENCIL.

This is University Roman.

This is Zapf Chancery.

Script fonts can offer an atmosphere of either elegance or informality. Often, the letters are connected, echoing the appearance of handwriting.

This is Brush Script.

This is Freestyle Script.

This is Zephyr Script.

You certainly wouldn't want to read text set in any of the above typefaces. Yet, when used appropriately, decorative type can draw attention and provide a pleasing contrast to the serif or sans-serif type it introduces.

Dingbats

Use asterisks, bullets and other dingbats, or symbols, for visual punctuation and interest.

Dingbats—decorative marks such as bullets, check marks and square boxes—can be used to embellish page design.

They can also call attention to items in a list in which all items are equally important.

Dingbats can be used to embellish page design.

Ingredients of a healthy diet include representatives of all major food groups, including:

- Butter
- Eggs
- Meat
- Fish
- Milk
- Corn
- Cereal
- Pop Tarts

Dingbats can be used for end signs, symbols that indicate the ends of articles.

Symbols can further reinforce publication identity: for example, a gavel for a newsletter distributed to judges or a small airplane for an aviation-oriented newsletter.

The seminar will consider ideas and methods for increasing safety levels in the aviation environment, such as

- ✈ Structures
- ✈ Performance
- ✈ Power Plants
- ✈ Navigation
- ✈ Airports

Other typefaces are available for engineering, mathematical, architectural and other technical applications. These faces include specialized symbols and fractions. Composers can even choose typefaces that create musical notes!

Some software programs allow you to create your own custom equations and symbols.

TYPE STYLE

Type style refers to the modifications that lend contrast or emphasis to each typeface.

On most desktop publishing systems, style options include bold, italic, bold italic and small capitals. Shadow, outline and underline styles are also offered.

Bold • *Italic* • ***Bold Italic*** • SMALL CAPS

Characters set in boldface type have thicker strokes and add authority or emphasis to a typeface. Bold type is frequently used for subheads that break up long expanses of text.

Type styles lend contrast or emphasis to a particular typeface.

Lend Contrast to Your Publication

Sans-serif type is, literally, what the name says: type without serifs. The simplicity and elegance of many sans-serif typefaces make them ideal for large headlines and other display treatments.

Serif type, on the other hand, works well in smaller sizes, particularly for a text face, and can look busy and cluttered when set in large sizes for display purposes. For this reason, you rarely encounter serif type on road signs.

Add Authority to Your Page

However, while sans-serif type in small doses can add impact to documents, it's often difficult to read in long blocks of text. Serifs help the reader recognize the shapes of the letters. Take away the serifs and there's less letter-to-letter differentiation.

Sans-serif typefaces look best when surrounded by plenty of white space, as in headlines or widely spaced lines of text.

Sans-serif type is, literally, what the name says: type without serifs. The simplicity and elegance of many sans-serif typefaces make them ideal for large headlines and other display treatments.

Break Up Long Blocks of Text

Serif type, on the other hand, works well in smaller sizes, particularly for a text face, and can look busy and cluttered when set in large sizes for display purposes. For this reason, you rarely encounter serif type on road signs.

However, while sans-serif type in small doses can add impact to documents, it's often difficult to read in long blocks of text. Serifs help the reader recognize the shapes of the letters. Take away the serifs and

there's less letter-to-letter differentiation.

Use Boldface Type Carefully

Sans-serif typefaces look best when surrounded by plenty of white space, as in headlines or widely spaced lines of text.

Serif type, on the other hand, works well in smaller sizes, particularly for a text face, and can look busy and cluttered when set in large sizes for display purposes. For this reason, you rarely encounter serif type on road signs.

However, while sans-serif type in small doses can add impact to documents, it's often difficult to read in long blocks of text. Serifs help the reader recognize the shapes of the letters. Take away the serifs and there is letter-to-letter differentiation.

Boldface type must be used carefully. In small sizes, the counters—enclosed spaces within letters like e and o—often become filled in on laser-printed output. A lot of boldface type also darkens a page.

A lot of bold type can darken a page.

Bold Not Always Better

Characters set in boldface type have thicker strokes and add authority or emphasis to a typeface. Bold type is frequently used for subheads that break up long expanses of text.

Close-Up of Typefaces
Boldface type must be used carefully. In small sizes, the counters-enclosed spaces within letters like e and o – often become filled in on laser printed output. A lot of boldface type also darkens a page. **Setting isolated words in boldface type in the middle of a block of text can draw more attention to a word than it warrants** and can also create a "checkerboard" appearance on the page. Characters set in boldface type have thicker strokes and add authority or emphasis to a typeface. Bold type is frequently used for subheads that break up long expanses of text. Boldface type must be

Letters Move In
Setting isolated words in boldface type in the middle of a text can draw more attention to a word than it warrants and can also create a "checkerboard" appearance on the page.
Characters set in boldface type have thicker strokes and add authority or emphasis to a typeface. Bold type is frequently used for subheads that break up long expanses of text. Boldface type must be used carefully. In small sizes, the counters - enclosed spaces within letters like e and o - often become filled in on laser printed output. A lot of boldface type also darkens a page. Setting isolated words in boldface type in the middle of a block of text can draw more attention to a word than it warrants and can also create a "checkerboard" appearance on the page. Characters set in boldface type have

thicker strokes and add authority or emphasis to a typeface. Bold type is frequently used for subheads that break up long expanses of text. Boldface type must be used carefully. In small sizes, the counters often fill in on laser printed output. Characters set in boldface type have thicker strokes and add authority or emphasis to a typeface. Bold type is frequently used for subheads that break up long expanses of text. **Boldface type must be used carefully. In small sizes, the counters – enclosed spaces within letters like e and o – often become filled in on laser printed output. A lot of boldface type also darkens a page. Setting isolated words in boldface type in the mid-dle of a block of text can draw more attention to a word than it warrants and can also create a "checkerboard" appearance on the page.**

Setting isolated words in boldface type in the middle of a block of text can draw more attention to a word than it warrants and can also create a "checkerboard" appearance on the page.

Type style refers to the modifications that lend **contrast** or emphasis to each typeface. On most desktop publishing systems, *style options* include bold, italic, bold-italic and small capitals. Shadow, outline and underline styles are also offered. Use *italic* for emphasis or when irony or humor is intended. It can also imply a conversational *tone* or indicate a quote. It's often used to set *captions.* Use *bold italic* to make a point really stand out.

Use italic for emphasis or when irony or humor is intended. It can also imply a conversational tone or indicate a quote. It's often used to set captions.

Not only was he late, he was *very* late.

Use bold italic to make a point really stand out.

And he forgot it was her *birthday*!

Italics can be used to imply a conversational tone.

Small caps are approximately 20 percent smaller than regular caps. Small caps let you emphasize the titles of books or poems without darkening the page with boldface or drawing attention with large caps. You can use large and small caps together to indicate sentence beginnings and proper nouns, however.

REGULAR CAPS VS. SMALL CAPS

Shadowed and outlined type should be used with discretion—and rarely in small sizes, since these styles can seriously hinder legibility.

LOOKS GREAT.
But, not so great in small sizes.

Likewise, underlining interferes with the reader's ability to recognize the shapes of words.

<u>Lines of emphasis can become lines of annoyance.</u>

Word shapes are recognized by the interplay of ascenders, descenders and intermediate vowels like a, e, i, o and u. Underlining obscures the descenders.

TYPE WEIGHT

Weight—letter width and stroke thickness—gives you further flexibility in lightening or darkening your page.

For example, in the Helvetica family, Helvetica Black has more impact than Helvetica Bold. Helvetica Black is an ideal choice for short, high-impact headlines.

BOLD WINS

Helvetica Light gives headlines a delicate appearance and "lightens" a page.

The Prima Ballerina

Condensed weights offer a narrower "footprint." This increases the number of letters that can fit on a line.

Helvetica Condensed, for example, preserves the essential attributes of Helvetica, but the letters are narrower. It's ideal for business forms where space is at a premium.

Combinations are also available. Helvetica Condensed, for example, is available in both Light and Black variations.

Helvetica Condensed

Helvetica Light Condensed

Helvetica Black Condensed

Condensed type increases the number of letters that can fit on a line.

These typeface variations offer you extra flexibility in giving your publication a "voice" without your having to introduce competing typefaces.

Stress

Stress refers to variations in the thickness of the strokes that make up a letter.

Serif type tends to have more stress than sans-serif; that is, it usually contains vertical and horizontal strokes of varying thickness.

Times Roman is characterized by moderate amounts of stress. Notice how the vertical strokes are thicker than the horizontal strokes.

This typeface is Times Roman.

Bookman, another frequently used serif typeface, has strokes of a more even thickness.

This typeface is Bookman.

By contrast, most sans-serif typefaces tend to exhibit the same thickness at all points of a character (although there are some notable exceptions).

Univers, for example, lacks stress.

This typeface is Univers.

Serif type tends to have more stress than sans-serif faces.

However, one of the reasons for Helvetica's popularity is its slight stress, which gives it a bit of visual interest. Notice how the horizontal strokes get smaller as they approach the points where they join vertical strokes.

This typeface is Helvetica.

TYPE SIZE

Type size should be proportionate to both the importance of the message and its surroundings.

When choosing type size, consider the amount of white space available.

Small type adrift in a sea of white space appears to be lost.

Where am I?

Large type squeezed into a small area is hard to read and is visually disturbing and claustrophobic.

Type size should be proportionate to the importance of the message.

Over Here,
Taking Up All
Available
Space!

Type is measured in points (72 points to the inch). And most desktop programs let you adjust type size in half-points.

X-Height

Alphabets set in different typefaces in the same type size can vary widely in apparent size and in line length.

Consider these two typefaces. Both are set in 18-point type. One looks significantly larger than the other. In addition, its lowercase alphabet occupies far more space than the other.

One, Two, Three, Four, Five
One, Two, Three, Four, Five

This is because it has a larger x-height. X-height refers to the height of lowercase letters that don't have ascenders (for example, a, o, e and, of course, x).

You can manipulate type to create special effects.

X-height plays a major role in the density, or grayness, of pages containing a lot of text. Alphabets with a low x-height increase word density while preserving "lightness," because of the extra white space between the top of the ascender and the main body of the letter.

low x-height high x-height

This is why you often want to increase leading between lines of type with high x-heights.

On the other hand, typefaces with a large x-height may enhance legibility, enabling you to use a smaller type size.

GRAPHIC DEVICES

In addition to the wealth of available typefaces, styles and sizes, you can also manipulate type to achieve special effects on most desktop publishing programs. These devices, when used with restraint, can transform type into artwork.

Initial Caps

Use a display-size initial letter, known in graphic design lingo as an initial cap, in the first word of a headline, first sentence of an article or new section of an article.

Initial caps at the beginning of an article provide visual transition between headline and text. They also can be placed in different places on a printed page to add interest to an otherwise-gray page of text. However, be sure initial caps placed in the text don't fall at the very top or bottom of a text column or line up with initial caps in adjoining columns. Also be sure initial caps don't inadvertently spell out a word.

Initial caps can add interest to a page.

Initial caps can be either dropped, raised or freestanding.

Consequat. Duis autem veleum iriure dolo in hendrerit in

Consequat. Duis autem vel eu iriure dolor in hendrerit in vulputate

Consequat. Duis tem vel eum iriure dolor in hendrerit vulputate velit es

Raised initial caps extend above the baseline into the white space above the text they introduce. Drop caps are set into the paragraphs they introduce. In either case, the baseline of the initial letter should rest on the appropriate baseline of text, depending on whether it's a raised or dropped cap.

Freestanding caps extend into the left-hand margin, adding an interesting visual element while not altering the adjoining text block.

Adjacent text and initial caps should be set as snug as possible to enhance the visual effect.

In addition, setting the first line of text or the first word or two in small caps or a larger type size can provide a smooth visual transition between the initial cap and regular text type size.

Onsequat. Duis autem vel eum iriure dolor in hendrerit in vulputate velit esse

FEW THINGS vel eum iriure dolor in hendrerit in vulputate velit esse molestie consequat, vel il-

Always set initial caps significantly larger than the type size of the paragraphs they introduce. Undersized initial caps are more a distraction than a design enhancement.

Runarounds

Runarounds are lines of text that "profile" or wrap around photographs, illustrations, initial caps and so on.

Runarounds use space efficiently.

Runarounds are an effective way to tie artwork and text together cohesively. They are also an artistic and efficient use of space.

However, be careful not to overdo it and create a text block that's difficult to read.

Distortion

Stretch or compress type to create special effects, such as on name-plates and logos.

Most desktop publishing programs let you stretch or compress individual letters or even words and sentences. Stretching and compressing type can convert words into graphic elements.

Distorted type is an option for words that are "recognized" instead of "read."

Like shadows and outlines, distortion should be used with discretion. It's acceptable for creating nameplates or department heads, which are "recognized" more than "read," but should be avoided in text.

Rotating Type

Type does not have to be laid out parallel to the top and bottom margins of a page.

Most desktop publishing programs are capable of rotating type, which lets you run a photo credit along the side of a photograph, for example.

PHOTO CREDIT HERE.

You can set a banner at an angle, such as an "Inside this issue!" announcement.

You can also attach text to arcs or circles, useful for creating logos or association seals.

Rotating type can be used effectively for attention-getting display type.

Although the above techniques are useful, they are best reserved for special effects—such as attention-getting display type.

TYPOGRAPHIC REFINEMENTS

Attractive, effective documents are based on typographic consistency and restraint.

In general, avoid using more than two typefaces on a page—three if you include a symbol typeface for lists and end signs. Many great-looking documents are based on a single sans-serif typeface for heads and subheads with a second serif typeface for text and captions.

Effective typography is based on restraint and consistency.

Avoid last-minute compromises, like reducing type size, line spacing or letter spacing to "squeeze in" text.

Likewise, avoid increasing text specifications to fill space.

The keys to effective typography are based on consistency, restraint and attention to detail.

Refining Punctuation

Replace "typewritten" characters with "typeset" punctuation whenever possible.

For example, replace two hyphens with a single long dash called an Em dash.

```
Although the techniques are useful, they are
best reserved for special effects--such as
attention-getting display type.
```

Although the techniques are useful, they are best reserved for special effects–such as attention-getting display type.

Replace a single hyphen—used for compound words—with an En dash, which is slightly longer than a hyphen.

Also, be sure to use "open" and "close" quotation marks instead of vertical ones. Some programs automatically make the substitution; others rely on you to do it.

Strive to approximate the look of traditional typesetting.

MOVING ON

Typography is a time-honored craft and an important one for every desktop publisher to learn.

By taking advantage of the wide variety of typeface alternatives available on desktop publishing systems and using the full range of spacing controls at your disposal, you can avoid a "desktop-published" look, and more closely approximate the work of traditional typesetters.

In the next chapter, we'll explore the importance of such visuals as photos, illustrations, charts and graphs that can be used to emphasize and/or enhance your message.

4 | ADDING EFFECTIVE VISUALS

Visual images in a document communicate your message at a glance.

The three major categories of visuals—photographs, illustrations and information graphics—can significantly enhance the effectiveness of your message and the overall attractiveness of your page.

Artwork enhances the attractiveness of your page.

Desktop publishing offers numerous features that can help you manipulate and modify your artwork to suit your page layout and overall design.

PHOTOGRAPHS

Photographs are the most literal form of visual communication.

Photography can capture with unerring accuracy the minute details and fleeting human emotions of a moment in time.

Photos capture fleeting emotions and minute details.

This is its greatest strength and at the same time its most frustrating weakness.

Photographic accuracy can become a problem when the camera captures unwanted elements that the photographer didn't notice—or failed to filter out. However, today's desktop publishing programs often let you selectively remove portions of the photo. (See "Cropping" and "Silhouetting" in this chapter.)

Photos prove the time-honored adage that seeing is believing.

For many documents, such as newsletters and sales brochures, photos add a sense of familiarity by letting readers see the faces of individuals or groups being written about. A "mug shot"—a head-shot photo—of a regular columnist or VIP also creates a more personal relationship with the reader.

In sum, quality photographs add interest as well as credibility to your document. As the old adage goes, seeing is believing.

Cropping

Eliminate unimportant details by cropping.

Cropping involves removing unwanted details by cutting off part of the top, bottom or sides of the photo, and having it still retain a rectangular or square shape.

Cropping a photo lets you focus on what's most important.

Silhouetting

Emphasize important details and introduce an interesting visual shape to your document by silhouetting a photo.

Silhouetting eliminates unimportant background details and reshapes the remaining portion of the photograph.

You can reshape a photo to add emphasis and interest.

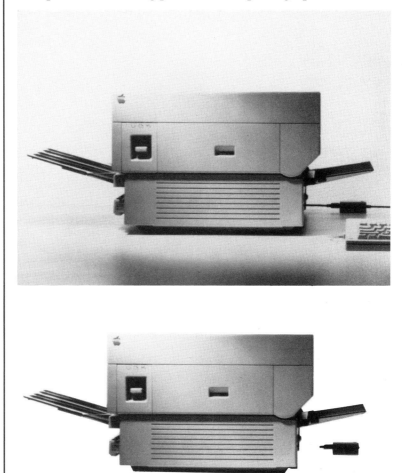

Partial silhouetting can be very effective. For example, a hand can extend beyond the boundaries of an otherwise square or rectangular photograph.

Silhouetting can provide a sense of motion.

Silhouetting the bow of this white-water raft creates a sense of motion—of escape from the confines of its space on the page.

Airbrushing and Photo Manipulation

Many software programs let you modify scanned photographic images on your computer screen. You can lighten shadowed areas or tone down distracting highlights.

You also can use these sophisticated tools to airbrush, or "paint out," distracting details, like eliminating a fire hydrant in front of the boss's new Porsche or removing unduly prominent lettering above a subject.

Airbrushing lets you "paint out" distracting details.

Often portions of two or more photographs can be "cut and pasted" together.

Airbrushing and cut-and-paste tools, of course, must be used with discretion and restraint, avoiding the temptation to misinform or mislead readers.

Organizing Photographs

When several photographs are used together, establish a hierarchy of importance that determines the size and placement of each photo on the page.

Smaller photographs can provide contrast and support the message of the primary photograph.

Photo placement should reflect a hierarchy of importance.

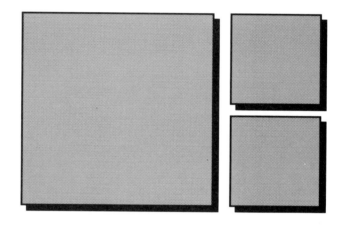

When no single photograph is more important than the others, arrange them in a repeating sequence.

This sequence can be organized vertically …

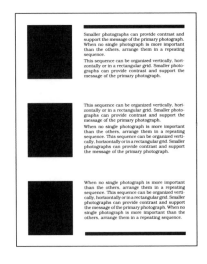

horizontally …

or in a rectangular grid ...

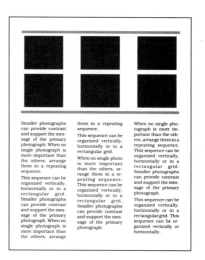

ILLUSTRATIONS

Illustrations consist of drawings, either hand- or computer-generated.

Illustrations can place aesthetic considerations before accuracy.

Illustrations offer far more opportunities for interpretation than photos do. The artist can selectively organize and emphasize information. Therefore, artwork can convey both accuracy and atmosphere or substitute accuracy for aesthetics.

For example, a draw-type program can be used to render an image of a person's hand, either literally or abstractly.

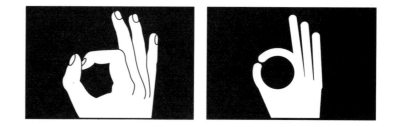

In this age of computer graphics, cutaways (line diagrams) of objects are often used in technical manuals and documents. These illustrations can show the structure of an object with more clarity than photographs of the various components of the object.

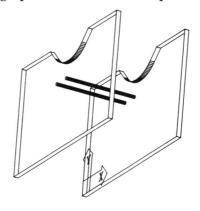

Clip Art

Use clip art to add pizazz and professionalism to ads, brochures, menus and newsletters.

"Canned" art can save you the time and money involved in creating original artwork.

Clip art consists of files of existing artwork that can be dropped into your desktop-published documents. Clip art can save you lots of time and money, by letting you "brighten" your publication without having to create your own illustrations.

A variety of clip art is available for just about every occasion. For example, some clip art packages are based on holiday or party themes, graduations and other special events.

Other clip art reflects occupational categories or fields of interest. Special packages are available for financial, legal, medical and religious publications.

Maps are also a popular and useful form of clip art.

Clip art is often used for borders. Border treatments run the gamut from Art Deco to the Wild West.

Clip art can be disguised by some special techniques.

Clip art doesn't have to be used "as is." You can often disguise its origins by using some special techniques.

For example, you can use just a portion of a clip-art image, but greatly increase its size.

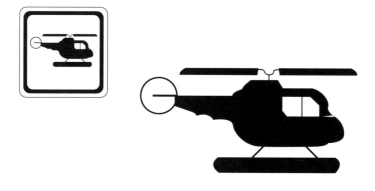

Another technique involves combining several clip-art images. For example, individual clip-art items can be brought together to form a dynamic visual, such as the still life superimposed on a geometric feature in the following example.

Manipulating Illustrations

Illustrations are even more adaptable to manipulation than photos.

Like photographs, art can be cropped, boxed or silhouetted. It can be placed against screened backgrounds or allowed to bleed (or extend) to the edge of the page.

Illustrations created with draw-type programs also can be distorted. For example, you can stretch the illustration vertically to make it taller.

Dramatic effects can be achieved by stretching an illustration.

Or, you can stretch it horizontally to make it wider.

Illustrations created with draw-type programs also can be compressed horizontally or vertically.

Enlarging dot patterns can create an impressionistic effect.

The most dramatic effects can be achieved with paint-type programs. As paint-type or scanned illustrations are increased in size, the pattern of the dots they're composed of becomes more and more apparent. This can be used to create attention-getting impressionistic effects, which often have more impact than the original illustration.

The basis for an impressionistic drawing might be a scanned photograph.

INFORMATION GRAPHICS

Information graphics can inform and draw attention to trends, comparisons and organizational structures.

Information graphics combine the communicating power of charts, diagrams and tables with the aesthetic appeal of drawings. They can be created easily using clip art and your desktop publishing program's drawing tools. Or, you can create them with separate drawing programs.

Information graphics combine communication with aesthetic appeal.

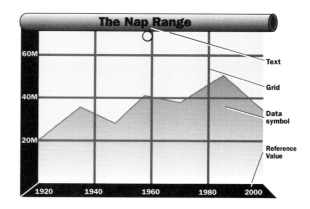

The widespread use of information graphics in publications such as *USA Today* and *Time* has shown that charts, diagrams and tables can be presented in visually exciting ways. As multi-color printing becomes easier and more affordable, you're likely to be using information graphics more and more in your publications and presentations.

You'll be surprised at the way you can assemble impressive graphics from nothing more than combinations of circles, straight lines, fill patterns (such as parallel lines or dots) and clip art.

Charts and Diagrams

Charts translate numbers and values into images.

Charts quickly communicate comparisons, relationships and trends. The first step in choosing the appropriate type of chart is to define its purpose and identify the most effective chart to present that concept to the reader or viewer.

Pie charts display part-to-whole relationships.

Charts quickly convey trends and comparisons.

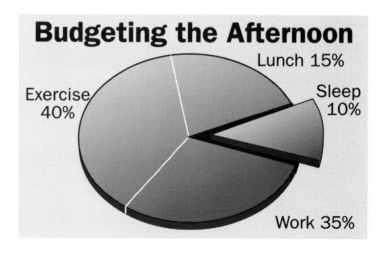

Budgeting the Afternoon

Lunch 15%
Sleep 10%
Exercise 40%
Work 35%

Bar charts make comparisons.

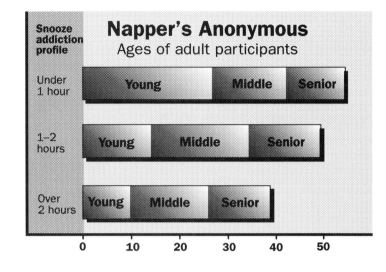

Line charts show trends.

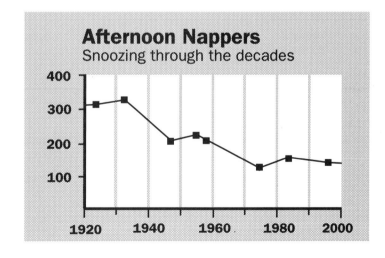

You can also combine chart types. Compound charts can show both total yearly sales and departmental contributions to the total.

Diagrams communicate relationships rather than numbers.

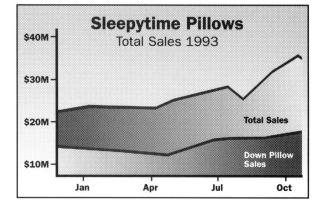

Choose diagrams rather than charts when you want to emphasize relationships and sequences, rather than numbers.

Organizational diagrams are one of the most frequently encountered types of diagrams. These display dominant/subordinate, "who reports to whom," relationships.

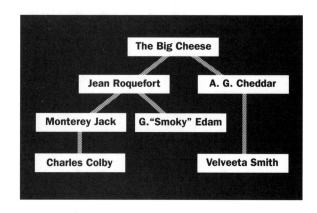

Flow, or process, diagrams are used to display sequences—what must be done first, what must be done second, and so on.

Flow diagrams display a sequence of events.

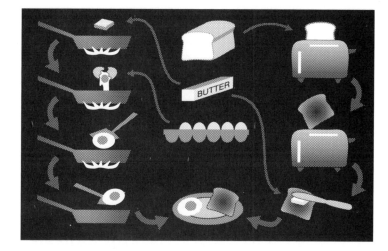

Choose a PERT—Program Evaluation Review Technique—diagram when you want to display both sequence and the length of time it will take to accomplish each step. PERT diagrams communicate both sequence and time because all elements are drawn to the same scale.

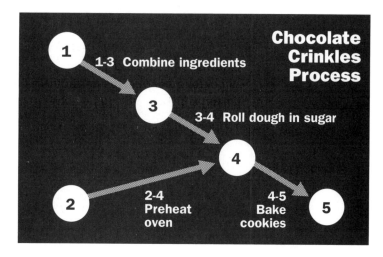

Timelines help you visually communicate historical perspectives. You can show when certain events occurred as well as how much time elapsed between them.

Timelines convey a historical perspective.

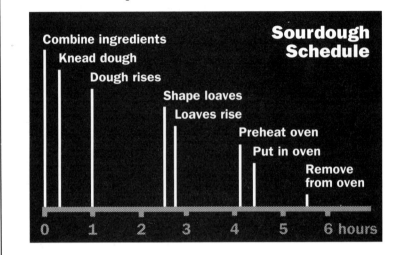

Diagrams can also be used to display spatial relationships. Floor plans, cutaway product drawings and maps are examples.

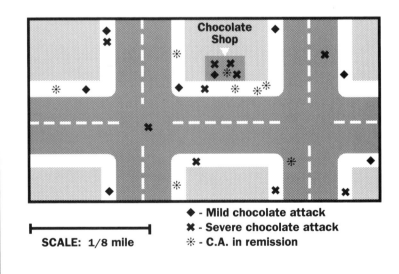

Add impact to your diagrams by using size and color. Size can be used, for example, to indicate time, and color can be used to draw attention to critical parts. You can also enhance your drawings by "exploding" them—isolating the most important part.

Use size and color to add impact to a diagram.

You can increase the impact and communicating power of your charts and diagrams by adding…

… a title that summarizes the purpose or importance of the information being displayed.

This title lacks impact:

1992 Sales by Region

But this title commands more attention:

Projected 1992 Sales Increases

... labels to indicate the exact amounts displayed in each chart segment or bar graph column...

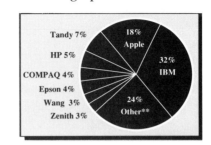

Grids provide a frame of reference by showing numeric divisions.

... background grids that provide a frame of reference by indicating the major numeric divisions...

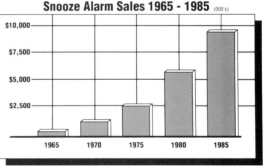

... tick marks that define subdivisions...

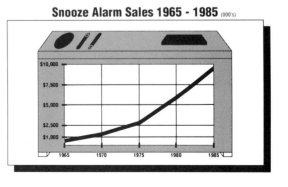

… a legend that identifies symbols, units of measure, etc., used in a chart or diagram…

… shades, patterns and colors that complement each other. Avoid adjacent colors that "fight" or blend together…

Legends indicate symbols and units of measure.

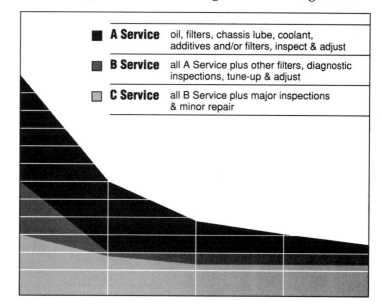

A Service	oil, filters, chassis lube, coolant, additives and/or filters, inspect & adjust
B Service	all A Service plus other filters, diagnostic inspections, tune-up & adjust
C Service	all B Service plus major inspections & minor repair

Three-dimensional effects can draw the reader's attention to charts and diagrams.

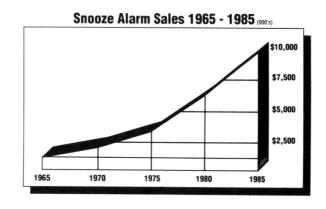

Snooze Alarm Sales 1965 - 1985 (000's)

Tables

Tables present a lot of information in a concise and orderly way.

Tables are useful when you want to focus your reader's attention on the data itself rather than on representations of it.

Tables focus on data rather than graphic representations of it.

Preferred Morning Beverage (1,000s)				
COFFEE	**1960**	**1970**	**1980**	**1990**
Instant	540	562	580	590
Perk	453	444	420	410
Drip	622	690	725	950
TEA				
Black	325	320	315	250
Herbal	105	110	160	200

Whereas charts and diagrams show trends and comparisons, tables let you easily read down or across to compare specific information in adjacent rows and columns.

A table can often replace several sentences. Tables are frequently used in proposals and reports to buttress arguments and conclusions. Tables are also used in slides and overheads.

When placing information in tables, be sure to leave enough "breathing room" around the text or numbers. Row and column headings should be significantly larger, or bolder, than the information they introduce. Screens can also be used to set off header information.

Sometimes, several sentences can be replaced by a table.

Preferred Morning Beverage (1,000s)				
COFFEE	**1960**	**1970**	**1980**	**1990**
Instant	540	562	580	590
Perk	453	444	420	410
Drip	622	690	725	950
TEA				
Black	325	320	315	250
Herbal	105	110	160	200

Preferred Morning Beverage				
COFFEE	**1960**	**1970**	**1980**	**1990**
Instant	540,291	562,190	580,410	590,125
Perk	453,210	444,009	420,130	410,023

Avoid including more detail than necessary. Instead of including all digits in large numbers, round the numbers off to the nearest hundred, thousand or million. (Be sure you prominently indicate the scale you're using.)

Although column headings are often centered, flush-right alignment can be used for row identifiers. This "locks" the information together.

Preferred Morning Beverage (1,000s)				
COFFEE	**1960**	**1970**	**1980**	**1990**
Instant	540	562	580	590
Perk	453	444	420	410
Drip	622	690	725	950

When tables contain numbers, decimal alignment ensures that the numbers will line up, regardless of the size of the number or the number of decimal points after it.

1,567.98	1,567.98
127.09	127.09
1,278.11	1,278.11
1,259.8	1,259.80
2,005.96	2,005.96

Avoid using thick rules that darken a table and overwhelm the information inside. Notice that the horizontal and vertical rules can be of different thicknesses, as can the border rules.

Preferred Morning Beverage (1,000s)				
COFFEE	**1960**	**1970**	**1980**	**1990**
Instant	540	562	580	590
Perk	453	444	420	410
Drip	622	690	725	950
TEA				
Black	325	320	315	250
Herbal	105	110	160	200

Data in a table can be overwhelmed by very thick rules.

Screen Captures

Computer documentation often contains a specialized form of line art, called "screen captures." These reproduce the images seen on a computer screen.

Screen captures reproduce the image seen on a computer.

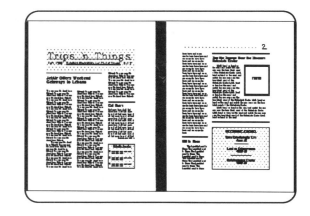

MOVING ON

Visuals add an important dimension to a document. Use them whenever possible to add "color" to your overall page and to support and communicate your message. The various manipulation features included in desktop publishing programs can be a mixed blessing. Overdoing it is a hazard every designer should be wary of. When used with restraint these features can transform ho-hum visuals into exciting ones.

Now let's focus on some of the most important graphics tools that can help your designs look good in print.

5 | BUILDING BLOCKS OF GRAPHIC DESIGN

The building blocks of graphic design add interest and color to your document, thereby enhancing its communicating power.

However, these tools must be used with restraint. Otherwise, the exceptional becomes the norm, making it difficult to separate the important from the unimportant.

White space provides a resting point for readers' eyes.

WHITE SPACE

White space—or blank space free of text or artwork—is one of the most undervalued tools of graphic design.

White space provides contrast, as well as a resting point for readers' eyes, as they begin moving through the publication. White space can take many forms:

A. The open area surrounding a headline—The attention-getting power of a headline may be enhanced more by extra white space around it than by larger type.

B. The page margins of an advertisement or publication—Wide margins direct the reader's attention into the center of the page.

C. The vertical space between columns of type—The wider the columns, the more space needed between them.

D. The space created by ragged line endings of unjustified type—This space relieves the monotony of large expanses of evenly measured text.

E. Paragraph indents and extra line space between paragraphs—These small but effective increments of space can open up a page layout.

F. The horizontal space, or leading, between lines of type—Tightly packed lines of type "darken" a publication page.

Note that "white space" doesn't have to be white. If your publication is printed on colored paper stock (e.g., ivory or tan), white space lets more of the background color appear.

White space is one of the most undervalued tools of graphic design.

Drops

One of the easiest ways to enliven your publication is to include a drop—a band of white space, also called a "sink"—at the top of each page.

This white space draws attention to the text below by adding contrast. It can also dramatize headlines.

A drop calls attention to the text below.

You can place photographs so that they slightly extend into the drop, rather than align with the top text margin.

A consistent drop provides important page-to-page continuity throughout your publication. Notice how publication unity is destroyed when the text begins at a different level on each page.

Vertical White Space

Vertical white space can really open up a page.

One of the best ways you can improve the appearance of a newsletter is to build a significant amount of vertical white space into each page—perhaps by omitting a column of text. Ideally, most of this area should remain open, but it can provide space to extend a front-page table of contents, publishing information or pull-quotes.

RULES

Rules are lines that can be used to emphasize or frame various page elements (headlines, pull-quotes, headers, etc.) or to separate items or parts of a publication from one another.

Rules can be horizontal or vertical, thick or thin.

Use rules to organize text and emphasize subheads.

Vertical rules, called downrules, are often used to separate columns, particularly when type isn't justified.

Horizontal rules can be used to separate topics within a column or to draw attention to subheads.

Horizontal rules often are used to draw attention to "pull-quotes" (short sentences or phrases that summarize the key points of an article).

Choose rules that harmonize with the "color" of your document.

Choose rules that harmonize with the "color" of your document. Thick rules "darken" a document and are most effective when set off by white space.

Thin rules are often appropriate for documents with a lot of copy.

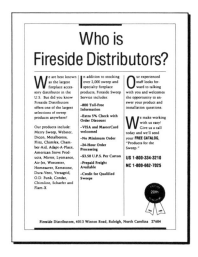

Another useful technique is to use rules similar in width to the thickness of the strokes of the letterforms used in a newsletter nameplate or an ad headline. This can add an interesting graphic element to the type treatment.

Thick rules are most effective when set off by white space.

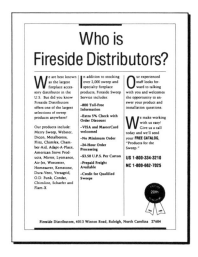

BORDERS

Use borders to frame and draw attention to the "live area"—the space in which text, display type and artwork appear.

Borders work with white space to determine publication "color" and "tone." Borders can be tangible or assumed.

Tangible borders are rules or graphics that outline a document. Assumed borders aren't visible but are created subconsciously as the reader encounters the edge of the live area of a document.

The basic tangible border is a large frame surrounding the contents of a page. With most desktop publishing programs, it's easy to create one by using the box-drawing tool. Either single or double lines, thick or thin, can be used.

All four borders don't have to be the same, however. Different styles can be used for the vertical or horizontal sides.

Borders can frame the "live area" of a page.

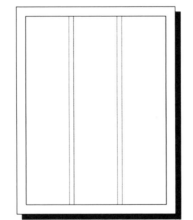 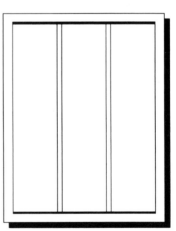

Thick borders can be created by using the box-drawing tool and filling the frames with solid (100 percent) black or shades of gray (see pages 119-121).

Borders don't have to extend the full height or width of a publication's "live area."

Assumed borders are created in the mind's eye.

With assumed borders, the edges of text columns and artwork create the illusion of borders.

BOXES

Use boxes for emphasis or to separate parts of a publication.

Sidebars (short articles that supplement longer feature articles) are often set in boxes.

A box can distinguish a list from the other text on a page.

Boxes can also be used to isolate the table of contents or masthead (a list of publication staff members and their titles).

Boxes can be used to create reader-response coupons. Most desk-top publishing programs let you create boxes with dashed borders to clearly identify the coupon.

Boxes can define the boundaries of a visual, especially impor-tant when the edges of the photograph or illustration are light-colored or indistinct. Remove the thin box from the photograph below, and the photograph looks unfinished, blending into the background.

Boxes create clear boundaries for a light-colored photo.

Box borders can be as thick or thin as you like.

Avoid thick boxes, however; they darken the page and tend to look like obituaries.

DROP SHADOWS

Use drop shadows to draw attention to boxes or visuals.

Drop shadows can create dramatic, three-dimensional effects.

Skillfully used, drop shadows can create attention-getting three-dimensional effects. They can help emphasize a photo or illustration by isolating it from its background.

However, like all desktop publishing tools, drop shadows should be used with discretion. Because they are easily created, they tend to be overused.

REVERSES

Emphasize headlines, subheads or other display type by using white type against a black background.

Because they are such an obvious contrast to conventional type, reverses call attention to the text.

Reversed type is particularly effective for short lines set in large, sans-serif uppercase and lowercase type.

Because they have magnetic appeal, reverses are an ideal way to draw attention to subheads or organizers—such as department headings.

Always surround reversed text with sufficient background. When there are equal amounts of black background and white type, the reader's eye will become confused and unable to focus on the text.

FROM THE PRESIDENT

Several reverses on one page can create a "Morse-code" effect.

Reverses also lose impact if they're hard to read, which can occur if type is too small. Avoid reversing small boldface type. The insides of letters like b, c, d and o can easily fill in, making it difficult to decipher the words.

Notice how the words run together and are difficult to read when reversed type is set too small

Be cautious when using serif typefaces with reverses. The serifs tend to lose definition, creating a blurred effect.

Reverses should be used with restraint. Several small reverses on a page can create a staccato, "Morse-code" effect on the page, attracting more attention than they warrant.

Screens

Distinguish headlines and important passages from surrounding text by placing them against a gray background.

Whereas reversed backgrounds are 100 percent black, screens are created by printing backgrounds in percentages of black. These percentages are usually in 20 percent increments. The greater the percentage, the darker the background.

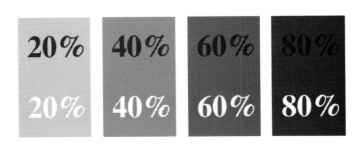

Screens can add contrast to and enhance the readability of your publication in many ways.

For example, use white type against a dark-gray background.

Or, use black type against a light-gray background.

> **Reduced Contrast**
> **Is Sometimes a**
> **Virtue**

Screens add contrast, turning text into a graphic element.

Screens are particularly effective when used with rules or boxes. Screens also help call attention to sidebars.

When using screens, be aware of the limitations of your output device. Screens created by some laser printers exhibit a grainy, or coarse, quality.

Screens often work best when your publication is produced on a high-resolution phototypesetter.

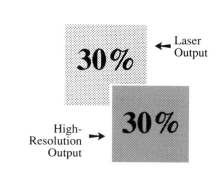

Another alternative is to indicate the placement of screens and have your commercial printer add them.

Bleeds

A printed image that extends beyond the text margin to the edge of a page is called a bleed.

Bleeds add impact to page design by emphasizing building blocks such as text, visuals or graphics.

An oversize initial cap, or chapter number, can bleed to the top or side edges of a title page of a manual or book.

Bleeds can add emphasis to text and visuals.

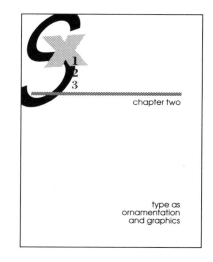

A photograph can gain "motion" when it extends to the edge of a page.

A photo gains motion when it bleeds to the edge of the page.

Horizontal rules that bleed to one, or both, sides of a page can add continuity to the pages.

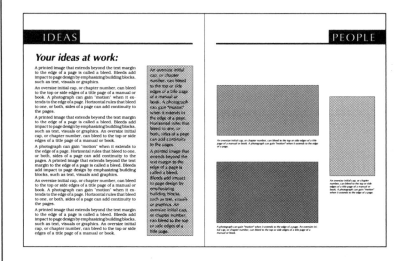

Newsletter nameplates gain impact when their backgrounds bleed to the top and/or sides of the page.

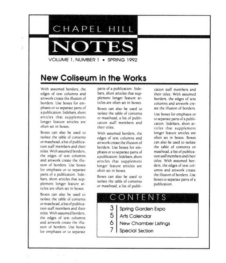

A nameplate gains impact when its background bleeds to the top of a page.

Bleeds work particularly well with two-color brochures, in which the entire front and back covers are printed in a second color, with headlines reversed out.

Check your budget and hardware resources before using bleeds. Because your commercial printer has to use an oversize sheet of paper and trim it to actual publication size after printing, bleeds increase costs. In addition, the printing area of most laser printers is approximately a half-inch smaller than the physical size of the paper. (High-resolution output devices do not have this limitation.) If necessary, you can print your pages at slightly reduced size and instruct your printer to increase them.

Color

When budget allows, color can be used to organize the contents of your publication.

Different parts of your publication—for instance, the various sections of a training document—can be color-coded.

Color can be used to highlight important advice.

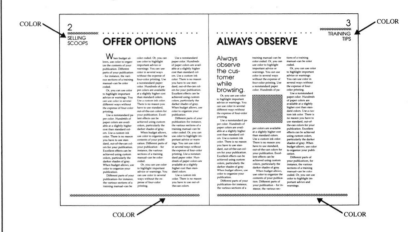

Or, you can use color to highlight important advice or warnings.

You can use color in several ways without the expense of four-color printing:

1) Use a nonstandard paper color. Hundreds of paper colors are available at a slightly higher cost than standard colors.

2) Use a custom ink color. There's no reason you *have* to use standard, out-of-the-can colors for your publication. Excellent effects can be achieved using custom colors, particularly the darker shades of gray. (See Appendix A.)

3) Add a second color to your publication. Use the second color for selected parts of your publication—borders, rules, subheads, nameplate or logo. Choose a second color that creates a pleasing contrast to the primary ink color. Avoid overuse of a second ink color. When it comes to color, less is often more.

4) Use blocks of color to provide a background for an entire page with reversed headlines or blocks of text.

When it comes to color, less is often more.

MOVING ON

In the previous chapters, you've learned how to use text and graphics to organize and give emphasis to your documents. The next chapter covers common misapplications of these tools, which can compromise your publication's message and design.

6 | TWENTY-FIVE COMMON DESIGN PITFALLS

The following illustrations are typical examples of "desktop publishing overkill." These samples show that using too many desktop publishing devices, compounded by a lack of attention to detail, can work against the goals of straightforward, effective communication.

RIVERS OF WHITE SPACE

Watch out for "rivers" of white space that can develop vertically or diagonally through justified text.

Rivers are caused by gaps between words; they occur often when large type is justified in narrow columns. They're especially likely to occur when two spaces instead of one are inserted after periods.

"Rivers" of white space in justified text can be distracting.

> feugait nulla facilisi. Lorem ipsum dolor sit amet, consectetuer adipiscing elit, sed diam nonummy nibh. Euismod tincidunt ut laoreet dolore magna aliquam erat volutpat. Ut wisi enim ad minim veniam, quis nostrud exerci tation. Ullamcorper suscipit lobortis nisl ut aliquip ex ea commodo consequat.

The cure is to alter type size and/or column width, as well as get in the habit of leaving only one space between sentences. You can also choose flush-left/ragged-right type alignment.

INAPPROPRIATE COLUMN SPACING

Column spacing should be proportionate to type size.

As type size increases, more space between columns is needed to prevent the reader's eyes from moving horizontally, across columns, instead of progressing down to the next line.

The larger the type, the more space between columns is required.

As type increases, more space between columns is needed to prevent the reader's eyes from moving horizontally, across columns, instead of progressing down to the next line. Be careful that you do not overdo it, however. Overly generous column spacing causes distracting vertical bands of white space.

As type increases, more space between columns is needed to prevent the

Be careful not to overdo it, however. Overly generous column spacing causes distracting vertical bands of white space. (The default column spacing for most desktop publishing programs may be too large or small for the specific typeface and type size you're using.)

TOMBSTONING

Avoid parallel headlines, subheads or initial caps in adjacent columns.

Tombstones are created when headlines or other display type items appear next to each other in adjacent columns. Readers may take them for a line of copy instead of separate elements. In

addition, tombstone headlines sometimes form a strong visual
that can unbalance and overwhelm the page.

*Adjacent lines of display type can create
a "tombstone" effect.*

Solutions include changing the typeface, type size, type style or
alignment, or editing the text in one column so headlines or
other display type treatments are staggered.

TRAPPED WHITE SPACE

Avoid "holes" in publications.

Trapped white space occurs when a "hole" appears between a headline and an adjacent photograph, or when an article is too short to fill the column down to the next headline.

Occasionally, white space can be too much of a good thing.

Solutions include increasing the size of the headline type or enlarging the visual.

Trapped white space often develops along the right-hand edge of a silhouetted photograph that has a runaround on the left-hand side.

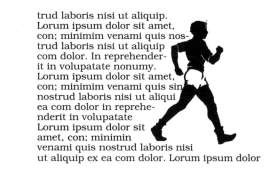

trud laboris nisi ut aliquip.
Lorum ipsum dolor sit amet,
con; minimim venami quis nostrud laboris nisi ut aliquip
com dolor. In reprehenderit in volupatate nonumy.
Lorum ipsum dolor sit amet,
con; minimim venami quis sin
nostrud laboris nisi ut aliqui
ea com dolor in reprehe-
nderit in volupatate
Lorum ipsum dolor sit
amet, con; minimin
venami quis nostrud laboris nisi
ut aliquip ex ea com dolor. Lorum ipsum dolor

The solution is to square off the silhouetted photograph by placing it in a box, perhaps against a gray background.

CLAUSTROPHOBIC PAGES

Always provide sufficient breathing room around columns of text.

Claustrophobic pages result when columns of text crowd each other and the edges of the page.

Be sure to give text columns breathing room.

[Illustration: mock newsletter page titled "PET PAPERS", Quarterly Newsletter, FREE, with headlines "DOGS MARCHING FOR MORE BONES", "BIRDS SINGING TOO MANY SONGS", and "TURTLES CROSSING TOO MANY ROADS".]

Claustrophobic pages also result when text is squeezed into boxes or wrapped too tightly around illustrations or silhouetted photographs.

A VERY TIGHT FIT	MUCH MORE COMFORTABLE
Lorum ipsum dolor sit amet, con; minimim venami quis nostrud laboris nisi ut aliquip ex ea com dolor. In reprehenderit in volupatate nonumy. Lorum ipsum dolor sit amet, con; minimim venami quis nostrud laboris nisi ut aliquip ex ea com dolor in reprehenderit in vo-	Lorum ipsum dolor sit amet, con; minimim venami quis nostrud laboris nisi ut aliquip ex ea com dolor. In reprehenderit in volupatate nonumy. Lorum ipsum dolor sit amet, con;

WHISPERING HEADLINES

Headlines should be significantly larger, and often bolder, than the text they introduce.

Give headlines the attention they deserve.

Gray pages result where there's not enough contrast between headlines and text. Whispering headlines fail to attract attention to the text they introduce.

JUMPING HORIZONS

Start text the same distance from the top of each page throughout a multipage document.

Jumping horizons occur when text columns start at different locations on a page. The up-and-down effect is disconcerting to the reader and destroys publication integrity.

Jumping horizons create a disconcerting up-and-down effect.

PRODUCTS IN THE NEWS   23

Lorum ipsum dolor sit amet, con; minimim venami quis nostrud laboris nisi ut aliquip ex ea com dolor. In reprehenderit in volupatate nonumy. Lorum ipsum dolor sit amet, con; minimim venami quis nostrud laboris nisi ut aliquip ex ea com dolor in reprehenderit in volupatate nonumy. Lorum ipsum dolor sit amet, con. Minimim venami quis nostrud laboris nisi ut aliquip ex ea com dolor in reprehenderit in volupatate nonumy.

Lorum ipsum dolor sit amet, con; minimim venami quis nostrud.

Plastic Products

Lorum ipsum dolor sit amet, con; minimim venami quis nostrud laboris nisi ut aliquip ex ea com dolor. In reprehenderit in volupatate nonumy. Lorum ipsum dolor sit amet, con; minimim venami quis nostrud laboris nisi ut aliquip ex ea com dolor in reprehenderit in volupatate nonumy. Lorum ipsum dolor sit amet, con.

Minimim venami quis nostrud laboris nisi ut aliquip ex ea com dolor in reprehenderit in volupatate nonumy.

Ipsum dolor sit amet, con; minimim venami quis nostrud laboris nisi. Lorum ipsum dolor sit amet, con; minimim venami quis nostrud laboris nisi ut aliquip ex ea com dolor in reprehenderit in volupatate nonumy. Lorum ipsum dolor sit amet, con; minimim venami quis nostrud laboris nisi ut aliquip ex ea com dolor.

In reprehenderit in volupatate nonumy. Lorum ipsum dolor sit amet, con; minimim venami quis nostrud laboris nisi ut aliquip ex ea com dolor in reprehenderit in volupatate nonumy. Lorum ipsum dolor sit amet, con. Minimim venami quis nostrud laboris nisi ut aliquip ex ea com dolor in reprehenderit in volupatate nonumy. Lorum ipsum dolor sit amet, con; minimim venami quis nostrud laboris nisi. Lorum ipsum dolor sit amet, con; minimim venami

quis nostrud laboris nisi ut aliquip ex ea com dolor in reprehenderit in volupatate nonumy. Lorum ipsum dolor sit amet, con; minimim venami.

Metal Products

Lorum ipsum dolor sit amet, con; minimim venami quis nostrud laboris nisi ut aliquip ex ea com dolor.

In reprehenderit in volupatate nonumy. Lorum ipsum dolor sit amet, con; minimim venami quis nostrud laboris nisi ut aliquip ex ea com dolor in reprehenderit in volupatate nonumy. Lorum ipsum dolor sit amet, con.

Minimim venami quis nostrud laboris nisi ut aliquip ex ea com dolor in reprehenderit in volupatate nonumy. Lorum ipsum dolor sit amet, con; minimim venami quis nostrud laboris nisi. Lorum ipsum dolor sit amet, con; minimim venami quis nostrud com dolor visi et laboris nisi ut aliquip ex ea com dolor in reprehenderit.

STRETCHED CAPTIONS

Avoid using small type sizes for captions that extend across more than one column.

Stretched captions in small type sizes are difficult to read because the reader's eyes tend to get lost between the end of one line of type and the beginning of the next, particularly when the alignment is justified.

Long captions set in small type can be difficult to read.

In reprehenderit in volupatate nonumy. Lorum ipsum dolor sit amet, con; minimim.

Avoid small type sizes for captions that extend across more than one column. Stretched captions in small type sizes are difficult to read because the reader's eyes tend to get lost between lines.

Lorum ipsum dolor sit amet, con. Minimim venami quis nostrud laboris nisi ut aliquip ex ea com dolor in reprehenderit in volupatate.

Solutions include editing the captions, using flush-left/ragged-right alignment and shortening the length of the line.

Another solution is to place the caption to the side of the photograph instead of below it.

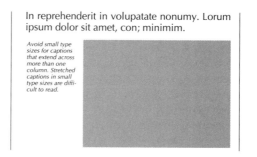

In reprehenderit in volupatate nonumy. Lorum ipsum dolor sit amet, con; minimim.

Avoid small type sizes for captions that extend across more than one column. Stretched captions in small type sizes are difficult to read.

LACK OF CONTRAST BETWEEN TEXT AND BACKGROUND

Strive for as much contrast between type and background as possible.

This is especially important when designing color slides and overhead transparencies. Without sufficient contrast, it's hard to distinguish the text from the background, especially if viewed from the back of the room.

OVERLY DETAILED CHARTS

Combine and simplify information presented in charts.

To highlight the important message of a chart, combine and simplify less important information. A pie chart, for example, with more than six slices is confusing.

Consolidate data to highlight what's most important.

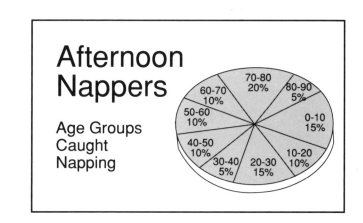

When the smaller slices are grouped together, more attention is directed to important segments.

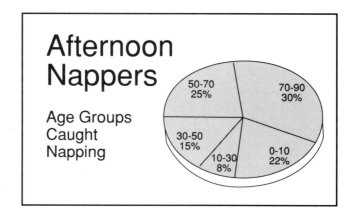

EXCESSIVE SPACING AFTER PUNCTUATION

Avoid placing two spaces after a period at the end of a sentence.

Two spaces following periods are needed for typewritten text. But in desktop-published type, the extra space creates unsightly "holes" between sentences, which is especially noticeable in justified text.

```
  Ipsum dolor sit amet,
con.   Minimim venami quis
nostrud laboris nisi ut.
Aliquip ex ea com dolor in
reprehenderit in volupata-
te nonumy.   Ipsum dolor
sit amet, con; minimim ve-
nami quis nostrud.   Labor-
```

Ipsum dolor sit amet, con. Minimim venami quis nostrud laboris nisi ut. Aliquip ex ea com dolor in reprehenderit in volupatate nonumy. Ipsum dolor sit amet, con; minimim venami quis nostrud. Laboris nisi lorum ipsum dolor sit. Aliquip ex ea com dolor in repre-

Since habits are hard to break, the easiest way to overcome this one is to use the Search and Replace command in your word processing or desktop publishing program to replace the two spaces with one space throughout your publication.

In long documents with paragraphs containing several sentences, you may be surprised at the difference this can make.

FLOATING HEADS AND SUBHEADS

Be sure headlines and subheads are closer to the text they introduce than to the preceding text.

The impact of a heading is weakened if it isn't immediately clear which text it belongs to.

Use appropriate line spacing to link subheads with text.

Aliquip ex ea com dolor in reprehenderit in volupatate nonumy. Ipsum dolor sit amet, con.

Sensitivity to variations in spacing

Minimim venami quis nostrud. Laboris nisi lorum ipsum dolor sit. Aliquip ex ea com dolor in reprehenderit in volupatate nonumy.

Com dolor in reprehenderit in volupatate nonumy. Minimim venami quis nostrud.

Sensitivity to variations in spacing

Laboris nisi lorum ipsum dolor sit. Aliquip ex ea com dolor in reprehenderit in volupatate.

BURIED HEADS AND SUBHEADS

Avoid headlines and subheads isolated near column bottoms.

Buried headlines can break readers' concentration.

Buried headlines and subheads are those followed by only one or two lines of type at the bottom of a page. This is not only unsightly but distracting. The reader's concentration may be broken by the jump to the top of the next column. This is especially troublesome when column bottoms are lined up.

Solutions include editing text or using uneven (scalloped) column bottoms.

BOX-ITIS AND RULE-ITIS

Avoid overusing boxes and rules.

Too many bordered elements on a page lead to overly compartmentalized pages. This can easily occur in newsletters if you use a box to frame each page, then add internal boxes around elements (e.g., nameplates, mastheads, pull-quotes, sidebars and the table of contents).

The result is a "busy" effect that interferes with easy reading.

To avoid a "busy" design, use rules and boxes with restraint .

Likewise, too many horizontal rules can break up the natural flow of the page.

Heavy rules next to headlines of approximately the same height can overwhelm the headlines.

SIMILAR TYPEFACES

Strive for maximum contrast when using more than one typeface on a page or within a publication.

Strive for contrast when choosing more than one typeface.

When using different typefaces for headlines and text, for example, go for contrast. Avoid typefaces that are similar in appearance. They can distract readers, rather than enhance a page design.

This is Bookman.	This is Helvetica Bold.
The copy is set in Times. The copy is set in Times. The copy is set in Times. The copy is set in Times. The copy is set in Times. The copy is set in Times. The copy is set in Times. The copy is set in Times.	The copy is set in Times. The copy is set in Times. The copy is set in Times. The copy is set in Times. The copy is set in Times. The copy is set in Times. The copy is set in Times. The copy is set in Times.

COPY-FILLED SLIDES AND OVERHEADS

Use as few words as possible in your presentation visuals.

Slides and overheads should support your oral presentation, not replace it.

The more words you use, the smaller your type will have to be, and this reduces the readability of your slides and overheads.

Use presentation graphics to enhance your spoken words.

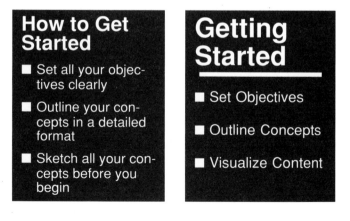

IRREGULARLY SHAPED BLOCKS OF COPY

Avoid the temptation to show off your desktop publishing program's ability to set type in irregular shapes.

Desktop publishing programs may tempt you to ignore the precept that readers read—or decode—words from left to right. It might be fun to set text in the shape of a diamond, cloud or reindeer, but chances are those special effects diminish the overall effectiveness of your communication.

Special effects can diminish the overall effectiveness of your message.

Flush-left type is easiest to read. Lines without a consistent starting point take more time to read and may cause readers to lose track.

Other irregular shapes include lines set on a diagonal margin. Varying indention requires more effort to read.

ANGLED TYPE

Angled type works best in short banners or "teasers," placed in the upper corner of the front page of a magazine or newsletter.

But type that goes uphill or downhill can also interrupt the normal flow of reading. Readers are forced to tilt their heads, tilt the page… or move on without reading.

Lorum ipsum dolor sit amet,
venami quis nostrud laboris
aliquip ex ea com dolor in rep

UNDERLINING

Underlining undermines readability.

Try to use boldface or italic type instead of underlining. More than a few underlined words cause visual clutter and confusion. Also, it takes more time for readers to separate the words from the horizontal lines.

In addition, portions of the descenders often become lost in the underlining, making the letters harder to identify.

WIDOWS AND ORPHANS

Watch for widows and orphans, which can cause unsightly gaps in text columns.

Widows can often be eliminated by editing the text.

A widow is a syllable, word or less than one-third of a line isolated at the bottom of a column, paragraph or page.

> Con minimim venami quis nostrud laboris nisi ut aliquip ex ea com dolor in in nostrud ami quis nostrud laboris nisi ut aliquip ex ea com do minimim venami quis nostrud laboris iquip ex ea com dolor in in nostrud ami quis nostrud laboris nisi ut aliquip.

An orphan is a word isolated at the top of a column or page.

> lorum ip.
>
> Con minimim venami quis nostrud laboris nisi ut aliquip ex ea com dolor in in nostrud ami quis nostrud laboris nisi ut aliquip ex ea com do minimim venami quis nostrud laboris nisi ut aliquip ex ea com

Widows and orphans can usually be eliminated by editing the text. Often, adding or subtracting a word or two is enough to adjust line endings and eliminate those awkward lines.

UNEQUAL SPACING

Strive for consistent spacing between the elements that make up an advertisement or publication.

The human eye is extremely sensitive to small variations in spacing. Inconsistent spacing can brand your work as careless and unworthy of serious notice, and give the impression that your message isn't very important.

Consistent spacing is key to quality design.

Pay particular attention to the space between headlines in relation to top and side borders, and headlines and text:

An Analysis of the Factors That Influence the Cost of Living Index

Rising Fuel Costs Increase Heating and Transportation Costs

Lorum ipsum dolor sit amet, con; minimim venami quis nostrud laboris nisi ut aliquip ex ea com dolor in reprehenderit in voluptate nonumy. Minimum veniam quis nostrud laboris nisi ut aliquip ex ea com dolor in reprehenderit in voluptate nonumy.

Lorum ipsum dolor sit amet, con; minimim venami quis nostrud laboris nisi ut aliquip ex ea com dolor in nderit in voluptate nonumy reprehenderit in voluptate nonumy.

Lorum ipsum dolor sit amet, con;

nisi ut aliquip ex ea com dolor in reprehenderit in voluptate nonumy. Minimum veniami quis nostrud laboris nisi ut aliquip ex ea Veniami quis nostrud laboris nisi ut aliquip ex ea com dolor in reprehenderit in volup tate nonumy.

Food Shortages Abroad Can Raise Domestic Food Prices

Laboris nisi ut aliquip ex ea com dolor in reprehenderit in voluptate nonumy.

Lorum ipsum dolor sit amet, con; minimim venami quis nostrud laboris

Faculty Pay Raises Increase Education Costs

Lorum ipsum dolor sit amet, con; minimim venami quis nostrud laboris nisi ut aliquip ex ea com dolor in reprehenderit in voluptate nonumy.

rehenderit in voluptate nonumy. Minimum veniami quis nostrud laboris nisi ut aliquip ex ea com dolor in reprehenderit in voluptate nonumy.

Lorum ipsum dolor sit amet, con; minimim venami quis nostrud laboris nisi ut aliquip ex ea com dolor in reprehenderit in voluptateveniami quis nostrud laboris nisi ut aliquip ex ea com dolor in reprehenderit in vo

Subheads and text:

Captions and artwork:

Spacing affects the impact of headings and artwork.

Lorum ipsum dolor sit amet, con; minimim venami quis nostrud laboris nisi ut aliquip ex ea com dolor in reprehenderit in voluptate nonumy.

Artwork and text:

Column endings and bottom margins:

EXAGGERATED TABS AND INDENTS

Default tabs and indents in word-processed text files should be altered to be proportionate with the type size and column width.

Adjust tabs to make them proportional to column widths.

Without modification, the first lines of each paragraph are often indented too deeply. (Standard five-space paragraph indents commonly used for word-processed documents often create distracting gaps in desktop-published multicolumn text.) Wide columns with large type usually require deeper tabs and indents than narrow columns with small type.

EXCESSIVE HYPHENATION

Switch to manual hyphenation or adjust the hyphenation zone when too many words are hyphenated.

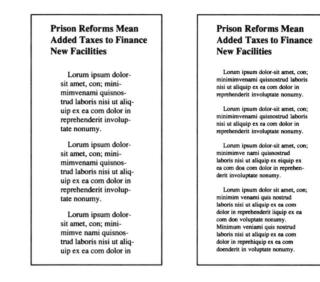

Excessive hyphenation occurs in narrow columns of type. Solutions include reducing type size, increasing column width or choosing flush-left/ragged-right alignment.

Increasing the hyphenation zone allows longer words at the end of each line (although excessive word spacing might result).

Manual hyphenation gives you control over which words are hyphenated and which are moved intact to the next line.

CRAMPED LOGOS AND ADDRESSES

Design your advertisements from the bottom up.

Often, a firm's logo, address, phone number and other buying information are difficult to read because they're treated as if they were an afterthought. To avoid that, build your documents around the logo and other vital information.

Treat your logo and address as primary design elements.

The logo and address in the first example below look like they were added at the last minute. The address and phone number are hard to read. In the second example, however, the logo and address are more readable.

(You might create a separate graphic file with a drawing program, consisting of your firm's logo, address and other information that will appear in every issue of your publication. That file can be easily added in a single step each time.)

Avoid the "ransom note" school of typography.

Use only enough type styles to organize your text.

TOO MANY TYPEFACES

Avoid a potpourri of typefaces, type sizes and weights.

One of the most common desktop publishing mistakes is to include too many typefaces on a single page. The effect is amateurish and confusing.

Discipline yourself to practice restraint. Use the minimum number of typefaces, type sizes and weights necessary to organize your information and create a hierarchy of importance. Each variation in typeface, size or weight slows down the reader.

MOVING ON

Now that you're familiar with the basic philosophy of practical desktop design and the basic tools of organization and emphasis, it's time to apply that knowledge to specific advertisements, brochures, newsletters and other projects.

The examples in Section Two illustrate successful applications of the tools of graphic design. They also show how the appearance and communicating power of an advertisement or publication can be improved by simply rearranging the elements or providing greater contrast between them.

SECTION TWO

Makeovers:
Putting Your Knowledge to Work

7 | PUTTING YOUR KNOWLEDGE to WORK

This section offers a gallery of graphic design examples that have been "made over," giving you a before-and-after perspective and the opportunity to examine first-hand the ingredients of successful page design. You may be surprised to see how a common problem can be resolved with a few minor changes.

As you read this section, try to focus on concepts rather than specific document types. For example, a three-column layout for an advertisement also might work well for your newsletter. A more creative logo placement in a brochure may provide a solution for improving the appearance of your letterhead.

The original samples and makeovers should help you understand how basic elements of graphic design work together to produce attractive printed materials.

Brochures (Original)

This brochure presents the reader with competing messages because of an inappropriate combination of typefaces, type styles and type sizes. Which message is most important? Which should be read first?

Ordering information comes too soon—it precedes the product information.

Too many type sizes and styles create confusion.

Inconsistent margin treatments (sometimes centered, sometimes flush-left) interrupt the continuity and slow the reading process.

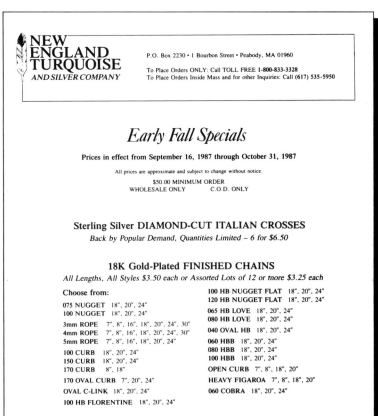

Brochures (Makeover)

White space is essential in pieces that contain a lot of detailed information. Note how white space has been reorganized to direct the eyes to important body copy.

The logo, address and ordering information are moved to the bottom of the page, allowing the "Early Fall Specials" a prominent place at the top.

A three-column grid gives readers easier access to product categories and descriptions.

Each item is introduced by a subhead set in a heavier weight.

Ordering information is emphasized in a screened box at the bottom of the page.

The "call-to-action" phone number is set in larger type.

Advertisements (Original)

When illustrations and type styles in ads and flyers conflict with one another, the intended message can get lost in the confusion.

Drawings of individuals busy answering phones don't project the image of a centralized, national answering service.

Unnecessary duplication of telephone numbers further detracts from the message.

Advertisements (Makeover)

This piece is strengthened dramatically by focusing on a single dominant visual and restructuring it into a three-column format.

The ad has been rebuilt around a drawing with true communicating power—a U.S. map.

The map has been stylized to reduce unnecessary detail.

A drop shadow effectively "pops" the map from the screened area.

Captions detailing the benefits of a nationwide 800 number prominently surround the illustration.

The bottom of the ad is weighted by Network Express's enlarged 800 numbers. Phone numbers and addresses should always appear prominently in ad copy.

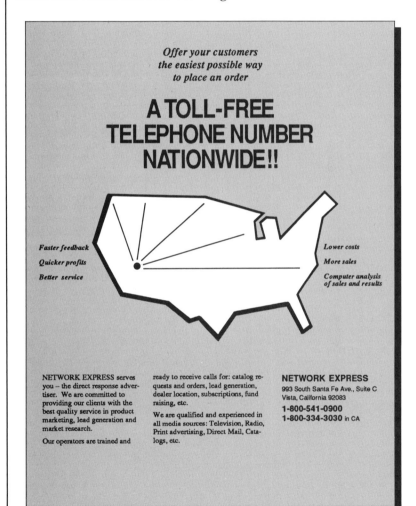

Advertisement (Original)

All the text is treated with equal strength. As a result, no concept or benefit clearly emerges.

The rhetorical question the copy begins with will probably turn off all but the most determined reader.

The page border lacks definition and character.

(Makeover)

Reducing the border and extending the keypad visual to break out of the box above and below make the ad appear larger.

The most important word has been significantly increased in size and shadowed, giving a three-dimensional effect.

Important words and the phone number, the call to action, are significantly larger than subordinate information.

Text alignment reflecting the diagonal shape of the graphic integrates text and visual.

Advertisement (Original)

The image of a house being struck by lightning may cause a negative reaction, making the advertisement more a hindrance than a help to this business.

A potpourri of type styles and sizes creates confusion in this small ad.

The small, underlined headline looks like the most insignificant line of copy in the ad.

(Makeover)

Simple graphic accents and a typographic overhaul create a more cohesive, appealing effect.

Similar type sizes link the headline and phone number, the most important items in the ad.

Screens of different values in the lightning image create interesting effects.

Catalogs (Original)

Catalogs and price lists without illustrations present a unique set of design challenges. Type must be handled skillfully to avoid visual monotony.

Often, a symmetrical type treatment provides too little contrast to fully engage the reader.

Note how undifferentiated spacing creates a run-on effect, further discouraging readers.

NORMAN ROCKWELL
323 MAGAZINE COVERS
By Finch. 456 pages. Huge. 12 x 15¼. This magnificent, large-format, full color volume spans the artist's long and prolific career, reproducing 332 of his cover paintings for the SATURDAY EVENING POST, LADIES HOME JOURNAL and other magazines. Published at **$85.00**. Only **$45.00**.

GREAT MAGAZINE COVERS OF THE WORLD
By Kery. 384 pages. 9¼ x 12. A panorama of more than 500 great magazine covers (most reproduced in full color) from 20 countries, spanning a century-and-a-half of magazine publishing around the world. Including examples from 200 19th and 20th century magazines. Published at **$65.00**. Only **$45.00**.

VASARELY
150 pages. 9¾ x 13. 180 illustrations, including 64 full color plates. Masterful reproductions and a text by the artist combine to form an authoritative yet personal study of one of the major figures of modern art. Published at **$60.00**. Only **$35.00**.

CHAGALL BY CHAGALL
Sorlier. 262 pages. 11¼ x 12. 285 illustrations, including 83 full color plates. Illustrated autobiography. Published at **$50.00**. Only **$40.00**.

MAXFIELD PARRISH
By Ludwig. 223 pages. 9 x 12. 184 illustrations, 64 in full color. Published at **$25.00**. Only **$18.00**.

THE GREAT BOOK OF
FRENCH IMPRESSIONISM
By Kelder. 448 pages. 12 x 15¼. Over 400 illustrations, including 200 full color plates and 16 spectacular full color fold-outs. Huge, exquisitely produced treasury of French Impressionist art, packed with full-page reproductions. Examines the lives and works of all the major Impressionists and Post-Impressionists. Published at **$100.00**. Now **$59.95**.

CARL FABERGE
Goldsmith to the Imperial Court of Russia
By Snowman. 100 pages. 8¼ x 10½. Over 185 photos, 111 in full color. Originally Published at **$35.00**. Only **$22.00**.

CONTEMPORARY PAINTING
By Vogt. 135 pages. 7½ x 10½. Over 50 in full color. Penetrating analysis of post World War II European and American art. Including paintings by Jaspar Johns, Andy Warhol, Roy Lichtenstein, Jackson Pollock, others. **$19.95**. Now — **$14.95**.

TWENTIETH CENTURY MASTERS
OF EROTIC ART
By Smith. 212 pages. 9 x 12. 190 full color plates presents erotic works by such top-ranking artists as Picasso, Segal, Dali, Ernst, Rauschenberg, Rivers, Warhol, Schiele and others, many of which have never been displayed in public exhibitions. **$30.00**. Now — **$20.00**.

LEONARDO DA VINCI
538 pages. 11 x 14½. Huge. 1,635 illustrations, including many large full color plates. Originally published in Italy by the Instituto Geografico De Agostini, this new edition is the most lavish, authoritative ever produced. Published at **$60.00**. Only **$50.00**.

REMBRANDT PAINTINGS
By Gerson. 527 pages. 11 x 14½. Huge. Over 730 illustrations, including many large full color plates. Complete, authoritative and beautiful presentation of the great master's work. Written by one of the world's foremost Rembrandt authorities. The book was thirty years in the making in Amsterdam, and is lavishly illustrated with spectacular reproductions. Published at **$60.00**. Only **$50.00**.

ENGLISH CAMEO GLASS
By Grover. 480 pages. 8 x 11. A wealth of rare firsthand material and over 1,000 color and black and white plates makes this book an invaluable reference. Published at **$50.00**. Now **$25.00**.

20,000 YEARS OF WORLD PAINTING
By Jaffe. 416 pages. 9 x 13. Historical survey from early to modern art. 1,000 reproductions in full color. Was **$50.00** Now **$27.00**.

STAINED GLASS
By Seddon & Stephens. 205 pages. 473 full color photos. 11 x 14. Covers stained glass from the beginning to the present. Was **$39.95** Now **$19.95**.

THE COMPLETE BOOK OF EROTIC ART
By Kronhausen. 781 black and white plates. Extraordinary collection of the world's erotic art from Japan, China, India, Renaissance masters and modern greats. Originally Published in 2 Volumes at **$50.00**. New, Complete 1 Volume Editon Only **$25.00**.

COLLECTING POLITICAL AMERICANA
By Sullivan 1980. 250 pages. 8 x 11. 400 illustrations. Packed with reading. Out of print. **$15.95**. Now **$10.00**.

DIAMONDS
Myth, Magic and Reality Revised Edition. Over 420 full color illustrations. Beautiful and informative look at the world's most magnificent and mysterious stone. Tells how to recognize and appreciate quality stones, more. 288 pages. Large. 10¼ x 12. Originally Published at **$50.00**. Only **$29.95**.

THE GREAT BOOK OF JEWELS
By Heininger. 206 full color plates. 94 black and white photos. The most spectacular, lavishly illustrated, comprehensive volume ever published on jewels and jewelry. Nearly 300 photos specially made for this volume, many gems never available for public inspection before. Includes bibliography, table of gemstones; much more. Huge 11¾ x 13¾. Published at **$69.50**. Now **$29.95**.

10

Catalogs (Makeover)

Subtle changes in spacing and typeface create contrast and promote readability.

The two-column format is retained, but body copy is set ragged-right (instead of justified) to add contrast and break up type.

Titles now appear in sans-serif type, which provides more contrast to body copy.

The "Reference Art Books" logo (taken from the front cover) has been reversed and repeated on each page.

The firm's toll-free phone number is repeated on each page, creating a consistent response mechanism.

Norman Rockwell: 323 Magazine Covers
By Finch, 456 pages. Huge. 12 x 15 1/4. This magnificent, large-format, full color volume spans the artist's long and prolific career, reproduction 332 of his cover paintings for the SATURDAY EVENING POST, LADIES HOME JOURNAL and other magazines. Published at $85.00. Only $45.00.

Great Magazine Covers of the World
By Kery. 384 pages. 9 1/4 x 12. A panorama of more than 500 great magazine covers (most reproduced in full color) from 20 countries, spanning a century-and-a-half of magazine publishing around the world. Examples from 200 19th and 20th century magazines. Published at $65.00. Only $45.00.

Vasarely
150 page. 9 3/4 x 13. 180 illustrations, including 64 full color plates. Masterful reproductions and a text by the artist combine to form an authoritative yet personal study of one of the major figures of modern art. Published at $60.00. Only $35.00.

Chagall by Chagall
Sorlier. 262 pages. 11 1/4 x 12. 285 illustrations, including 83 full color plates. Illustrated autobiography. Published at $50.00. Only $40.00.

Maxfield Parrish
By Ludwig. 223 pages. 9 x 12. 184 illustrations, 64 in full color. Published at $25.00. Now $20.00.

The Great Book of French Impressionism
By Kelder. 448 pages. 12 x 15 1/4. Over 400 illustrations, including 200 full color plates and 16 spectacular full color fold-outs. Huge, exquisitely produced treasury of French Impressionist art, packed with full-page reproductions. Examines the lives and works of all the major Impressionists and Post-Impressionists. Published at $100.00. Now $59.95.

Carl Faberge
Goldsmith to the Imperial Court of Russia
By Snowman. 100 page. 8 1/4 x 10 1/2. Over 185 photos, 111 in full color. Originally Published at $35.00. Only $22.00.

Contemporary Painting
By Vogt. 135 pages. 7 1/2 x 10 1/2. Over 50 in full color. Penetrating analysis of post World War II European and American art. Including paintings by Jaspar Johns. Andy Warhol, Roy Lichtenstein, Jackson Pollock, others. $19.95. Now $14.95.

Twentieth Century Masters of Erotic Art
By Smith. 212 pages. 9 x 12. 190 full color plates presents erotic works by such top-ranking artists as Picasso, Dali, Ernst, Rauschenberg, Rivers. Warhol, and others, many of which have never been displayed in public exhibitions. Only $25.00.

Leonardo Da Vinci
538 page. 11 x 14 1/2. Huge. 1,635 illustrations including many large full color plates. Originally published in Italy by the Instituto Geografico De Agostini, this new edition is the most lavish, authoritative ever produced. Published at $60.00. Only $50.00.

Rembrandt Paintings
By Gerson. 527 pages 11 x 14 1/2. Huge. Over 730 illustrations, including many large full color plates. Complete, authoritative and beautiful presentation of the great master's work. Written by one of the world's foremost Rembrandt authorities. The book was thirty years in the making in Amsterdam, and is lavishly illustrated with spectacular reproductions. Published at $60.00. Only $50.00.

English Cameo Glass
By Grover. 480 pages. 8 x 11. A wealth of rare first-hand material and over 1,000 color and black and white plates makes this book an invaluable reference. Published at $50.00. Now $30.00.

20,000 Years of World Painting
By Jaffe. 416 pages. 9 x 13. Historical survey from early to modern art. 1,000 reproductions in full color. Was $50.00. Now $19.95.

Stained Glass
By Seddon & Stephens. 205 pages. 473 full color photos. 11 x 14. Covers stained glass from the beginning to the present. Was $39.95 Now $19.95.

The Complete Book of Erotic Art
By Allen. More than 300 Paintings and Drawings. Over 100 in full color. Many never before reproduced. 9 x 12. Originally Published at $29.95. Now $19.95.

Collecting Political Americana
By Schrade. 93 illustrations. 40 hand tipped plates in color. First major survey on the subject in English. Rare out of print. 137 pages. Only $25.00.

Diamonds
By McCracken. A biography and picture gallery of the dean of Indian painters. 170 color and black and white illustrations. He lived and worked among 48 Indian tribes. Catlin's paintings are authentic depictions of daily life of the native Americans. 9 x 11. Out of print. $18.50.

The Great Book of Jewels
By Rawls. 488 pages. 11 3/4 x 15 format. Over 400 large reproductions, including over 300 full color plates. Presents the largest number of Currier & Ives prints ever reproduced in a single volume. Huge. Published at $100.00. Only $55.00.

Reference Art Books   Phone TOLL-FREE 1-800-238-8288

Correspondence (Original)

Letters produced on a typewriter lack the professional appearance of desktop-typeset output.

There are too many words on the page. Margins are minuscule.

Indented items are indistinct from each other and from body copy.

The uniform type size throughout lacks color and dynamics.

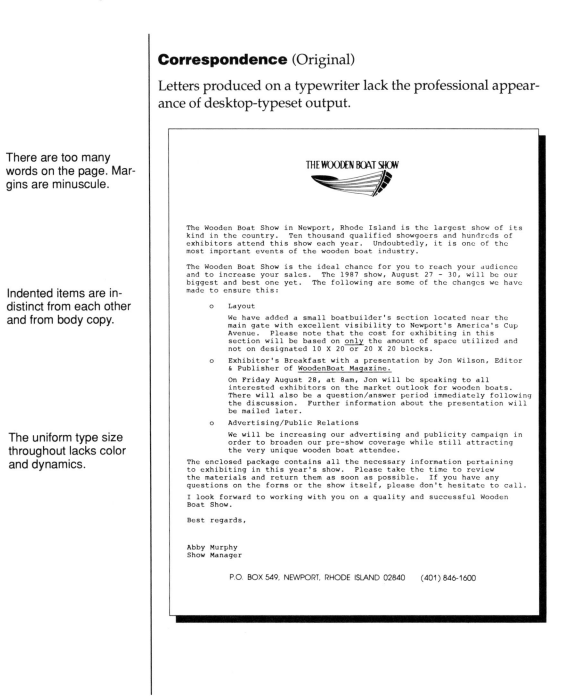

THE WOODEN BOAT SHOW

The Wooden Boat Show in Newport, Rhode Island is the largest show of its kind in the country. Ten thousand qualified showgoers and hundreds of exhibitors attend this show each year. Undoubtedly, it is one of the most important events of the wooden boat industry.

The Wooden Boat Show is the ideal chance for you to reach your audience and to increase your sales. The 1987 show, August 27 - 30, will be our biggest and best one yet. The following are some of the changes we have made to ensure this:

   o   Layout

      We have added a small boatbuilder's section located near the main gate with excellent visibility to Newport's America's Cup Avenue. Please note that the cost for exhibiting in this section will be based on <u>only</u> the amount of space utilized and not on designated 10 X 20 or 20 X 20 blocks.

   o   Exhibitor's Breakfast with a presentation by Jon Wilson, Editor & Publisher of <u>WoodenBoat Magazine.</u>

      On Friday August 28, at 8am, Jon will be speaking to all interested exhibitors on the market outlook for wooden boats. There will also be a question/answer period immediately following the discussion. Further information about the presentation will be mailed later.

   o   Advertising/Public Relations

      We will be increasing our advertising and publicity campaign in order to broaden our pre-show coverage while still attracting the very unique wooden boat attendee.

The enclosed package contains all the necessary information pertaining to exhibiting in this year's show. Please take the time to review the materials and return them as soon as possible. If you have any questions on the forms or the show itself, please don't hesitate to call.

I look forward to working with you on a quality and successful Wooden Boat Show.

Best regards,

Abby Murphy
Show Manager

P.O. BOX 549, NEWPORT, RHODE ISLAND 02840   (401) 846-1600

Correspondence (Makeover)

Even the simplest desktop publishing techniques can greatly improve letters to selected recipients.

To unify the letterhead, the illustration has been moved to the left and integrated with the address.

A salutation engages the reader.

A highly readable Times Roman serif typeface condenses the message.

Boldface type contrasts subheads with text.

The copy for indented sections is set smaller, with reduced leading.

The letter ends by returning to a single wide column that matches the first paragraph.

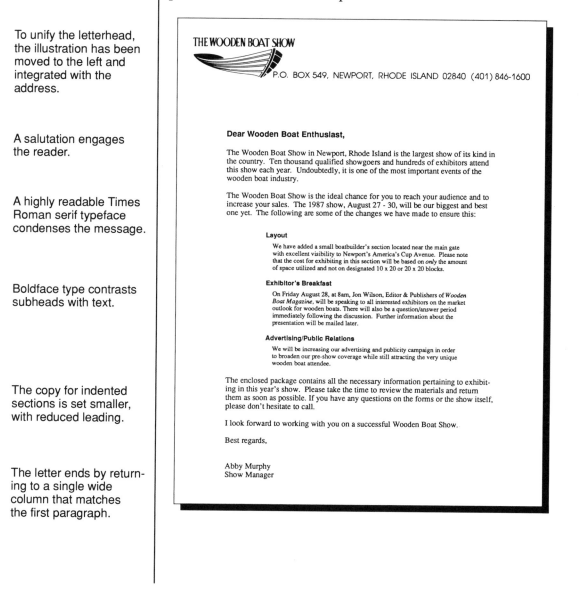

THE WOODEN BOAT SHOW

P.O. BOX 549, NEWPORT, RHODE ISLAND 02840 (401) 846-1600

Dear Wooden Boat Enthusiast,

The Wooden Boat Show in Newport, Rhode Island is the largest show of its kind in the country. Ten thousand qualified showgoers and hundreds of exhibitors attend this show each year. Undoubtedly, it is one of the most important events of the wooden boat industry.

The Wooden Boat Show is the ideal chance for you to reach your audience and to increase your sales. The 1987 show, August 27 - 30, will be our biggest and best one yet. The following are some of the changes we have made to ensure this:

Layout

We have added a small boatbuilder's section located near the main gate with excellent visibility to Newport's America's Cup Avenue. Please note that the cost for exhibiting in this section will be based on *only* the amount of space utilized and not on designated 10 x 20 or 20 x 20 blocks.

Exhibitor's Breakfast

On Friday August 28, at 8am, Jon Wilson, Editor & Publishers of *Wooden Boat Magazine*, will be speaking to all interested exhibitors on the market outlook for wooden boats. There will also be a question/answer period immediately following the discussion. Further information about the presentation will be mailed later.

Advertising/Public Relations

We will be increasing our advertising and publicity campaign in order to broaden our pre-show coverage while still attracting the very unique wooden boat attendee.

The enclosed package contains all the necessary information pertaining to exhibiting in this year's show. Please take the time to review the materials and return them as soon as possible. If you have any questions on the forms or the show itself, please don't hesitate to call.

I look forward to working with you on a successful Wooden Boat Show.

Best regards,

Abby Murphy
Show Manager

Flyers (Original)

On this and the next three pages, two similar "question-and-answer" motifs are manipulated to produce different but effective results.

The question marks are redundant because the headline and content clearly communicate the Q&A format.

The text and visuals are crowded.

Answers beginning with a single, boldface word (e.g., "Yes!") look as if they might belong with the preceding boldface question.

Answers to Questions Frequently Asked about Tri-Steel Homes

1. What is the Tri-Steel concept and why is it different from conventional wood frame construction?

The Tri-Steel concept is based upon the utilization and superior quality and strength of steel to form the "frame" or "shell" of a home. This allows the home to be "stick built" on site, but with steel instead of wood and with bolts and fasteners instead of nails and staples.

The superior strength of steel means that frame spacing can be on 6-foot and 8-foot centers instead of 16-inch and 24-inch centers. Plus, we can utilize 9 inches of insulation on the sides and also provide consistent quality, less maintenance, and much greater strength than is possible with conventional construction. In addition, this gives you much greater flexibility inside the home since none of the walls need to be load bearing. **Also important, the entire shell can often be dried-in within 4 to 5 days by an inexperienced crew.**

2. How are Tri-Steel homes unique?

Our homes utilize an engineered and computer designed steel structural system. You can choose from a wide selection of contemporary slant wall designs which stand out among conventional wooden structures or numerous conventional-looking straight wall designs ranging from conservatively gabled roof lines to ultra-modern units allowing clerestory window placement.

3. What are some of the advantages of Tri-Steel homes?

Tri-Steel homes can cost less to erect and can go up much faster. They are exceptionally energy efficient, require almost no exterior maintenance, and are tremendously flexible in their design. In addition to these areas of savings, they offer the strength and durability of steel to withstand extreme weather conditions, termites and fire. The quality of steel is consistently high. Pre-engineered framing components ensure your home goes up one way — **the RIGHT way!** Special snow or wind loads are possible with very little extra cost. They also meet Seismic 4 earthquake specifications - the highest rating required.

4. Have these homes been tried and proven?

Absolutely! In terms of the history of home building, Tri-Steel homes are a new and unique concept; however, these homes have been in use throughout the South for over ten years. Tri-Steel has thousands of structures all across the nation and we are constantly receiving letters from satisfied homeowners attesting to the beauty, strength and energy savings of Tri-Steel structures.

5. Can I put up one of these homes myself and is construction assistance available?

Yes! The home is actually designed to be constructed independently by the buyer. No heavy lifting equipment or special tools are required. The steel beams are designed to bolt together — A to B, B to C — with prepunched holes so you are basically working with a giant erector set. No cutting or welding is required on the job site and complete instructions and drawings are included with the package. Tri-Steel can provide your choice of construction assistance. As part of the assistance available, we can consult with you over the phone, have your shell erected, or provide on-site supervision on a daily or weekly basis.

6. How much flexibility do I have in choosing a home size?

Infinite! A virtually unlimited variety of home sizes are offered from 800 square feet on up. Our homes come in one, two or three level designs with slant or straight walls. We have hundreds of plans drawn and available for immediate mailing and we can also draw custom designs to meet virtually any floor plan or size requirements.

7. Can I add to the home at a later date?

Yes! Additional space may be added in the future at low cost and relative ease allowing you to enlarge your home economically as your needs and income requires.

Flyers (Makeover)

This informative "magazine style" format uses creative type treatments to lure the reader into the piece.

Question marks and illustrations have been omitted to allow larger type and more white space.

Numbers in drop-cap style create further contrast and visual tension that attract attention.

Answers now appear in a different typeface, which helps distinguish them from the questions.

The Tri-Steel logo feature is now larger and more readable.

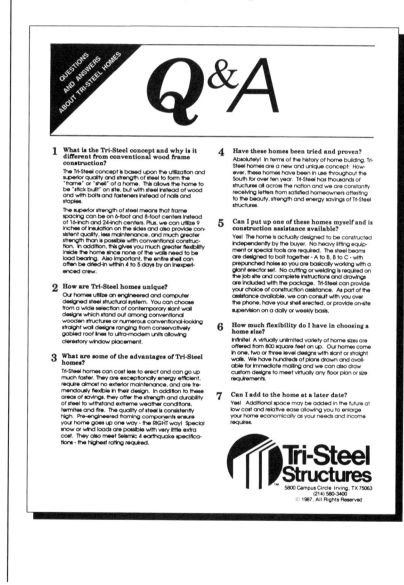

QUESTIONS AND ANSWERS ABOUT TRI-STEEL HOMES

Q&A

1 What is the Tri-Steel concept and why is it different from conventional wood frame construction?

The Tri-Steel concept is based upon the utilization and superior quality and strength of steel to form the "frame" or "shell" of a home. This allows the home to be "stick built" on site, but with steel instead of wood and with bolts and fasteners instead of nails and staples.

The superior strength of steel means that frame spacing can be on 6-foot and 8-foot centers instead of 16-inch and 24-inch centers. Plus, we can utilize 9 inches of insulation on the sides and also provide consistent quality, less maintenance, and much greater strength than is possible with conventional construction. In addition, this gives you much greater flexibility inside the home since none of the walls need to be load bearing. Also important, the entire shell can often be dried-in within 4 to 5 days by an inexperienced crew.

2 How are Tri-Steel homes unique?

Our homes utilize an engineered and computer designed steel structural system. You can choose from a wide selection of contemporary slant wall designs which stand out among conventional wooden structures or numerous conventional-looking straight wall designs ranging from conservatively gabled roof lines to ultra-modern units allowing clerestory window placement.

3 What are some of the advantages of Tri-Steel homes?

Tri-Steel homes can cost less to erect and can go up much faster. They are exceptionally energy efficient, require almost no exterior maintenance, and are tremendously flexible in their design. In addition to these areas of savings, they offer the strength and durability of steel to withstand extreme weather conditions, termites and fire. The quality of steel is consistently high. Pre-engineered framing components ensure your home goes up one way - the RIGHT way! Special snow or wind loads are possible with very little extra cost. They also meet Seismic 4 earthquake specifications - the highest rating required.

4 Have these homes been tried and proven?

Absolutely! In terms of the history of home building, Tri-Steel homes are a new and unique concept. However, these homes have been in use throughout the South for over ten year. Tri-Steel has thousands of structures all across the nation and we are constantly receiving letters from satisfied homeowners attesting to the beauty, strength and energy savings of Tri-Steel structures.

5 Can I put up one of these homes myself and is construction assistance available?

Yes! The home is actually designed to be constructed independently by the buyer. No heavy lifting equipment or special tools are required. The steel beams are designed to bolt together - A to B, B to C - with prepunched holes so you are basically working with a giant erector set. No cutting or welding is required on the job site and complete instructions and drawings are included with the package. Tri-Steel can provide your choice of construction assistance. As part of the assistance available, we can consult with you over the phone, have your shell erected, or provide on-site supervision on a daily or weekly basis.

6 How much flexibility do I have in choosing a home size?

Infinite! A virtually unlimited variety of home sizes are offered from 800 square feet on up. Our homes come in one, two or three level designs with slant or straight walls. We have hundreds of plans drawn and available for immediate mailing and we can also draw custom designs to meet virtually any floor plan or size requirements.

7 Can I add to the home at a later date?

Yes! Additional space may be added in the future at low cost and relative ease allowing you to enlarge your home economically as your needs and income requires.

Tri-Steel Structures

5800 Campus Circle Irving, TX 75063
(214) 580-3400
© 1987, All Rights Reserved

Flyers (Original)

Too much copy crammed into a small space creates a "dark" look that discourages reading.

The company name, SPORT IT, disappears into the headline.

Questions set in bold, uppercase type are hard to read.

Answers are also difficult to read because the type size is too small in proportion to the line length.

Justified type creates exaggerated word spacing and often produces widows.

THE MOST FREQUENTLY ASKED QUESTIONS ABOUT A SPORT IT DEALERSHIP

1. **WHAT IS THE INITIAL INVESTMENT FOR A SPORT IT DEALERSHIP?**

   $1,500.

2. **IS THERE A ROYALTY OR SERVICE FEE?**

   There is no royalty fee, however, there is a minimal $25.00 service fee to cover the following: monthly newsletters, toll free consultation service and on-going research for obtaining new suppliers. This $25.00 service fee is due the 10th of each month and can not fluctuate during the five year term of the Sport It Dealer Agreement.

3. **ARE THERE ANY OTHER FEES OR CHARGES?**

   Yes. There is a $100.00 renewal fee at the end of the five year term of the Agreement which will renew the Agreement for an additional five year period. Also, if you elect to sell your dealership or transfer to a new location a $100.00 transfer fee is needed to cover the cost of changes and modifications to our records, files, et cetera.

4. **WHAT QUALIFICATIONS ARE NEEDED TO BECOME A SPORT IT DEALER?**

   The Sport It Home Office receives over 1,600 inquiries per month. From these inquiries nearly 400 applications are received. The evaluation committee selects approximately 40 applicants that will become Sport It Dealers. These applicants must have a good credit standing, positive references and have potential to represent Sport It as professional dealers.

5. **WHAT DO I RECEIVE FOR MY INITIAL INVESTMENT OF $1,500?**

   The initial $1,500 investment provides you with a business opportunity allowing immediate access to brand name merchandise at very competitive prices which would not be available to you as an independent dealer. The Sport It Dealership puts you in business immediately. You will receive catalogs, price lists, purchase order forms, an Operations Manual and miscellaneous samples in your initial box of materials.

6. **WHAT IS THE TERM OF THE SPORT IT DEALERSHIP AGREEMENT?**

   Five years.

7. **MAY I HAVE A PARTNER OR PARTNERS WITH MY SPORT IT DEALERSHIP?**

   Yes. You may have as many partners as you wish.

8. **ARE THERE ANY TAX ADVANTAGES WITH MY SPORT IT DEALERSHIP?**

   There are many tax advantages available for your home operated business. A portion of your rent, house payment, electricity, heat, insurance, taxes, et cetera, can be used as deductions. In addition, automobile expenses and depreciation may be deducted according to the percentage that your vehicle is used for business.

9. **CAN I FINANCE MY INITIAL INVESTMENT OF $1,500?**

   The initial $1,500 investment can be charged to your MasterCard or Visa credit card enabling you to make monthly payments for your Sport it Dealership.

10. **CAN I SELL MY SPORT IT DEALERSHIP?**

    Yes. Some Dealers, due to unforeseen circumstances, have had to sell their Dealership. Most Dealers who have sold their Dealership have done so at a substantial profit.

Flyers (Makeover)

A three-column format clearly separates questions and answers, letting readers pick and choose according to their specific interests.

The company name is reversed and enlarged for greater impact and recognition.

A "friendlier" typeface and flush-left/ragged-right alignment have been used for all text.

A three-column format, with questions appearing in the narrow left-hand column, provides better organization and more white space.

Shorter lines set in narrower columns make the answers more readable.

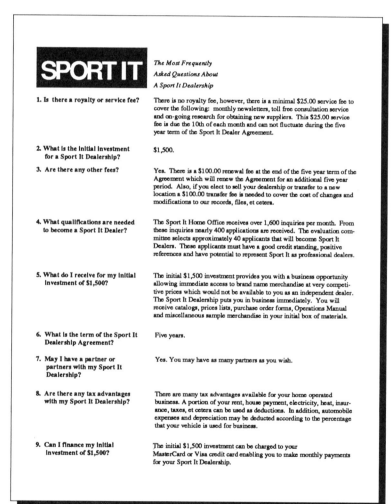

SPORT IT

The Most Frequently Asked Questions About A Sport It Dealership

1. **Is there a royalty or service fee?**

   There is no royalty fee, however, there is a minimal $25.00 service fee to cover the following: monthly newsletters, toll free consultation service and on-going research for obtaining new suppliers. This $25.00 service fee is due the 10th of each month and can not fluctuate during the five year term of the Sport It Dealer Agreement.

2. **What is the initial investment for a Sport It Dealership?**

   $1,500.

3. **Are there any other fees?**

   Yes. There is a $100.00 renewal fee at the end of the five year term of the Agreement which will renew the Agreement for an additional five year period. Also, if you elect to sell your dealership or transfer to a new location a $100.00 transfer fee is needed to cover the cost of changes and modifications to our records, files, et cetera.

4. **What qualifications are needed to become a Sport It Dealer?**

   The Sport It Home Office receives over 1,600 inquiries per month. From these inquiries nearly 400 applications are received. The evaluation committee selects approximately 40 applicants that will become Sport It Dealers. These applicants must have a good credit standing, positive references and have potential to represent Sport It as professional dealers.

5. **What do I receive for my initial investment of $1,500?**

   The initial $1,500 investment provides you with a business opportunity allowing immediate access to brand name merchandise at very competitive prices which would not be available to you as an independent dealer. The Sport It Dealership puts you in business immediately. You will receive catalogs, prices lists, purchase order forms, Operations Manual and miscellaneous sample merchandise in your initial box of materials.

6. **What is the term of the Sport It Dealership Agreement?**

   Five years.

7. **May I have a partner or partners with my Sport It Dealership?**

   Yes. You may have as many partners as you wish.

8. **Are there any tax advantages with my Sport It Dealership?**

   There are many tax advantages available for your home operated business. A portion of your rent, house payment, electricity, heat, insurance, taxes, et cetera can be used as deductions. In addition, automobile expenses and depreciation may be deducted according to the percentage that your vehicle is used for business.

9. **Can I finance my initial investment of $1,500?**

   The initial $1,500 investment can be charged to your MasterCard or Visa credit card enabling you to make monthly payments for your Sport It Dealership.

User Manuals (Original)

Because of their practical and simple design, user guides, reference manuals and technical documents are ideal formats for desktop publishing.

The copy begins unceremoniously with "READ AND SAVE THESE INSTRUCTIONS."

The "UL" symbol is an unnecessary visual distraction. It is irrelevant by the time the customer gets to the instructions.

The code number (T-1), primarily an internal document tracking number, is given too much prominence. (Such identifiers should be placed in small type on the last page of a document.)

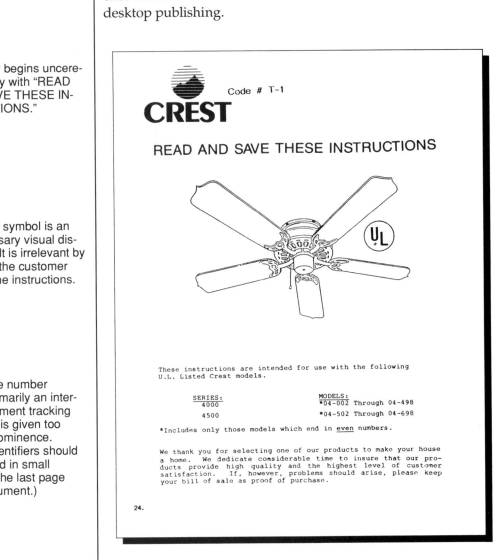

Code # T-1

CREST

READ AND SAVE THESE INSTRUCTIONS

These instructions are intended for use with the following U.L. Listed Crest models.

SERIES:
4000
4500

MODELS:
*04-002 Through 04-498
*04-502 Through 04-698

*Includes only those models which end in even numbers.

We thank you for selecting one of our products to make your house a home. We dedicate considerable time to insure that our products provide high quality and the highest level of customer satisfaction. If, however, problems should arise, please keep your bill of sale as proof of purchase.

24.

User Manuals (Makeover)

Note how a few modifications have made this document more inviting *and* more informative. The page is now usefully organized so that each element—body copy, illustration, table of contents, etc.—is distinguished by its own format.

The heading is now friendlier and not as intimidating.

The illustration has been touched up and screened, strengthening its impact.

Series and model numbers are set closer together at the upper right-hand corner, where the purchaser can quickly find them.

The Crest logo is moved to a bottom corner, where readers are accustomed to finding such information.

A small but complete table of contents balances the introductory paragraph and acts as a quick reference.

HOW TO INSTALL YOUR NEW CREST FAN

These instructions are intended for use with the following U.L. Listed Crest models. Save this manual for future reference.

Series: **4000**
Models: **04-001** through **04-499**

Series:**4500**
Models: **04-501** through **40-699**

TABLE OF CONTENTS:

We thank you for selecting one of our porducts to make your house a home. We dedicate considerable time to insure that our products provide high quality and the highest level of customer satisfaction. If, however, problems should arise, please keep your bill of sale as proof of purchase.

CREST

User Manuals (Original)

On the inside pages, formatting changes are in order, to improve the readability and appeal of the piece.

The wide column of type is gray and monotonous.

The illustration is buried, unconnected to the text.

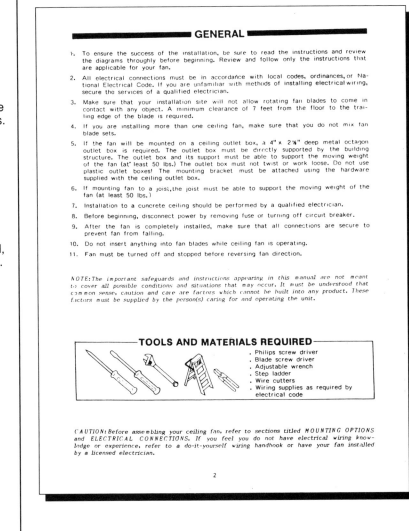

GENERAL

1. To ensure the success of the installation, be sure to read the instructions and review the diagrams throughly before beginning. Review and follow only the instructions that are applicable for your fan.

2. All electrical connections must be in accordance with local codes, ordinances, or National Electrical Code. If you are unfamiliar with methods of installing electrical wiring, secure the services of a qualified electrician.

3. Make sure that your installation site will not allow rotating fan blades to come in contact with any object. A minimum clearance of 7 feet from the floor to the trailing edge of the blade is required.

4. If you are installing more than one ceiling fan, make sure that you do not mix fan blade sets.

5. If the fan will be mounted on a ceiling outlet box, a 4" x 2⅛" deep metal octagon outlet box is required. The outlet box must be directly supported by the building structure. The outlet box and its support must be able to support the moving weight of the fan (at least 50 lbs.) The outlet box must not twist or work loose. Do not use plastic outlet boxes! The mounting bracket must be attached using the hardware supplied with the ceiling outlet box.

6. If mounting fan to a joist, the joist must be able to support the moving weight of the fan (at least 50 lbs.)

7. Installation to a concrete ceiling should be performed by a qualified electrician.

8. Before beginning, disconnect power by removing fuse or turning off circuit breaker.

9. After the fan is completely installed, make sure that all connections are secure to prevent fan from falling.

10. Do not insert anything into fan blades while ceiling fan is operating.

11. Fan must be turned off and stopped before reversing fan direction.

NOTE: The important safeguards and instructions appearing in this manual are not meant to cover all possible conditions and situations that may occur. It must be understood that common sense, caution and care are factors which cannot be built into any product. These factors must be supplied by the person(s) caring for and operating the unit.

TOOLS AND MATERIALS REQUIRED

. Philips screw driver
. Blade screw driver
. Adjustable wrench
. Step ladder
. Wire cutters
. Wiring supplies as required by electrical code

CAUTION: Before assembling your ceiling fan, refer to sections titled MOUNTING OPTIONS and ELECTRICAL CONNECTIONS. If you feel you do not have electrical wiring knowledge or experience, refer to a do-it-yourself wiring handbook or have your fan installed by a licensed electrician.

2

User Manuals (Makeover)

With text, illustrations and caution notes organized into appropriate formats, the user instructions are easier to follow.

Subheads are now set flush-left (flush-right on right-hand pages) so readers can quickly spot major information categories.

The illustration has been moved to the top and screened to call immediate attention to required items.

Horizontal rules have been thickened to match the type size of the headings.

Skillful layout of text and illustrations allows more information on each page.

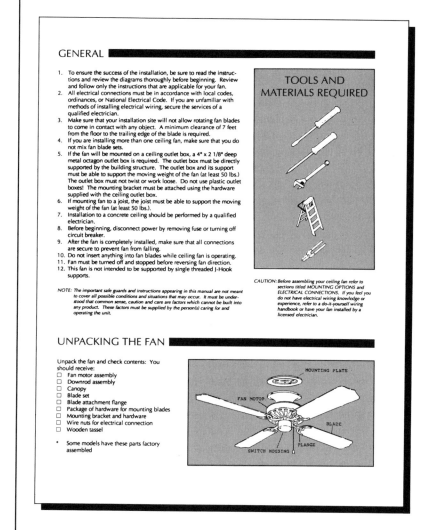

GENERAL

1. To ensure the success of the installation, be sure to read the instructions and review the diagrams thoroughly before beginning. Review and follow only the instructions that are applicable for your fan.
2. All electrical connections must be in accordance with local codes, ordinances, or National Electrical Code. If you are unfamiliar with methods of installing electrical wiring, secure the services of a qualified electrician.
3. Make sure that your installation site will not allow rotating fan blades to come in contact with any object. A minimum clearance of 7 feet from the floor to the trailing edge of the blade is required.
4. If you are installing more than one ceiling fan, make sure that you do not mix fan blade sets.
5. If the fan will be mounted on a ceiling outlet box, a 4" x 2 1/8" deep metal octagon outlet box is required. The outlet box must be directly supported by the building structure. The outlet box and its support must be able to support the moving weight of the fan (at least 50 lbs.) The outlet box must not twist or work loose. Do not use plastic outlet boxes! The mounting bracket must be attached using the hardware supplied with the ceiling outlet box.
6. If mounting fan to a joist, the joist must be able to support the moving weight of the fan (at least 50 lbs.).
7. Installation to a concrete ceiling should be performed by a qualified electrician.
8. Before beginning, disconnect power by removing fuse or turning off circuit breaker.
9. After the fan is completely installed, make sure that all connections are secure to prevent fan from falling.
10. Do not insert anything into fan blades while ceiling fan is operating.
11. Fan must be turned off and stopped before reversing fan direction.
12. This fan is not intended to be supported by single threaded J-Hook supports.

NOTE: The important safe guards and instructions appearing in this manual are not meant to cover all possible conditions and situations that may occur. It must be understood that common sense, caution and care are factors which cannot be built into any product. These factors must be supplied by the person(s) caring for and operating the unit.

TOOLS AND MATERIALS REQUIRED

CAUTION: Before assembling your ceiling fan refer to sections titled MOUNTING OPTIONS and ELECTRICAL CONNECTIONS. If you feel you do not have electrical wiring knowledge or experience, refer to a do-it-yourself wiring handbook or have your fan installed by a licensed electrician.

UNPACKING THE FAN

Unpack the fan and check contents: You should receive:
☐ Fan motor assembly
☐ Downrod assembly
☐ Canopy
☐ Blade set
☐ Blade attachment flange
☐ Package of hardware for mounting blades
☐ Mounting bracket and hardware
☐ Wire nuts for electrical connection
☐ Wooden tassel

* Some models have these parts factory assembled

MOUNTING PLATE
FAN MOTOR
BLADE
FLANGE
SWITCH HOUSING

Advertisements (Original)

Repetition can easily lead to confusion. In this page design, continuity and coherence are sacrificed.

Three repeating headlines waste valuable space and segment the ad unnecessarily.

Phone numbers and hotel information are repeated throughout the piece, creating visual "clutter."

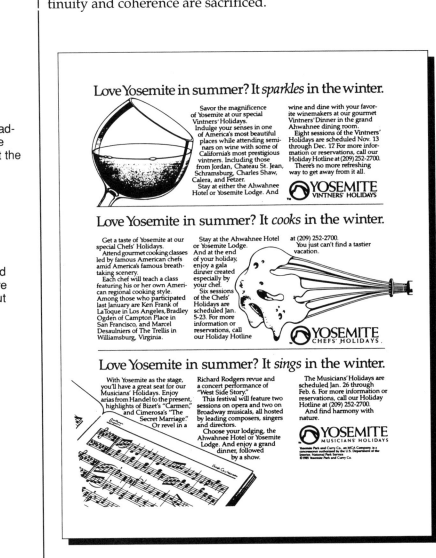

Advertisements (Makeover)

The ad is strengthened and unified considerably by the large headline and the more natural vertical orientation of the columns of body copy.

A single "master headline" now dominates the page.

The headlines from the original ad are retained but used as subheads within the copy.

The original illustrations are reduced and repositioned.

Runaround type effectively ties body copy to illustrations.

The bottom of the ad has been cleaned up and the response vehicle—Yosemite's Holiday Hotline phone number—is now a dominant visual element.

Newsletters (Original)

This piece demonstrates how design principles applied inappropriately can result in a poorly designed document.

The rules in the body copy fight with the illustration box and rules in the nameplate.

Nonproportional typefaces create uneven word spacing.

Indention within narrow columns often causes awkward blocks of white space.

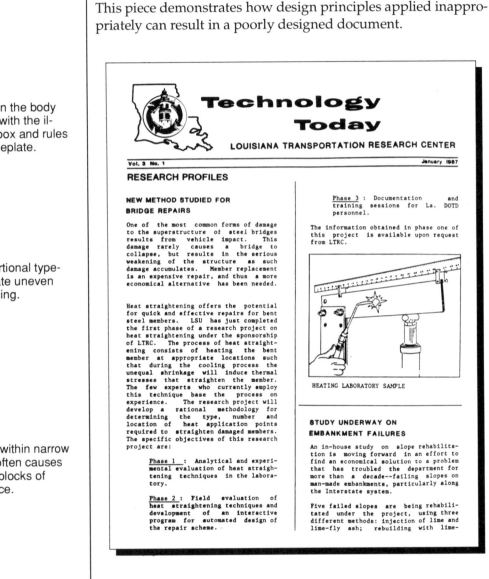

Technology Today

LOUISIANA TRANSPORTATION RESEARCH CENTER

Vol. 3 No. 1   January 1987

RESEARCH PROFILES

NEW METHOD STUDIED FOR BRIDGE REPAIRS

One of the most common forms of damage to the superstructure of steel bridges results from vehicle impact. This damage rarely causes a bridge to collapse, but results in the serious weakening of the structure as such damage accumulates. Member replacement is an expensive repair, and thus a more economical alternative has been needed.

Heat straightening offers the potential for quick and effective repairs for bent steel members. LSU has just completed the first phase of a research project on heat straightening under the sponsorship of LTRC. The process of heat straightening consists of heating the bent member at appropriate locations such that during the cooling process the unequal shrinkage will induce thermal stresses that straighten the member. The few experts who currently employ this technique base the process on experience. The research project will develop a rational methodology for determining the type, number and location of heat application points required to straighten damaged members. The specific objectives of this research project are:

Phase 1 : Analytical and experimental evaluation of heat straightening techniques in the laboratory.

Phase 2 : Field evaluation of heat straightening techniques and development of an interactive program for automated design of the repair scheme.

Phase 3 : Documentation and training sessions for La. DOTD personnel.

The information obtained in phase one of this project is available upon request from LTRC.

HEATING LABORATORY SAMPLE

STUDY UNDERWAY ON EMBANKMENT FAILURES

An in-house study on slope rehabilitation is moving forward in an effort to find an economical solution to a problem that has troubled the department for more than a decade—failing slopes on man-made embankments, particularly along the Interstate system.

Five failed slopes are being rehabilitated under the project, using three different methods: injection of lime and lime-fly ash; rebuilding with lime-

Newsletters (Makeover)

Contrasting typefaces and rules give the piece a contemporary feel appropriate to a technology newsletter.

The nameplate has been completely reworked.

A highly readable Times Roman typeface contrasts text with the sans-serif headline.

The caption is moved inside the illustration for better balance.

A 20 percent screen behind the illustration adds contrast and balances the nameplate with the text.

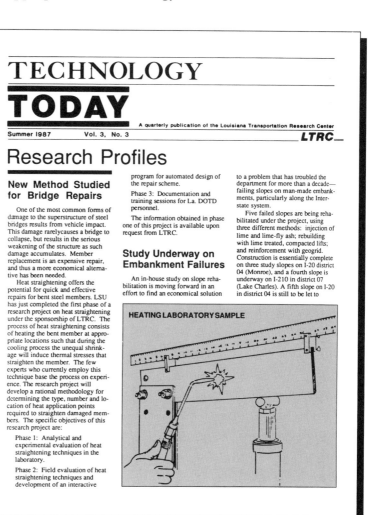

TECHNOLOGY
TODAY

A quarterly publication of the Louisiana Transportation Research Center

Summer 1987   Vol. 3, No. 3   *LTRC*

Research Profiles

New Method Studied for Bridge Repairs

One of the most common forms of damage to the superstructure of steel bridges results from vehicle impact. This damage rarely causes a bridge to collapse, but results in the serious weakening of the structure as such damage accumulates. Member replacement is an expensive repair, and thus a more economical alternative has been needed.

Heat straightening offers the potential for quick and effective repairs for bent steel members. LSU has just completed the first phase of a research project on heat straightening under the sponsorship of LTRC. The process of heat straightening consists of heating the bent member at appropriate locations such that during the cooling process the unequal shrinkage will induce thermal stresses that straighten the member. The few experts who currently employ this technique base the process on experience. The research project will develop a rational methodology for determining the type, number and location of heat application points required to straighten damaged members. The specific objectives of this research project are:

Phase 1: Analytical and experimental evaluation of heat straightening techniques in the laboratory.

Phase 2: Field evaluation of heat straightening techniques and development of an interactive

program for automated design of the repair scheme.

Phase 3: Documentation and training sessions for La. DOTD personnel.

The information obtained in phase one of this project is available upon request from LTRC.

Study Underway on Embankment Failures

An in-house study on slope rehabilitation is moving forward in an effort to find an economical solution

to a problem that has troubled the department for more than a decade—failing slopes on man-made embankments, particularly along the Interstate system.

Five failed slopes are being rehabilitated under the project, using three different methods: injection of lime and lime-fly ash; rebuilding with lime treated, compacted lifts; and reinforcement with geogrid. Construction is essentially complete on three study slopes on I-20 district 04 (Monroe), and a fourth slope is underway on I-210 in district 07 (Lake Charles). A fifth slope on I-20 in district 04 is still to be let to

HEATING LABORATORY SAMPLE

Newsletters (Original)

In-house newsletters and other time-sensitive documents often can be made more appealing at no additional cost.

Headlines "butt" each other at the top, creating too much uniformity and symmetry.

A lack of indention sets up a uniformity that leads to boredom when the readers' eyes aren't challenged by contrast.

Matching type styles in headlines and text create a "gray" look.

Similarly, the lack of contrast caused by large square blocks of text and excessive leading between paragraphs causes readers to lose interest.

COMPUTER CENTER
FACULTY BULLETIN

CALIFORNIA STATE UNIVERSITY, NORTHRIDGE   OCTOBER 1985

WHATEVER HAPPENED TO COMPUTER AIDED INSTRUCTION

by Kurt Webb

Computer Aided Instruction (CAI) had its moments in the sun several years ago and has since seemed to have faded from the academic computing scene. However, there are now indications that a resurgence in CAI is occurring. This renaissance may be due to two factors: (1) The increased availability of authoring systems on micros and mainframe computers; and (2) The increased awareness and utilization of computing among educators.

An authoring system is a software product that allows the educator: (1) to organize the subject material, to be presented to the student, in a systematic way; (2) to query the student taking the computerized lessons on their comprehension of the subject material; (3) to review the material previously presented or continue on with new material depending on how the student responded to the queries; and (4) to analyze student response to the lesson as a whole to help determine the next step in the learning process. Once such a CAI lesson has been prepared by using an authoring system, it can be presented to any number of students with each student taking the lesson at their convenience and at their own pace.

The Computer Center has recently purchased two authoring systems for the IBM PC. These are TENCORE and the McGraw-Hill Authoring System. These two systems do require that the author as well as students have access to IBM PC computers. A third authoring, Instructional Workbench, is available on the AT&T 385 mainframe computers. These computers can be accessed from virtually any terminal on campus.

More on CAI and authoring systems will be forthcoming. In the meantime, if you are interested in any of these products contact Kurt Webb at Extension 3966.

MICROCOMPUTER JOURNAL FOR INSTRUCTIONAL USERS

by J. S. Fleming

COLLEGIATE MICROCOMPUTER is "a quarterly journal devoted to all aspects of microcomputers in the higher education curricula." A sample copy received by the Computer Center included articles such as "The Use of Microcomputers in the Teaching of Calculus," "An Introductory Course in System Dynamics," "Using Microcomputers to Store and Evaluate Exam Items," and "Computer Literacy for Undergraduate Humanities and Social Majors."

If interested, this journal is published by COLLEGIATE MICROCOMPUTER, Rose-Hulman Institute of Technology, Terre Haute, IN 47803. Individual subscriptions are $28.00. A sample copy may be reviewed at the Computer Center, Engineering 121.

MICROCOMPUTER GRAPHICS BEGIN TO GROW UP

by Dave Crawford

Do you remember what life was like before computer graphics?

If you are old enough to be reading this you probably do, since computer graphics for popular consumption have been with us for only a few years. But computer-generated pictures have become so common in movies and on television that most of us no longer marvel at them. We accept them unthinkingly, as if they had always been with us.

We watch science fiction movies in which vivid alien landscapes have been created in a computer's memory without using models of any kind. We are perfectly accustomed to music videos in

Newsletters (Makeover)

Creative use of white space, indention and leading helps make the piece more readable.

A simple, appealing nameplate often is the best way to improve a newsletter or tabloid.

Rules between columns and in the margins tie the nameplate to the text.

Exaggerated indents at beginnings of paragraphs add contrast without the intricacies of drop caps.

A "rag bottom" format provides design flexibility and saves production time.

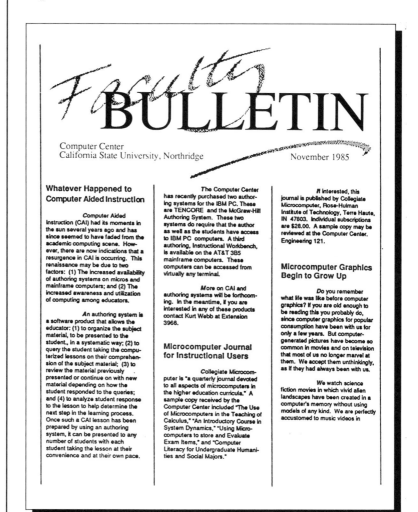

Newsletters (Original)

Lack of type size and typeface variety, and too much horizontal movement make for an undistinguished cover.

The nameplate lacks impact: the type size is too small, and it's set in a hard-to-read typeface. "Newsletter," set in a different typeface, clashes with the title.

The four parallel lines next to an undersized globe logo clutter the visual. The arrow icon is isolated rather than being integrated into the nameplate.

The type is too small for the width.

Reduced hyphenation in the justified text causes disconcerting gaps between words.

The photograph "floats" on the page, and its centered, italicized caption seems weak.

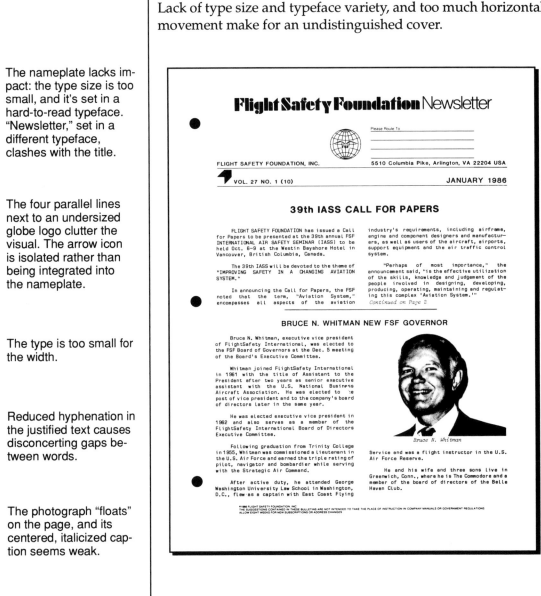

Flight Safety Foundation Newsletter

Please Route To

FLIGHT SAFETY FOUNDATION, INC.　　5510 Columbia Pike, Arlington, VA 22204 USA

VOL. 27 NO. 1 (10)　　　　　　　　　　　　JANUARY 1986

39th IASS CALL FOR PAPERS

FLIGHT SAFETY FOUNDATION has issued a Call for Papers to be presented at the 39th annual FSF INTERNATIONAL AIR SAFETY SEMINAR (IASS) to be held Oct. 6-9 at the Westin Bayshore Hotel in Vancouver, British Columbia, Canada.

The 39th IASS will be devoted to the theme of "IMPROVING SAFETY IN A CHANGING AVIATION SYSTEM."

In announcing the Call for Papers, the FSF noted that the term, "Aviation System," encompasses all aspects of the aviation industry's requirements, including airframe, engine and component designers and manufacturers, as well as users of the aircraft, airports, support equipment and the air traffic control system.

"Perhaps of most importance," the announcement said, "is the effective utilization of the skills, knowledge and judgement of the people involved in designing, developing, producing, operating, maintaining and regulating this complex 'Aviation System.'"

Continued on Page 2

BRUCE N. WHITMAN NEW FSF GOVERNOR

Bruce N. Whitman, executive vice president of FlightSafety International, was elected to the FSF Board of Governors at the Dec. 5 meeting of the Board's Executive Committee.

Whitman joined FlightSafety International in 1961 with the title of Assistant to the President after two years as senior executive assistant with the U.S. National Business Aircraft Association. He was elected to the post of vice president and to the company's board of directors later in the same year.

He was elected executive vice president in 1962 and also serves as a member of the FlightSafety International Board of Directors Executive Committee.

Following graduation from Trinity College in 1955, Whitman was commissioned a lieutenant in the U.S. Air Force and earned the triple rating of pilot, navigator and bombardier while serving with the Strategic Air Command.

After active duty, he attended George Washington University Law School in Washington, D.C., flew as a captain with East Coast Flying

Bruce N. Whitman

Service and was a flight instructor in the U.S. Air Force Reserve.

He and his wife and three sons live in Greenwich, Conn., where he is The Commodore and a member of the board of directors of the Belle Haven Club.

©1986 FLIGHT SAFETY FOUNDATION INC.
THE SUGGESTIONS CONTAINED IN THESE BULLETINS ARE NOT INTENDED TO TAKE THE PLACE OF INSTRUCTION IN COMPANY MANUALS OR GOVERNMENT REGULATIONS
ALLOW EIGHT WEEKS FOR NEW SUBSCRIPTIONS OR ADDRESS CHANGES

Newsletters (Makeover)

A vertical screen, rearranged elements and varied type sizes provide pleasing contrast and spotlight the name of the sponsoring organization.

The title gains character and impact set in a large, "safe" sans-serif type with tightly spaced letters.

A narrow, screened vertical column gives balance to the page and provides space for the logo, date, issue and contents listing.

The reversed type in the screened area adds balance and interest to the page design.

Column widths have been reduced and text size increased, allowing for a more comfortable relationship between type size and line length.

A frame helps anchor the photo and relate it to the text; a small aviation icon reversed out of a bullet enhances the boldface caption.

Flight Safety Foundation
N e w s l e t t e r

January 1990
Volume 27 Number 1 (10)

In this Issue
- Plans for Future IASS, CASS Sessions
- Deadlines for Seminar Submissions

Flight Safety Foundation, Inc.
5510 Columbia Pike
Arlington, VA 22204 USA

Bruce N. Whitman New FSF Governor

Bruce N. Whitman, executive vice president of FlightSafety International, was elected to the FSF Board of Governors at the Dec. 5 meeting of the Board's Executive Committee.

Whitman joined FlightSafety International in 1961 with the title of Assistant to the President after two years as senior executive assistant with the U.S. National Business Aircraft Association. He was elected to the post of vice president and to the company's board of directors later in the same year.

He was elected executive vice president in 1962 and also serves as a member of the FlightSafety International Board of Directors Executive Committee.

Following graduation from Trinity College in 1955, Whitman was commissioned a lieutenant in the U.S. Air Force and earned the triple rating of pilot, navigator and bombardier while serving with the Strategic Air Command.

After active duty, he attended George Washington University Law School in Washington, D.C., flew as a captain with East Coast Flying Service and was a flight instructor in the U.S. Air Force Reserve.

He and his wife and three sons live in Greenwich, Conn., where he is The Commodore and a member of the board of directors of the Belle Haven Club.

● Bruce N. Whitman

39th International Air Safety Seminar: Call for Papers

Flight Safety Foundation has issued a Call for Papers to be presented at the 39th annual FSF International Air Safety Seminar (IASS) to be held Oct. 6-9 at the Westin Bayshore Hotel in Vancouver, British Columbia, Canada.

The 39th International Air Safety Seminar will be devoted to the theme of *"Improving Safety in a Changing Aviation System."*

In announcing the Call for Papers, the FSF noted that the term, "Aviation System," encompasses all aspects of the aviation industry's requirements, including airframe, engine and component designers and manufacturers, as well as users of the aircraft, airports, support equipment and the air traffic control system.

"Perhaps of most importance," the announcement said, "is the effective utilization of the skills, knowledge and judgement of the people involved in designing, developing, producing, operating, maintaining and regulating this complex 'Aviation System.'"

It also noted that, with the currently changing environments and concepts in all segments

● See IASS Call for Papers on Page 2

Newsletters (Original)

Failure to organize white space and prioritize copy results in a smorgasbord effect.

Again, the text is not easy to read because of the small type set justified with almost no hyphenation. The unnaturally wide space between the two columns creates a distracting "landing strip."

Indention for paragraphs and listed information is too deep for the type size used.

Headlines "whisper" because they don't contrast enough with text.

Headlines and subheads aren't linked with their text by appropriate spacing above and below.

It also noted that, with the currently changing environments and concepts in all segments of aviation and the even greater changes anticipated for the future, the persons involved "will experience changing roles and responsibilities for making the Aviation System function with greater efficiency and improved margins of safety."

DISCUSSION AREAS

The seminar will consider ideas, concepts and methods for increasing the levels of safety in a changing aviation-system environment, including the potential impact of current and future technological developments in such areas as:

- Powerplants
- Structures
- Performance
- Communications
- Navigation
- Airway Traffic Control
- Airports
- Support Equipment

The roll of the human in the man/machine environment also will be considered at the seminar, including its impact upon:

- Safety Management
- Human Factors
- Training
- Communications

The Foundation encourages persons from all segments of the aviation industry, worldwide, to share their knowledge and experiences in these areas through active participation in the 39th IASS.

MARCH 15 DEADLINE

Authors/speakers wishing to present papers at the seminar should submit an abstract, proposed title and the name(s) of the author(s) and organization by March 15 to:

FLIGHT SAFETY FOUNDATION
Attn: L. Homer Mouden
Vice President-Technical Affairs
5510 Columbia Pike
Arlington, VA 22204-3194 USA
Telex: 901176 FSF INC AGTN

PLANS DRAFTED FOR FUTURE IASS, CASS SESSIONS

Detailed planning was conducted during the November 38th annual FSF INTERNATIONAL AIR SAFETY SEMINAR (IASS) in Boston, Mass., for the 1986, 1987 and 1988 international seminars and the Foundation's 1986 and 1987 CORPORATE AVIATION SAFETY SEMINARs (CASS).

During a meeting on Nov. 4, the FSF International Advisory Committee (IAC) completed plans for the 1986 IASS to be held Oct. 6-9,

Members of the FSF International Advisory Committee met in Boston during the 38th IASS to discuss plans for future Foundation International Air Safety Seminars.

FSF NEWSLETTER, JANUARY 1986

1986, at the Westin Bayshore Hotel in Vancouver, British Columbia, with the theme of "IMPROVING SAFETY IN A CHANGING AVIATION SYSTEM;" the 40th annual seminar to be held in late October of 1987 in Tokyo, Japan, and the 41st IASS to be held Oct. 4-7, 1988, in Sydney, Australia.

Following the IAC meeting, FSF President John H. Enders and Foundation Administrative Officer and Treasurer Luciana P. Frost discussed detailed planning for the Sydney seminar with Robert H. Naylor, of Ansett Airlines, and Capt. Trevor Jensen, of Qantas Airways, representing the 41st IASS host, the Australasian Airline Flight Safety Council.

Meeting on the same day, the FSF Corporate Advisory Committee (CAC) reviewed plans for the 31st annual CORPORATE AVIATION SAFETY SEMINAR to be held April 14-16, 1986, at the Omni Netherlands Hotel in Cincinnati, Ohio, and decided upon the St. Francis Hotel in San Francisco, Calif., as the site for the 32nd CASS in the spring of 1987.

At the conclusion of the session, Mrs. Frost met with 31st CASS Co-Chairman Robert Gray, chief pilot of Procter and Gamble Co., to discuss final planning for that seminar, whose theme will be "SAFETY IN OUR ENVIRONMENT."

Newsletters (Makeover)

The long, narrow, left-hand column is used again, reinforcing the newsletter's visual identity established on the front cover. This feature also serves as a convenient receptacle for the photograph's caption.

Larger headlines in the text typeface attract attention, while sans-serif subheads provide comfortable contrast.

Shallower indents and tighter spacing of list items remove excessive white space.

Airplane symbols used as bullets reinforce the aviation theme.

Important mailing address information, now set in boldface type, is easily located.

Publication information is relegated to the bottom of the page.

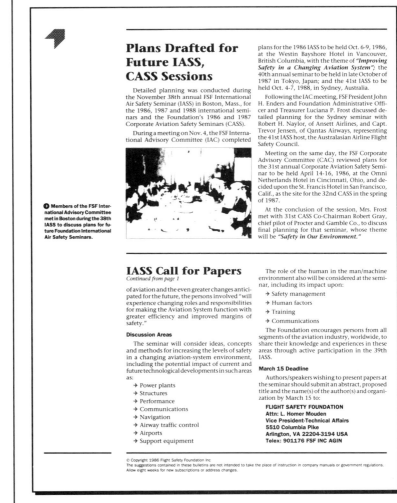

Plans Drafted for Future IASS, CASS Sessions

Detailed planning was conducted during the November 38th annual FSF International Air Safety Seminar (IASS) in Boston, Mass., for the 1986, 1987 and 1988 international seminars and the Foundation's 1986 and 1987 Corporate Aviation Safety Seminars (CASS).

During a meeting on Nov. 4, the FSF International Advisory Committee (IAC) completed

➤ Members of the FSF International Advisory Committee met in Boston during the 38th IASS to discuss plans for future Foundation International Air Safety Seminars.

plans for the 1986 IASS to be held Oct. 6-9, 1986, at the Westin Bayshore Hotel in Vancouver, British Columbia, with the theme of *"Improving Safety in a Changing Aviation System"*; the 40th annual seminar to be held in late October of 1987 in Tokyo, Japan; and the 41st IASS to be held Oct. 4-7, 1988, in Sydney, Australia.

Following the IAC meeting, FSF President John H. Enders and Foundation Administrative Officer and Treasurer Luciana P. Frost discussed detailed planning for the Sydney seminar with Robert H. Naylor, of Ansett Airlines, and Capt. Trevor Jensen, of Qantas Airways, representing the 41st IASS host, the Australasian Airline Flight Safety Council.

Meeting on the same day, the FSF Corporate Advisory Committee (CAC) reviewed plans for the 31st annual Corporate Aviation Safety Seminar to be held April 14-16, 1986, at the Omni Netherlands Hotel in Cincinnati, Ohio, and decided upon the St. Francis Hotel in San Francisco, Calif., as the site for the 32nd CASS in the spring of 1987.

At the conclusion of the session, Mrs. Frost met with 31st CASS Co-Chairman Robert Gray, chief pilot of Procter and Gamble Co., to discuss final planning for that seminar, whose theme will be *"Safety in Our Environment."*

IASS Call for Papers
Continued from page 1

of aviation and the even greater changes anticipated for the future, the persons involved "will experience changing roles and responsibilities for making the Aviation System function with greater efficiency and improved margins of safety."

Discussion Areas

The seminar will consider ideas, concepts and methods for increasing the levels of safety in a changing aviation-system environment, including the potential impact of current and future technological developments in such areas as:

→ Power plants
→ Structures
→ Performance
→ Communications
→ Navigation
→ Airway traffic control
→ Airports
→ Support equipment

The role of the human in the man/machine environment also will be considered at the seminar, including its impact upon:

→ Safety management
→ Human factors
→ Training
→ Communications

The Foundation encourages persons from all segments of the aviation industry, worldwide, to share their knowledge and experiences in these areas through active participation in the 39th IASS.

March 15 Deadline

Authors/speakers wishing to present papers at the seminar should submit an abstract, proposed title and the name(s) of the author(s) and organization by March 15 to:

**FLIGHT SAFETY FOUNDATION
Attn: L. Homer Mouden
Vice President-Technical Affairs
5510 Columbia Pike
Arlington, VA 22204-3194 USA
Telex: 901176 FSF INC AGIN**

© Copyright 1986 Flight Safety Foundation Inc
The suggestions contained in these bulletins are not intended to take the place of instruction in company manuals or government regulations. Allow eight weeks for new subscriptions or address changes.

Newsletters (Original)

The original *Executive* presents a confusing mixture of typefaces and graphic elements, all vying for the reader's attention.

Heavy horizontal rules separating articles in the second and third columns compete with the nameplate, head-lines, drop caps and article lead-ins.

In the nameplate, the type for the words "The Executive" is too flamboy-ant for a corporate image.

Underlining the "Shirt-sleeve Seminar March 7" kicker makes it difficult to read.

Default line spacing for "Turning Your Ideas…" wastes vertical space. The dollar sign is too cute—again, inappro-priate for executives.

The boxes at the ends of articles are overly prominent.

The box around the din-ner meeting announce-ment separates it from the article it relates to.

The Executive

MARCH '88
VOL. 1 NO. 3

Sales & Marketing Executives: "1988—A Positive Vision Towards Accomplishment"

"How To Get A Watermelon From A Seed"

Turning Your Ideas Into Million$ — An Eight-Step Process

Robert C. Boint, executive director of PLUS Business, Inc., in Huntington Beach, and a member of the National Speakers Association, will be the guest speaker at the Monday, March 7, 1988 dinner/meeting of Sales & Marketing.

Boint has served as the national sales leader for several major corporations, including Bell & Howell, Brunswick, G.A.F. and Sylvania.

Boint's presentation is entitled: "How To Get A Watermelon From A Seed — Turning Your Ideas Into Millions, An Eight-Step Process." He will address the ways to channel your creative energy in regards to your company's products or service to penetrate competitive markets and increase sales.

The PLUS Business Strategy identifies more than 117 areas of potential increased sales and how these can be analyzed as a check list for greater business performance. With Boint's system, you will see how to create and develop your own plans to aid you in a better understanding of the marketing tasks and field selling strategies ahead of you.

Boint's style of presentation, and the information made available, will make this a dinner meeting you don't want to miss.

The meeting at the Long Beach Airport Marriott begins with no-host cocktails at 6 p.m., with dinner served at 7:15 p.m. □

Thank You For Prizes

Special thank you to the Ramada Renaissance Hotel, Long Beach Airport Marriott, and the SME Board of Directors for providing prizes for the February 1 dinner meeting.

If your firm would like to donate prizes for our monthly raffle drawings, please call John Craig at 213/988-1239. □

Robert C. Boint
Executive Director
PLUS Business, Inc.

Shirtsleeve Seminar March 7

Money Management And Tax Planning

Our first SHIRTSLEEVE SEMINAR will be held Monday, March 7, prior to our monthly dinner meeting. "Money Management and Tax Planning" will be presented by Max and Linda DeZemplen of Preferred Financial Advisory Corp.

The shirtsleever runs from 4:45 to 6 p.m. and is free to members. There is a $20 cost to non-members and guests.

The DeZemplen's will emphasize retirement, tax and estate plans, protection and savings, and investment strategies. Please make reservations in advance by calling 213/988-1239.

This will be one of several forums during the year for discussion and input on issues of concern to you, the member. These shirtsleevers, led by recognized experts in their fields, will provide information that can be put to immediate use … another member benefit. □

Dinner Meeting

Date: Monday, March 7, 1988
Time: Cocktails 6 p.m.
        Dinner 7:15 p.m.
Place: Long Beach Airport Marriott
        4700 Airport Plaza Drive
Cost: Members $18 Guests $25

A NEW MEMBER BENEFIT!

As a new SME member, you receive a "free" table top display for your products or services…to be used at the next dinner meeting following your approval for membership.

Newsletters (Makeover)

The nameplate's condensed typeface and superimposed triangle now appropriately express the "positive vision" focus of the newsletter.

The subtitle emerges clear and strong. The four-column format, with headlines set in the left-hand column, opens up the layout and lets readers skim the titles.

Using fewer typefaces and type sizes contributes to consistency.

The Dinner Meeting information is now properly seen as part of the article.

The caption is now more informative and relates the photograph to the adjacent article.

Thick horizontal bars extending from the thin rules between articles help define the left-hand column. They also strengthen the headlines.

THE EXECUTIVE

VOLUME 1 NUMBER 3   MARCH 1988

SALES AND MARKETING EXECUTIVES
1988: A POSITIVE VISION TOWARDS ACCOMPLISHMENT

How to Get a Watermelon from a Seed

Robert C. Boint, executive director of PLUS Business, Inc., in Huntington Beach, and a member of the National Speakers Association, will be the guest speaker at the Monday, March 7, 1988 dinner/meeting of Sales & Marketing.

Boint has served as the national sales leader for several major corporations, including Bell & Howell, Brunswick, G.A.F. and Sylvania.

Boint's presentation is entitled: "How To Get A Watermelon From A Seed—Turning Your Ideas Into Millions, An Eight-Step Process." He will address the ways to channel your creative energy in regards to your company's products or service to penetrate competitive markets and increase sales.

The PLUS Business Strategy identifies more than 117 areas of potential increased sales and how these can be analyzed as a check list for greater business performance. With Boint's system, you will see how to create and develop your own plans to aid you in a better

Robert C. Boint, Executive Director, PLUS Business, Inc., will share his strategies for success on March 7.

understanding of the marketing tasks and field selling strategies ahead of you.

Boint's style of presentation, and the information made available, will make this a dinner meeting you don't want to miss.

The meeting at the Long Beach Airport Marriott begins with no-host cocktails at 6 p.m., with dinner served at 7:15 p.m.

Dinner Meeting

Date: Monday,
        March 7, 1988

Time: Cocktails 6 p.m.
        Dinner 7:15 p.m.

Place: Long Beach
        Airport Marriott
        4700 Airport
        Plaza Drive

Cost: Members $18
        Guests $25

Money Management and Tax Planning

Shirtsleeve Seminar March 7

Our first **shirtsleeve seminar** will be held Monday, March 7, prior to our monthly dinner meeting. "Money Management and Tax Planning" will be presented by Max and Linda DeZemplen of Preferred Financial Advisory Corporation.

The shirtsleever runs from 4:45 to 6 p.m. and is free to members. There is a $20 cost to non-members and guests.

The DeZemplens will emphasize retirement, tax and estate plans, protection and savings, and investment strategies. Please make reservations in advance by calling 213/988-1239.

This will be one of several forums during the year for discussion and input on issues of concern to you, the member. These shirt-sleevers, led by recognized experts in their fields, will provide information that can be put to immediate use... another member benefit.

Upcoming Meetings

March 7
Dinner/Meeting

May 16
Distinguished Sales
Awards Banquet

June 6
Dinner/Meeting

July 11
Coast!

Nameplates

The four illustrations on this spread show how nameplates can be reworked to set the proper tone for a newsletter's content.

(Original)

The map of Louisiana is too complex; it detracts from the message.

The outdated typeface doesn't effectively communicate "technology."

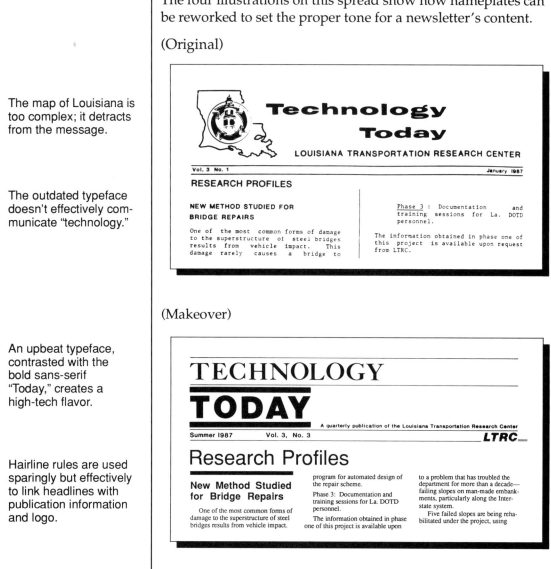

An upbeat typeface, contrasted with the bold sans-serif "Today," creates a high-tech flavor.

Hairline rules are used sparingly but effectively to link headlines with publication information and logo.

(Makeover)

Nameplates

Creating a good nameplate is often the best way to improve the look of a newsletter or tabloid.

(Original)

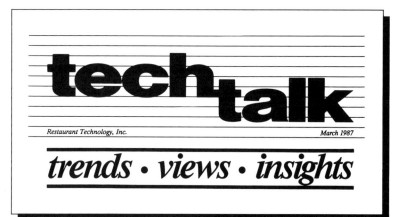

Excessively heavy type set against thin horizontal lines is distracting.

The subhead is far too large and contributes little to the message.

(Makeover)

Simple nameplates are best; slender, condensed, lowercase type creates valuable white space, punctuated by a thick rule above and thin rule below the name.

The subhead has been eliminated and replaced by the less obtrusive "Restaurant Technology" slugline.

Business Reports (Original)

The low-contrast, "gray" tone of business reports and memos often neutralizes the positive effects of good writing, persuasive argument and strong evidence.

Because busy managers have only a short time to read a lot of material, a page full of typewritten copy can be very un-appealing.

Although critical to the report, long blocks of supporting evidence tend to discourage readers.

Awkward spacing of data interrupts the flow of reading.

---

the average late riser, this product will revolutionize his or her sleeping habits.

CURRENT SNOOZE ALARM SALES

As stated previously, we believe that a high number of present users of snooze alarm technology will want to own TardiSnooz. Current sales of snooze alarms have never been higher, as the figures below show:

YEAR	# UNITS SOLD	$ RETAIL
1965	1,100	$ 12,000
1970	65,000	430,000
1975	220,000	2,800,000
1980	673,000	5,900,000
1985	1,220,000	11,670,000

A corresponding trend of employee tardiness has become evident, particularly in the last ten years. In fact, some researchers believe that snooze alarms have indeed played a large part in <u>causing</u> employee tardiness. According to Real Life Information in Palo Alto, California, "Snooze alarm technology is largely responsible for the dramatic rise in employee tardiness and late calls. Further, the admonishment thrust upon the average employee, compounded by the guilt, feelings of inadequacy and consequent resentment, creates an unresolved <u>authority-figure conflict</u>, resulting in sharply decreased productivity....One solution to this problem is a mechanism whereby the employee can at least call in late with a feeling of efficiency and accomplishment, instead of languishing in <u>commuter-frustrated dissonance</u> on his or her way to work."

Clearly, the above findings indicate the need for added features to snooze technology. This, coupled with the fall in wholesale modem chip prices, could make TardiSnooz our sale item of the decade.

PROJECTED TARDISNOOZ SALES

Based on a 1,000-piece consumer survey mailed last month (see attached data), we found consumers receptive, and indeed eager, to pay the slightly higher price that TardiSnooz would command. Below are projected sales figures, based on our survey:

PROJECTED TARDISNOOZ SALES

YEAR	# UNITS PROJECTED	$ RETAIL
1990	34,000	$ 430,000
1991	81,000	970,000
1992	239,000 (Break-even)	2,400,000
1993	310,000	3,700,000
1994	228,000 (Recession Projected)	2,200,000
1995	426,000	4,450,000

When you examine the above figures, and consider that all we have to do is add a $.93 modem chip to our present alarms, the conclusion is inescapable to all but the most ardent critics that our company should

Business Reports (Makeover)

Even the most basic layout software allows you to substitute interesting, informative charts, diagrams and other visuals for text-based data.

Charts and diagrams present information in easy-to-understand, interesting forms.

Diagonal lines in the bar chart add needed contrast to the page.

Research information is broken into several paragraphs and indented left and right for additional emphasis.

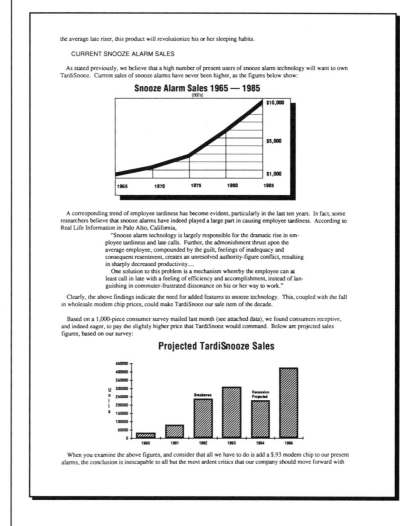

the average late riser, this product will revolutionize his or her sleeping habits.

CURRENT SNOOZE ALARM SALES

As stated previously, we believe that a high number of present users of snooze alarm technology will want to own TardiSnooz. Current sales of snooze alarms have never been higher, as the figures below show:

Snooze Alarm Sales 1965 — 1985
(000's)

A corresponding trend of employee tardiness has become evident, particularly in the last ten years. In fact, some researchers believe that snooze alarms have indeed played a large part in causing employee tardiness. According to Real Life Information in Palo Alto, California,

"Snooze alarm technology is largely responsible for the dramatic rise in employee tardiness and late calls. Further, the admonishment thrust upon the average employee, compounded by the guilt, feelings of inadequacy and consequent resentment, creates an unresolved authority-figure conflict, resulting in sharply decreased productivity....

One solution to this problem is a mechanism whereby the employee can at least call in late with a feeling of efficiency and accomplishment, instead of languishing in commuter-frustrated dissonance on his or her way to work."

Clearly, the above findings indicate the need for added features to snooze technology. This, coupled with the fall in wholesale modem chip prices, could make TardiSnooz our sale item of the decade.

Based on a 1,000-piece consumer survey mailed last month (see attached data), we found consumers receptive, and indeed eager, to pay the slightly higher price that TardiSnooz would command. Below are projected sales figures, based on our survey:

Projected TardiSnooze Sales

When you examine the above figures, and consider that all we have to do is add a $.93 modem chip to our present alarms, the conclusion is inescapable to all but the most ardent critics that our company should move forward with

Charts & Diagrams

Quantitative information can be comprehended quicker and more thoroughly with visual representations. The illustrations below show four ways the same information can be presented to make data more appealing.

A three-dimensional effect enhances a basic line chart.

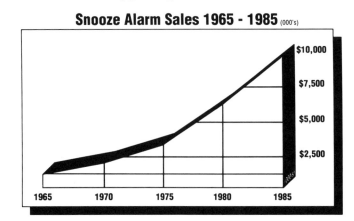

Snooze Alarm Sales 1965 - 1985 (000's)

Illustrations within a presentation graphic can add humor and further identify the content.

Snooze Alarm Sales 1965 — 1985 (000's)

Charts & Diagrams

You can use your layout software to make revisions and embellishments to charts and diagrams.

Rules, screens and drop shadows can make a simple bar chart more compelling.

Images that relate to the subject matter can form a chart or diagram's most important visual.

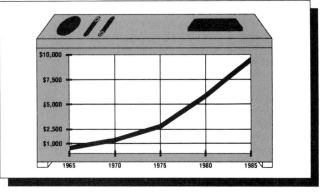

Business Reports (Original)

A conservative image does not dictate visual uniformity.

The combination of small, light type and wide columns reduces readability.

Distracting white space is created by the wide gap between columns of unhyphenated text set in small type, the extra space after periods and the two returns between paragraphs.

The three upper diagrams conflict with the two-column layout, and especially with the two diagrams at the bottom of the page.

The charts are hard to understand without legends or unit labels.

Lack of a jumpline at the end of the second column leaves the reader suspended in mid-sentence with no direction for continuation of the text.

McKenzie Management, Inc.

MARKET LETTER

VOLUME 2 - NUMBER 17   AUGUST 20, 1986

GOLD in U.S. DOLLARS   INFLATION WATCH INDICATOR Gold/U.S. Treasury Bond   OIL

Gold broke out of its long term trading range on August 8th. It achieved the $380 objective and then some before settling down this week in the 370s. Oil started moving higher earlier that week in response to the OPEC production cut agreement.

However, the most common reason cited for the action in gold was the prospective sanctions against South Africa by Western governments. Since that's not exactly a new item on the investment scene, I suspect that the balance between buying and selling over the past six months, which had resulted in a narrow trading range, had shifted to a position of net buying. In other words, technically, the gold market was ready to break out.

U.S. investors are naturally concerned with the price of gold in dollars. For a major bull market to evolve in gold, however, it is equally important for the price of the metal to be in uptrends in other major currencies.

As evidenced in the charts below, gold remains in long-term downtrends both in D-marks and yen. It does appear to be bottoming out against the West German currency and, on its recent strength, the current price

rose above the 30-week moving average.

Japan has bought 220 tons of gold since the beginning of the year. Much of that buying was done in order to mint a new coin celebrating Emperor Hirohito's 60 years reign.

Business Week in its August 25th issue reported that Zurich's Bank Julius Bär & Co. shifted 5% of its clients portfolios into gold. And also noted that Middle Eastern clients are flocking back.

Overall, sentiment regarding gold seems rather passive. There was some increase in public buying of gold-oriented mutual funds immediately after the move, but interest quickly subsided. This lack of enthusiasm tends to strengthen the technical outlook for the price of gold. It suggests that the uptrend will have to be further along before attracting a surge of buying interest.

The rise in gold prices had a big impact on the Inflation Watch Indicator. The indicator is a ratio of gold to Treasury bonds. The middle chart above shows that gold has been outperforming bonds since late April of this year. The indicator is now in a long-term uptrend

GOLD in WEST GERMAN D-MARKS   GOLD in JAPANESE YEN

Business Reports (Makeover)

Four narrower columns and smaller, heavier type increase information density and readability.

The most important word in the nameplate, "McKenzie," projects more strength and character when set in a significantly larger, more stylized serif type, in contrast to the smaller, more conservative treatment of "Management." The "i" has been dotted with a stylized logo.

Reversed headlines and subheads provide contrast and organization. Enlarged initial caps lead the reader from the headlines into the articles.

Charts are placed in a "contrast" column, defined at the top by the issue date. Shading makes the charts' trend lines easy to follow.

August 20, 1986

McKenzie
MANAGEMENT

GOLD
This Week

Gold broke out of its long term trading range on August 8th. It achieved the $380 objective and then some before settling down this week in the 370s. Oil started moving higher earlier that week in response to the OPEC production cut agreement.

However, the most common reason cited for the action in gold was the prospective sanctions against South Africa by Western governments. Since that's not exactly a new item on the investment scene, I suspect that the balance between buying and selling over the past six months, which had resulted in a narrow trading range,

Gold/U.S. Dollars

Gold/West German Marks

Gold/Japanese Yen

Gold/U.S. Treasury Bonds

had shifted to a position of net buying. In other words, technically, the gold market was ready to break out.

U.S. investors are naturally concerned with the price of gold in dollars. For a major bull market to evolve in gold, however, it is equally important for the price of the metal to be in uptrends in other major currencies.

As evidenced in the charts, gold remains in long-term downtrends both in D-marks and yen. It does appear to be bottoming out against the West German currency and, on its recent strength, the current price rose above the 30-week moving average.

Japan has bought 220 tons of gold since the beginning of the year. Much of that buying was done in order to mint a

new coin celebrating Emperor Hirohito's 60-year reign.

Business Week in its August 25th issue reported that Zurich's Bank Julius Bar & Co. shifted 5% of its clients' portfolios into gold. And also noted that Middle Eastern clients are flocking back.

Overall, sentiment regarding gold seems rather passive. There was some increase in public buying of gold-oriented mutual funds immediately after the move, but interest quickly subsided. This lack of enthusiasm tends to strengthen the technical outlook for the price of gold. It suggests that the uptrend will have to be further along before attracting a surge of buying interest.

INFLATION
Watch Indicator

The rise in gold prices had a big impact on the Inflation Watch Indicator. The indicator is a ratio of gold to Treasury bonds. The chart to the left shows that gold had been outperforming bonds since late April of this year. The indicator is now in a long-term uptrend indicating a shift in investor expectations from deflation to inflation.

Or is it? Conventional wisdom ties investor preference

of gold to an inflationary environment. But another possibility, given the sluggish U.S. economy and the persistent trade and budget deficits, may be a flight from the dollar. Gold may be in demand because the dollar is not. The Japanese, among other foreign investors, are awash in dollars and they have to invest in something. Perhaps we should turn the Inflation Watch Indicator upside down and call it "Interest in the Dollar"—a rising trend would indicate a favorable outlook for the dollar, a

declining trend would be adverse.

The other side of the equation is the bond market. It has remained near its high in anticipation of another discount rate cut by the Federal Reserve Board. If the Central Banks of Japan and West Germany go along with the prospective U.S. cut, the bond market would probably go to new highs bringing long-term rates lower. If the foreign banks resist stimulating their economies, the U.S. bond market would probably sell off.

Business Reports (Original)

Inconsistent spacing, sizing and organization create barriers to continuity.

The wide gutter collides with the "Buy Recommendations" box.

Headlines and subheads float, without clear linkage to the text they introduce.

The chart, expanded to match the column width, seems unnaturally large.

In the box, continuity is inhibited by column heads of undifferentiated weight and size.

---

indicating a shift in investor expectations from deflation to inflation.

Or is it? Conventional wisdom ties investor preference of gold to an inflationary environment. But another possibility, given the sluggish U.S. economy and the persistent trade and budget deficits, may be a flight from the dollar. Gold may be in demand because the dollar is not. The Japanese, among other foreign investors, are awash in dollars and they have to invest in something. Perhaps we should turn the Inflation Watch Indicator upside down and call it "Interest in the Dollar "- a rising trend would indicate a favorable outlook for the dollar, a declining trend would be adverse.

The other side of the equation is the bond market. It has remained near its high in anticipation of another discount rate cut by the Federal Reserve Board. If the Central Banks of Japan and West Germany go along with the prospective U.S. cut, the bond market would probably go to new highs bringing long-term rates lower. If the foreign banks resist stimulating their economies, the U.S. bond market would probably sell off.

The Stock Market

Prices

Prices improved on a broad front during the past two weeks. The Utility Average went to a new high reflecting lower interest rates. Short term price trends have reversed to the upside.

Volume

Volume has picked up slightly. This level of activity is fairly typical of August. Volume remains neutral.

Breadth

The breadth indicators have swung into line with the Averages. This set of indicators has been upgraded from negative to positive.

Sentiment

The sentiment indicators remain neutral.

Money and Interest Rates

Short term rates continue to ease to new lows in anticipation of a cut in the discount rate. The bond market remains near its high; i.e. long term rates are at their lowest levels in years. This indicator remains bullish.

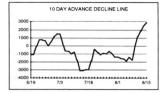
10 DAY ADVANCE DECLINE LINE

Momentum

A successful test of the selling wave in mid-July did take place in early August. In the previous issue, I suggested that it might be happening, but that it was too early to confirm it. The 10-Day Advance Decline Line above clearly shows that the greater selling pressure occurred in July even though the DJIA hit bottom on August 4th (the closing low was on Friday, August 1st). Momentum is upgraded to positive.

Summary of Stock Market Indicators

Long Term: Bullish
Intermediate Term: Bullish

The indicators have all improved during the past two weeks. The selling pressure of July has clearly subsided. We appear to be in a normal August environment of low volume. Post Labor Day activity will provide us with a better clue as to the potential power of this move.

Investment Strategy

Retain 12%-15% in cash reserves. Gold Mining and International Oils are among the best performing issues on this rally.

Buy Recommendations

Industry	Company	Symbol	Exchange	Recent Price	Buying Range	Date & Price Recomended		Sell if Price Closes Below
Computers	Evans & Sutherland	ESCC	OTC	22.2	21-23	8-6-86	22.0	19
Drugs	Johnson & Johnson	JNJ	NYSE	70.8	Hold	1-2-85	36.0	62
	Merck	MRK	"	116	"	"	47.0	96
Mining	Echo Bay Mines Ltd.	ECO	AMEX	18.5	17-20	7-23-86	15.5	14
Oil	Mobil	MOB	NYSE	34.5	31-34	7-23-86	31.0	29
Wood Products	Scott Paper	SPP	"	57.6	Hold	1-2-85	34.0	52

2

Business Reports (Makeover)

An illusion of spaciousness is created without sacrificing any information.

Reversed headlines, the prominent bar across the top of the box and generous white space around the charts add color, contrast and organizational value to the page.

A "drop" of white space at the top of the page framing the logo reinforces the publication's corporate identity.

Redistribution of white space above and below subheads and the addition of underline rules clearly relate each subhead to its text.

"Buy Recommendations" are now easier to read, with increased vertical spacing and added contrast between column heads and text.

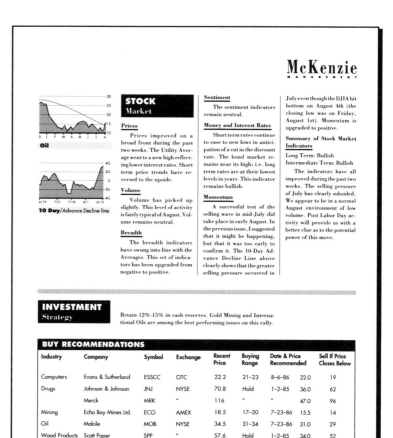

Consistency Versus Correctness

Rules are made to be broken.

You may be a bit concerned that the "before-and-after" examples featured in this section break many of the conventions presented in Section One. As mentioned before, there are no absolute rules in graphic design; solutions that work in some situations simply aren't appropriate in others.

The goal in Section Two and throughout this book is not to place restrictions but to increase your awareness of appropriate and inappropriate ways of applying design principles to your desktop publishing efforts. Although fundamentals of good design should never be ignored, many decisions are largely intuitive. The more responsive you become to your own design sense and intuition, the more you'll develop your own abilities.

Many design principles are largely intuitive.

By now, you should be more comfortable with the basic concepts outlined in Section One, after seeing how they can be applied in actual examples. But instead of passively accepting these makeovers as the definitive design solutions, you may feel motivated to do even better.

Take the time now to review those examples and create your own makeovers! You may even want to stop reading at this point, boot up your computer and develop alternative ways of solving the design problems presented in the previous pages.

A Note on Style

Style doesn't emerge overnight; it evolves gradually through discipline, hard work and persistence.

As you become increasingly familiar with the capabilities—and limitations—of your desktop publishing hardware and software, your unique style will develop as you explore various ways of solving design problems.

Style evolves as you find ways to solve design problems.

Remember, with desktop publishing you have unprecedented creative capabilities at your fingertips—more than any previous generation of graphic designers!

In the past, it would have been unthinkably extravagant for a graphic artist to set type and paste up a large document simply for learning purposes. Desktop publishing allows you to go through the same learning process at no charge—on the screen of your computer! And if you have access to a laser printer, you can have the tangible results of your efforts for pennies per copy.

MOVING ON

Now that you're acquainted with the basics of graphic design and know how those elements work together to produce successful design solutions, you'll want to begin work on a project. Section Three covers several major design categories and presents valuable tips and tricks for producing different kinds of documents.

SECTION THREE

Getting Down to Business

8 | DESIGNING EFFECTIVE NEWSLETTERS

Newsletters are major beneficiaries of the desktop publishing revolution. Highly specialized newsletters that once were impractical because of high typesetting and paste-up costs can now be produced using the most basic desktop publishing and word processing software.

Desktop-published newsletters also provide associations, retail and service establishments with a cost-effective advertising medium.

Although they may appear simple, newsletters are surprisingly complex. The typical newsletter contains numerous elements that must be successfully integrated—often under last-minute deadline pressure.

Here are some things to look for when examining a newsletter or planning your own:

REPEATING ELEMENTS

Successful newsletters are built around a number of elements that appear in every issue.

Repeating elements can be hallmarks of good design.

While the content changes, these features are always included: nameplate, logo, publication information, department heads, kickers, headlines, lead-ins, text, teasers, artwork, captions, jumplines, credits and mailing area.

Nameplate

Your nameplate should provide immediate visual identification and communicate your newsletter's purpose.

A great deal of thought should be devoted to the design of the nameplate and logo. They're the most noticeable and essential features for promoting identification and continuity.

Newsletter nameplates usually are placed at the top of the first page and often extend across the full width of the newsletter.

Nameplates should create a good first impression.

However, equally effective nameplates can be placed centered, flush-left or flush-right.

Although most nameplates are at the top of the page, they can be placed approximately a third of the way down from the top. This location leaves room for a feature headline and article to appear above it.

Vertical orientation, though less common, can draw more attention to an important headline.

A short motto may be incorporated into the nameplate to amplify the nameplate's meaning or target the newsletter's intended audience.

Grids

Creative column size and placement can breathe life into even the most text-heavy newsletters.

Vary column widths to add motion and color to the page.

Many newsletters look prosaic and dull because they're set up with two or three columns of equal width. Two-column formats are particularly static, because of the formal left-right balance.

One way of avoiding monotony is to reduce the width of the columns slightly and run a vertical band of white space along the left-hand side of each page. This white space can be used for a table of contents and publication data …

"Empty" left-hand columns can show-case display text.

visuals …

… or short features such as sidebars, and pull-quotes …

Vertical white space can enhance side-bars and illustrations.

When using an asymmetrical column layout, be consistent on each page.

There's nothing as disappointing as a newsletter with an attractive front cover based on an asymmetrical grid …

If you use an asymmetrical layout, carry it throughout your publication.

… that turns into a conventional, balanced, two-column grid when you turn the page …

Headlines

The number and length of articles included in each issue should be considered when designing the headlines.

If you plan to focus each issue on a single in-depth article plus a few short ones, you'll need a single, dominant headline.

Design the front page with headlines in mind.

On the other hand, if you feature several short articles, the front page must accommodate more than one significant headline.

Headlines typically are placed above the articles they introduce. However, they can be placed next to the article as well.

Headlines don't necessarily have to be placed above the text.

Teasers

Use teasers to invite readers inside your newsletter.

A short table of contents on the front cover can draw attention to articles and features inside or on the back cover.

The table of contents can beckon readers to look inside.

Make your newsletter's table of contents a focal point by placing it in a small shaded box …

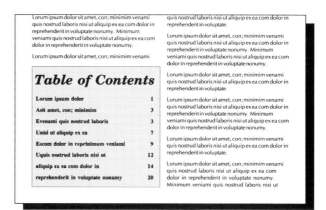

… in a narrow column adjacent to the text columns …

Place teasers where they'll draw the most attention.

… next to the nameplate …

… or centered below the body copy.

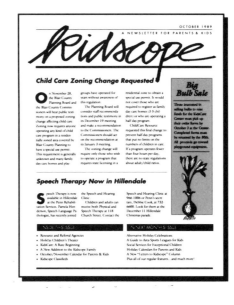

The entire front cover of your newsletter can serve as the table of contents.

Instead of merely consisting of titles and page numbers, your table of contents can include a frieze of photographs along the bottom of the cover page that relate to articles inside. The photo captions will lead the readers to the articles to find out more.

Your table of contents can include a frieze of photos.

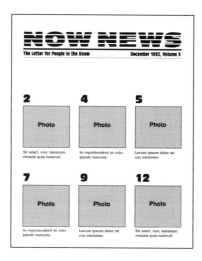

Because most newsletters appear in the reader's mailbox address label up, you may want to place the table of contents next to the mailing label area where it can't be overlooked.

Artwork and Captions

The availability of illustrations and photographs greatly influences your newsletter's design.

If the content of your newsletter is mostly factual or technical and you plan to add supporting illustrations, be sure to leave space for them. Also allow space for a caption to accompany each illustration.

Use artwork to strengthen your message.

On the other hand, if your newsletter articles are predominantly generic commentary and photographs aren't readily available, you can safely do without artwork or use illustrations without captions to strengthen your message.

Publication Information

Readers should be able to identify the source of the newsletter quickly and easily.

Be sure to leave space for your organization's logo, as well as your address and phone number.

Don't hesitate to tell readers who you are.

In most cases, the logo appears on the front cover. It should be large enough to be noticed but not large enough to compete with or overwhelm the nameplate.

Your logo also can be placed within the nameplate.

You can place the logo at the bottom of the front cover, relegate it to the back cover or totally eliminate it, as long as your organization is identified in some way.

The volume and issue numbers and date should be prominently featured if readers are likely to save and refer to your newsletter in the future.

Include issue numbers and dates if your newsletter will be used later as a resource.

Lead-Ins

Use subheads and short summaries to provide transition between headlines and body copy. (For example, this sentence is a lead-in to this subsection.)

Lead-ins can be placed between the headline and text.

Lead-ins take different forms but provide good reader cues.

Frequently, lead-ins span more than one column.

The lead-in is often placed within the text, set off by horizontal rules or some other device.

A lead-in also can take the form of a pull-quote.

Text

Your newsletter design must take into account the length of the articles likely to be included in each issue.

If long feature articles will be used, choose small type set in multiple narrow columns.

The appearance of multicolumn newsletters can be improved by placing thin vertical rules between the columns.

However, if shorter features are the rule, choose wider columns and larger type.

Credits

If your newsletter is designed to provide your employees with opportunities to express themselves, then identify authors by name, department and division or position.

If possible, personalize your newsletter by including a photograph or drawing of the author.

Thin vertical rules improve the looks of multicolumn publications.

Mailing Information

If your newsletter is a self-mailer, be sure to provide sufficient space for a mailing label and other mailing information.

A newsletter's mailing area normally appears at the bottom of the back page.

The mailing label area lets readers know where you are.

Be sure to include your organization's return address next to the mailing label. (Of course, if fulfillment—or mailing list maintenance and addressing—is handled by an outside firm, put that firm's return address in the mailing area.)

The mailing area also should clearly indicate whether your newsletter is First- or Third-Class mail. In either case, include your firm's postal permit number to avoid licking stamps.

Adding "Address Correction Requested" above the mailing label area helps you keep your customer or prospect mailing list up-to-date. If you include "Address Correction Requested" in the mailing area of your newsletter, you'll be informed of the new address when a newsletter recipient moves.

Many newsletter mailers choose to include "Address Correction Requested" only once or twice a year.

SIZE

Although smaller formats are possible, the standard newsletter is created by folding an 11- by 17-inch sheet of paper, called a signature, into four 8 1/2- by 11-inch pages.

Newsletters with 8, 12, 16 or so pages are assembled by using additional 11- by 17-inch sheets.

DISTRIBUTION

Distribution methods should be taken into account when you design your newsletter.

Design your newsletter with distribution methods in mind.

Newsletters can be mailed full size or folded; they can be self-mailers or stuffed into envelopes.

Decisions about distribution should be made early in your planning process. Self-mailers avoid the cost of envelopes but sacrifice valuable editorial or selling space to the address area.

A multiple-fold newsletter is inexpensive to mail, but the nameplate and headlines aren't visible until the folds are opened. In addition, the advantage of presenting the recipient with the "billboard effect" of a full-size 8 1/2- by 11-inch newsletter is lost.

EVALUATION CHECKLIST

By answering the following questions, you can check to see whether you've incorporated all the elements necessary for a successful newsletter.

1. Is your newsletter built around a distinctive nameplate that identifies subject matter and editorial focus?

2. Is the nameplate amplified by a phrase or motto that identifies its focus or intended audience?

3. Are volume number and issue dates clearly identified?

4. Do headlines compete with the nameplate or with each other?

5. Is the source of your newsletter clearly identified by a logo, address and telephone information?

6. Are there "teasers" or a table of contents on the front cover to direct the reader's attention inside?

7. Are articles clearly separated from each other?

8. Have you paid equal attention to the front and back covers?

9. Is there enough consistency between each issue of your newsletter to maintain its identity, yet enough variety to set each issue apart and maintain reader interest?

10. Are all photos accompanied by meaningful captions?

9 | TABLOIDS AND NEWSPAPERS

Designing tabloid-sized newsletters and newspapers represents a logical progression from 8 1/2- by 11-inch newsletters.

Many of the same principles involved in designing successful newsletters apply to tabloids and newspapers, particularly the need to maintain issue-to-issue consistency while accommodating a constantly changing mix of text and visuals.

For example, all three formats need high-impact headlines that don't compete with the nameplate or with each other.

And it's also important to organize photographs of varying size as effectively as possible.

TABLOIDS

Tabloids are similar to newsletters, except that their larger page size allows more design flexibility.

Tabloids' large size allows more design flexibility.

The typical tabloid page is 11 by 17 inches, although those dimensions vary from newspaper to newspaper and printer to printer. Some tabloids, for example, are 11 by 14 inches.

Tabloids often are printed on a web press, which feeds the paper to the press off a large roll. As a result, the actual image area of the tabloid is slightly smaller than 11 by 17 inches.

Laser printers can be used to prepare tabloids, since the coarse newsprint paper most tabloids are printed on absorbs ink and consequently reduces the high-resolution sharpness normally achieved in phototypeset images. In addition, desktop publishing allows revisions to be made easily up to deadline time.

Most desktop publishing software programs let you create tabloid pages. Most laser printers, however, are not designed to handle paper sizes larger than 8 1/2 by 11 inches. (Tabloid-sized laser printers are available, although fairly uncommon.)

To get around that limitation, desktop publishing programs offer a tiling feature that automatically overlaps, or tiles, a series of 8 1/2- by 11-inch pages that can then be pasted together to create one large tabloid page.

Front Cover

The tabloid page size can accommodate large, bold headlines and large photographs.

You can let one large photograph dominate the front cover of a tabloid.

Larger page sizes allow a bolder treatment for photos and display type.

THE GOLD
STANDARD
For Investors in Precious Metals

Or, you can combine a large photo with a grid of smaller photos.

The front page can feature text or visuals.
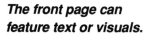

In some cases, the front cover consists mostly of headline type.

Inside Pages

Choose a consistent format for the inside pages of your tabloid.

Design your tabloid as a series of two-page spreads. Include your organization's logo at least once on every spread. Ideally, nameplate or firm name and tabloid title or theme are repeated in each spread. An ideal place for such items is in a drop (a deep top border).

Design your tabloid for two-page spreads.

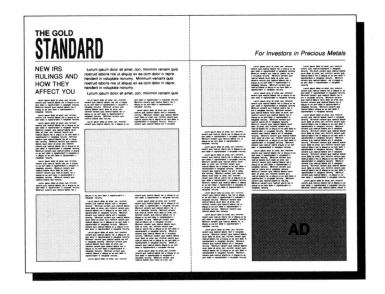

Choosing a three-column format lets you use a variety of photograph sizes.

The wider columns of a three-column format are more suitable for tabloids than for newsletters.

A five-column grid creates even more design flexibility, just as it does with newsletters.

Wider columns are better suited for tabloids than for newsletters.

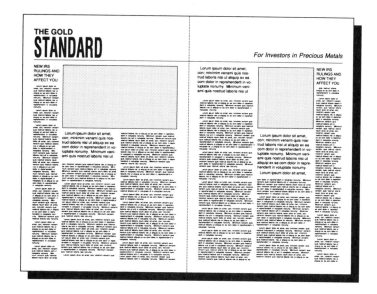

Content

Because of their size, tabloids let you creatively mix editorial and selling space.

Tabloids creatively mix editorial and selling space.

You can mix information and advertising in your tabloid to enhance your firm's credibility and image; pre-sell prospective customers on your firm's competence and professionalism; and expand the market for your products by answering basic questions first-time buyers might have.

There are several ways you can highlight editorial information:

Between parallel rules on the top half of each page …

Rules and white space can provide a framework for your message.

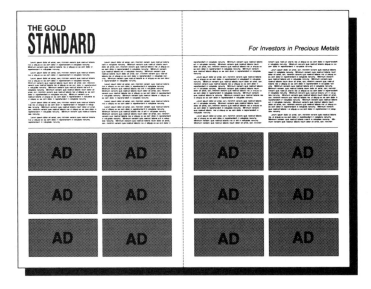

In vertical columns adjacent to the selling area …

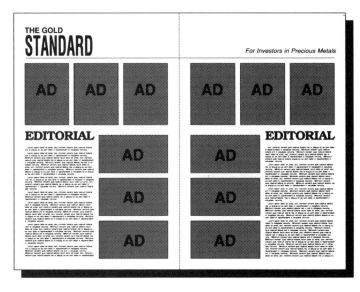

Between the selling areas …

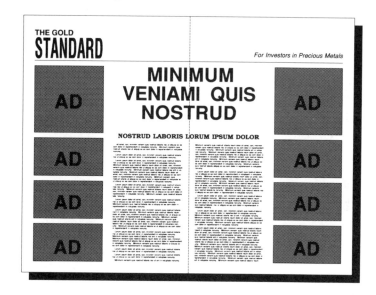

At the bottom of each page …

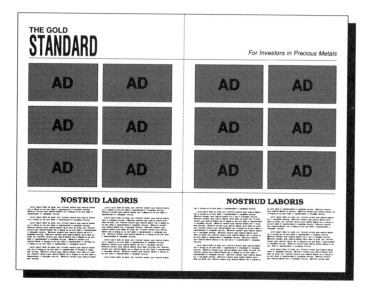

With a screen to integrate the editorial material into a unit...

Screens can unify blocks of editorial material.

Back Cover

Pay as much attention to the back cover as you do to the front.

Use the back cover as well as the front to promote your theme.

Many readers see the back of a newspaper before the front. Therefore, you should use the back as well as the front to promote your theme. One way is to summarize important points contained in the front-cover articles.

Another way is to repeat your best ads on the back cover, including special financing incentives and limited-time offers.

Previewing Your Tabloid

You can preview your finished tabloid by printing reduced-size pages.

To preview full pages of your tabloid, print them at 65 percent of actual size. You'll be able to see an entire 11- by 17-inch tabloid page on an 8 1/2- by 11-inch sheet of paper.

NEWSPAPERS

Once you're comfortable producing tabloid-size newsletters, you'll find it an easy step up to newspaper design.

One of the key differences between the two formats is the number of columns. Tabloids are usually set up on fewer, wider text columns.

Newspaper pages, however, are divided into many—often six or more—narrow text columns. The resulting shorter line lengths require smaller type sizes and more attention to hyphenation and letter and word spacing.

More columns mean smaller type sizes.

Headlines

An important challenge that faces newspaper designers is working out a hierarchical order among the various articles that will appear on the same page.

Confusion will reign if all articles are introduced by the same size headline.

The most important articles need larger headlines.

And if larger headlines are placed too low on the page, the result is an unbalanced, bottom-heavy layout.

Let the top of the page carry most of the weight.

The solution is to arrange headlines in a way that clearly identifies their importance without allowing them to overpower subordinate articles.

Photographs

Newspapers must accommodate a wide variety of photographs of differing size, and degree, of importance.

In a typical newspaper, the front page alone often contains more photos than are found in an entire newsletter issue.

When arranging multiple photographs, each should be placed appropriately in relation to the others and to the page design as a whole.

Whereas many newsletter photographs are often simple head shots, newspaper photos include a variety of subjects, shapes and sizes.

Teasers

Because of a newspaper's greater size and complexity, it's even more important to provide front-page teasers to attract readers inside.

Attention must be drawn to special features and high-interest articles inside. Readers also want clear direction to specific items such as classified listings, a calendar of events, etc.

Draw readers inside with hints of what's to come.

Standing Elements

The front page of a newspaper usually includes repeating features, such as stock market highlights and weather and sports summaries.

These have to be accessible to the casual reader but not so prominent that they detract from the current events of the day.

Don't let repeating features compete with the news.

All these elements have to coexist with the newspaper's nameplate and subtitle.

Article Jumplines

Another peculiarity of newspapers is the large number of articles continued on inside pages.

Long articles are often broken into several segments placed on succeeding pages. Each segment requires jumplines to help the reader locate the continuation. Jumplines present a challenge to the designer: they must be easily noticed but also easily distinguished from headlines and subheads.

Jumplines help readers locate continuing articles.

Advertisements

Advertising is a necessary ingredient and, in fact, pays the bills for most newspapers!

It's often impossible to be sure of the number and sizes of advertisements you'll run until the last minute.

Advertisements must neither compete with nor be overshadowed by adjacent editorial material.

Lorum ipsum dolor sit amet, con; minimim venami quis nostrud laboris nisi ut aliquip ex ea com dolor. In reprehenderit in volupatate.

Lorum ipsum dolor sit amet, con; minimim venami quis nostrud laboris nisi ut aliquip ex ea com dolor in reprehenderit in voluptate nonumy. Lorum ipsum dolor sit amet, con. Minimim venami quis nostrud laboris nisi ut aliquip ex ea com dolor in reprehenderit in voluptate.

Lorum ipsum dolor sit amet, con; minimim venami quis nostrud laboris nisi. Lorum ipsum dolor sit

amet, con; minimim venami quis nostrud laboris nisi ut aliquip ex ea com dolor in reprehenderit in voluptate nonumy. Quis nostrud laboris nisi ut aliquip com dolor. In reprehenderit in voluptate.

Lorum ipsum dolor sit amet, con; minimim venami quis nostrud laboris nisi ut aliquip ex ea com dolor in reprehenderit in voluptate nonumy. Lorum ipsum dolor.

Minimim venami quis nostrud laboris nisi ut aliquip ex ea com dolor in reprehenderit in voluptate nonumy. Lorum ipsum dolor sit

amet, con; minimim venami quis nostrud laboris.

Lorum ipsum dolor sit amet, con; minimim venami quis nostrud laboris nisi ut aliquip ex ea com dolor in reprehenderit in voluptate nonumy. Lorum ipsum dolor sit amet, con; minimim venami quis nostrud laboris nisi ut aliquip ex com dolor.

Lorum ipsum dolor sit amet, con; minimim venami quis nostrud laboris nisi ut aliquip ex ea com dolor . In reprehenderit in voluptate nonumy. Lorum ipsum dolor sit minimim.

Venami quis nostrud laboris nisi ut

Lorum ipsum dolor sit amet, con; minimim venami quis nostrud laLorum ipsum dolor sit amet, con; minimim venami quis nostrud la-

BIGGEST SALE EVER!

Lorum ipsum dolor sit amet, con; minimim venami quis nostrud laboris nisi ut aliquip ex ea com dolor. In reprehenderit in voluptate nonumy. Lorum ipsum dolor sit minimim.

Terry's Tire Service
988 W. Rolling Road
Treadtown, NY 77000

Many newspapers are adhering to Standard Advertising Units specifications to simplify page makeup (check this with your local newspaper). These include a variety of standard ad sizes that can be used as building blocks in assembling pages.

EVALUATION CHECKLIST

Use the following questions to test your tabloids and newspapers in terms of the elements discussed in this chapter.

1. Is the front page of your tabloid assembled around a single major story or idea?

2. Have you designed the front cover with elements that invite readers inside?

3. Do the inside tabloid pages contain a pleasing mixture of dominant and subordinate articles?

4. Are newspaper headlines sized and placed in a way that shows their relative status yet also lets readers quickly locate articles?

5. Can readers quickly locate article continuations on inside pages?

6. Is each photograph sized and placed to reflect its importance?

7. Have you used a single grid and consistent graphic accents throughout your newspaper or tabloid?

8. Have you reinforced your publication's image by repeating the nameplate on inside pages?

10 | MAGAZINE AND NEWSPAPER ADVERTISEMENTS

Desktop publishing is ideally suited to producing newspaper advertisements. In addition, important recent advances in desktop publishing hardware and software, including the ability to enhance color photographs on your computer screen and prepare color separations, now allow you to produce high-quality, professional-looking magazine ads.

Although we begin this chapter by analyzing factors that contribute to successful newspaper ads, you can use many of the same techniques to improve your magazine ads.

NEWSPAPER ADVERTISEMENTS

Even with the typically short lead times you're given and the inevitability of content changes, you can produce newspaper ads quickly and cost-effectively with templates prepared in advance.

Making Maximum Use of Grids

The best way to design effective advertisements is to make maximum use of the grid as a planning tool.

Grids make it easy to plan for the approximate number of products and text blocks necessary for your marketing and promotional needs.

Start creating a flexible grid by dividing a vertical rectangle— the shape of many ads—into six equal vertical columns. Then divide each column into 13 equal squares.

A grid can provide a versatile framework for your ads.

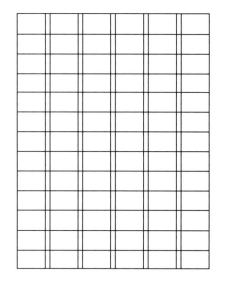

From this simple grid, a number of ways of mixing text and graphics become possible. For example, you can divide the space from top to bottom into four areas: a two-unit-high headline area extending across the top of the page; below that, an area for visuals also extending the width of the page; then three two-column-wide text blocks four units high; and at the bottom of the page, a two-unit-high response area along the bottom of the ad. The response area would contain your firm's logo, address and perhaps a coupon.

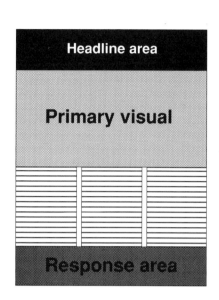

Without changing any of the proportions, notice how you can completely alter the appearance of the ad by relocating the headline below the visual.

Relocating one element can give your ad a whole new look.

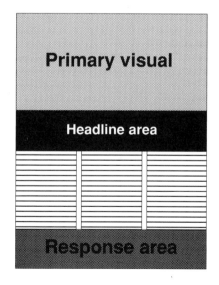

If you wanted to use a smaller amount of body copy, you could set the text in larger type and use only two parallel text blocks, each three columns wide.

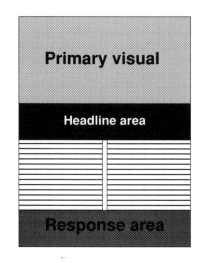

Another way to divide the space is to arrange the text in an L-shaped block wrapped around a vertical photograph. You might choose an "atmosphere" photo showing the benefits of the product or service you're advertising.

In an alternate arrangement, you could subdivide the space by using a box containing a smaller photograph accompanied by a two-column caption and a large price.

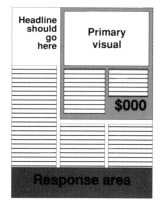

Introducing Variety

Basing your layout on a grid makes it easy to vary the size, shape and placement of text and visual elements.

Things get interesting when you include both dominant and subordinate visual elements: for example, the combination of a large "atmosphere"—or "premise"—photograph, a column of "premise" copy, plus three boxes, each containing the photo, caption and price of a specific product.

Dominant and subordinate visuals can create interest.

Headline should go here

Premise visual

Premise copy

Photo Photo Photo

$000 $000 $000

Response area

To include *more* products, you could reduce the primary photo and add another row of product photos.

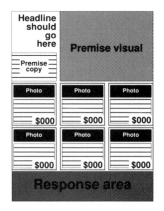

Ten products—one dominant, nine subordinate—are included in the layout example below.

Grids don't limit but, in fact, liberate space.

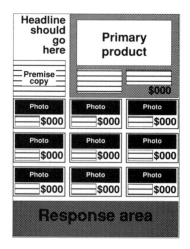

As the preceding examples show, grids don't limit your creative freedom; they actually *liberate you* to utilize space in more creative and cost-effective ways!

Pyramid Ad Layouts

Choose a pyramid ad layout when you want to emphasize some products more than others.

A multicolumn "pyramid" ad allows a hierarchical organization. Place a large photograph of your most competitive product at the top of the ad. Immediately below it, place the next two or three most competitive products. Below this, add several columns of product listings.

Pyramid layouts establish a hierarchy of importance.

More Grid Options

When your products are of equal importance, organize product offerings in equal-sized boxes.

As an alternative, photos, captions and prices can be contained within a grid of equal-sized boxes. Although the boxes are the same, a great deal of flexibility is still possible.

A grid of equal-sized boxes creates a lot of flexibility.

The columns and rows of your grid can be organized horizontally or vertically by reversed-out category dividers.

EASY-LIVING
YEAR-END CLOSE OUT

Sofas	Chairs	Tables	Beds
description of inventory here description of inventory here	description of inventory here description of inventory here	description of inventory here description of inventory here	description of inventory here description of inventory here
10% SAVINGS	**20%** SAVINGS	**30%** SAVINGS	**40%** SAVINGS
list of styles and retail price here list of styles and retail price here	list of styles and retail price here list of styles and retail price here	list of styles and retail price here list of styles and retail price here	list of styles and retail price here list of styles and retail price here
10% SAVINGS	**20%** SAVINGS	**30%** SAVINGS	**40%** SAVINGS
list of styles and retail price here list of styles and retail price here	list of styles and retail price here list of styles and retail price here	list of styles and retail price here list of styles and retail price here	list of styles and retail price here list of styles and retail price here
10% SAVINGS	**20%** SAVINGS	**30%** SAVINGS	**40%** SAVINGS
list of styles and retail price here list of styles and retail price here	list of styles and retail price here list of styles and retail price here	list of styles and retail price here list of styles and retail price here	list of styles and retail price here list of styles and retail price here

Featured items in a two-page ad can be placed in larger boxes.

To break up the monotony, featured items can be placed in double-wide or double-high boxes.

Featured item boxes can also be four times normal size. This technique can be used to balance ads running on facing pages of a two-page spread.

Column Ads

Choose a column-based ad structure when your competition is using pyramid or grid-based ads.

Multiple products can be organized by category, using vertical columns with subheads at the top of each column.

Your ad should set you apart from the competition.

When a wider ad is designed, however, horizontal organization works just as well. Subheads can be placed in a column to the left.

Templates for Newspaper Ads

Templates can save you time and effort in designing and producing newspaper ads.

For example, create and save ad templates for various sizes—full-page, half-page, one-third-page and one-quarter-page. Design them all to reflect a strong family resemblance, with consistent treatments of headlines, borders, artwork and buying information.

By letting you predetermine the number of items you can use, grids make your planning sessions easier.

Key elements can be saved in templates for use in other ads.

Borders

Because most newspaper advertisements occupy less than a full page, pay special attention to borders and white space.

Strong borders separate your newspaper ad from the "clutter" of other page elements that surround it. The type of border you choose will often be determined by the shape of the ad.

A wide, vertically oriented ad should have strong top and bottom rules.

Strong borders make an ad stand out on the page.

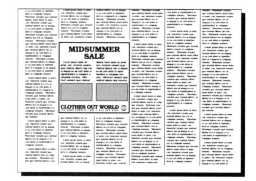

Thinner side rules can make small advertisements look taller than they actually are.

A small, square advertisement should be bordered with rules of equal thickness.

White Space

Use white space to further isolate your newspaper advertisement from its surroundings.

The impact of your ad can be increased by providing sufficient "breathing room" within the ruled borders of the ad to set off artwork and text.

One way to do that is to place the borders of your ad within the space allotted. As a result, there will be white space around your borders, clearly separating your copy from its surroundings.

Leave enough "breathing room" within the borders of an ad.

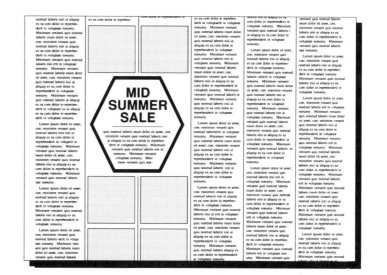

Using this technique, you can make small ads look larger by letting part of the ad break through the border into the surrounding interior white space.

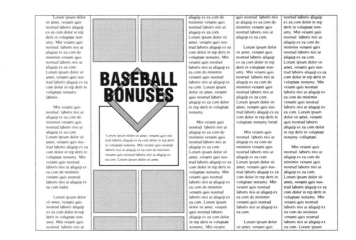

White space within ads can be created by using a multicolumn grid, indenting body copy and allowing headlines to begin in the vertical band of white space to the left of the ad.

Headlines draw more attention when set off with white space.

JOIN US FOR A GREAT FUTURE.

White space within small ads can be created by using a multicolumn grid, indenting body copy and allowing headlines to begin in the vertical band of white space to the left of the ad. White space within small ads can be created by using a multicolumn grid, indenting body copy and allowing headlines to begin in the vertical band of white space to the left of the ad.

Worldwide Imports   Anytown, USA

Headlines

Use the same headline treatment for all the ads in your newspaper, regardless of their size.

A common technique is to reverse the headline out of the upper one-fourth to one-third of the area occupied by the ad.

Reverse headlines can be attention-getting.

Avoid reversing headlines out of long, narrow boxes. This creates "frowning" ads that obscure the headline.

Another effective technique is to place a graduated dark-to-light screen behind the headline and primary photograph or illustration. This allows the headline to be reversed and the text to be set in black type against a light background.

Adding a graduated screen behind headlines can be effective.

Headlines are often centered in newspaper ads, although that doesn't have to be the case.

An alternate technique is to balance a strong flush-right head-line with a smaller flush-left subhead. This draws the reader into the ad by speeding the transition from "premise" headline to "supporting" subhead.

Base your ad layout on product visuals.

Handling Artwork

In multiproduct ads, base your layout on the number of products you want to include in your advertisement.

Your ad design and layout should evolve out of the number and size of the products you want to include, and should also be in-fluenced by the appearance of your competitors' ads.

Screens

Screens add a "two-color" effect to your ads.

Screens within boxes, for example, can unify horizontal and ver-tical elements of the ad.

Or you can place the screens behind the whole ad, which adds contrast to the boxes because of their "whiteness."

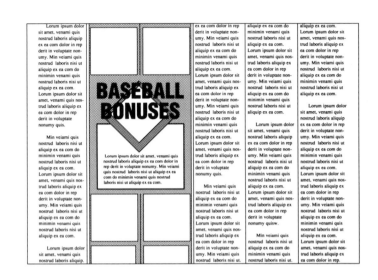

Callouts

Use callouts to draw attention to the most important selling features of your products.

A callout is a graphic arrow that connects a visual to a brief description of product features and benefits. Callouts give readers a concise "educational" message about why they should buy a particular product.

Add an educational tone to your ad by highlighting a product's key features.

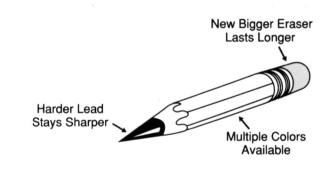

Prices, Buying Information and Logos

Every ad should include all necessary purchasing information.

The logo of the firm running the ad should be very prominent. This can be achieved by either size or contrast.

In this ad, the logo is relatively small, yet it's easily identified because it's surrounded by white space.

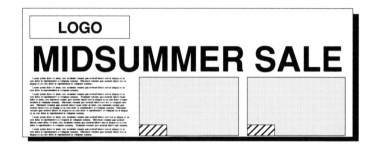

Make it easy for readers to respond to your ad.

Clearly visible addresses, phone numbers and buying information make it easy for the reader to respond to the ad.

The type size used for captions and prices should be proportional to the size of the photograph or artwork used to illustrate the product. Set prices in large type for large photographs, in small type for small photographs.

Likewise, the size of a manufacturer's logo should be in correct proportion to the size of the visual it relates to and its surrounding information.

Consistency

Prices and manufacturer logos should always be placed in the same location.

In grid-type ads, all logos and prices should be the same size and, whenever possible, placed in the same relative position in each box.

Not every advertised product needs to be illustrated.

Practice restraint when choosing typefaces and type sizes. Avoid using a different type size for each product. Even the most product-filled ad needs no more than a few type sizes. One size for "primary" products and a second size for secondary products may be all the variety you need.

Remember that not every product advertised needs to be illustrated. Often, the best-looking ads simply list the products, along with a few representative photographs or drawings.

Smaller Newspaper Ads

Desktop publishing is ideally suited for preparing newspaper ads that cover one, two or three columns.

It's often harder to produce an effective small newspaper ad than a full- or half-page ad.

Large ads attract attention simply because of their size. Smaller ads have to be designed more carefully, so they'll emerge from the many competing elements around them.

One of the most effective designs for single-column newspaper ads reverses the headline out of solid black, focuses the ad around a single product and balances the reversed-out headline and product visual with a bulleted list of product benefits, concluding with a screened logo and address at the bottom.

It's often harder to create an effective small advertisement than a large one.

This technique provides visual interest, because the strong reversed area at the top of the ad is balanced by the screened area at the bottom. Notice how the introductory paragraph is wrapped around the visual, integrating text and illustration.

The indention and flush-left, ragged-right alignment of the bullet items create white space to the left and right of the ad, providing separation from surrounding elements.

Smaller ads require both simplicity and attention to detail.

Small ads require restraint and attention to detail. It's all too easy to make them complex and hard to read. Small ads gain impact to the extent they're focused—and frequently repeated.

Classified Ads

Desktop publishing can produce attractive classified ads.

Advertisers often don't realize they can submit their own camera-ready copy, rather than leaving the ad preparation to the newspaper.

The addition of a strong, high-contrast headline and prominent border can make a big difference in the response you get to your "Help Wanted" ad.

A strong headline can increase response to "Help Wanted" ads.

venami quis nostrud laboris nisi ut aliquip ex ea com dolor in reprehenderit in voluptate nonumy. Minimum

DESKTOP PUBLISHING

art/production person to help out three tired cowboys and one cowgirl who are working day and night to finish a graphic design book. Must have DTP experience, willing to work long hours, meet hot deadlines and like pizza. Must relocate to Denver Colorado ASAP. Send résumé to Laser Writing Inc. "World Head quarters."

VENIAMI QUIS nostrud laboris erit in voluptate nonumy. Minimum veniami quis nostrud laboris nsum dolor sit amet, con; minimim

NOSTRUD LABORIS nisi ut aliquip ex ea com dolor in reprehenderit in voluptate nonumy. Minimum veniami quis nostrud Laboris erit in voluptate nonumy. Minimum veniami quis nostrud laboris nsum dolor sit amet, con; minimim veniami quis nostrud

Indenting body copy can also draw attention to your ad by incorporating a strong vertical band of white space into an otherwise gray page.

Lorum ipsum dolor sit amet, venami quis nostrud laboris aliquip ex ea com dolor in rep derit in voluptate nonumy. Min veiami quis nostrud laboris nisi ut aliquip ex ea com do minimin venami quis nostrud laboris nisi ut aliquip ex ea com. Lorum ipsum dolor sit amet, venami quis nostrud laboris aliquip ex ea com dolor in rep derit in voluptate nonumy.

Min veiami quis nostrud laboris nisi ut aliquip ex ea com do minimin venami quis nostrud laboris nisi ut aliquip ex ea com. Lorum

ipsum dolor sit amet, venami quis nostrud laboris aliquip ex ea com dolor in rep derit in voluptate nonumy. Min veiami quis

SALES MANAGER
FOR EXPANDING
COMPUTER SOFTWARE
COMPANY
Supervisory or extensive
retail experience required.
CALL TODAY!
1-800-333-4444

nostrud laboris nisi ut aliquip ex ea com do minimin venami quis nostrud laboris nisi ut aliquip ex ea com nostrud.

Lorum ipsum dolor sit amet, venami quis nostrud laboris aliquip ex ea com dolor in rep derit in voluptate nonumy. Min veiami quis nostrud laboris nisi ut aliquip ex ea com do minimin venami quis nostrud laboris nisi ut aliquip ex ea com. Lorum ipsum dolor sit amet, venami quis nostrud laboris aliquip ex ea com dolor in rep derit in voluptate nonumy.

Min veiami quis nostrud laboris nisi ut aliquip ex ea com do minimin venami quis nostrud laboris nisi ut aliquip ex ea com.

Quality Considerations

It's entirely appropriate to prepare camera-ready newspaper ads using your laser printer.

The quality of photo-typesetting is often lost on newsprint.

It's usually not necessary to go to the expense of having newspaper ads phototypeset, because the relatively coarse newsprint absorbs the ink to such a degree that the quality advantage offered by phototypesetting is lost.

Another advantage of desktop publishing is that you can build a library of scanned line-art illustrations to use in your ads, when appropriate, in place of photographs.

The new generation of 1,000-dot-per-inch plain-paper laser printers makes it even easier to prepare high-quality newspaper ads in your office.

As newspapers continue to improve their reproduction quality, the added clarity of images and type prepared with 1,000-dot-per-inch laser printers will become readily apparent.

In addition, scanners and desktop publishing programs are rapidly improving in their ability to handle photographs. The quality produced on a laser printer will soon approach the quality of newspaper photo reproduction. Thus, it's entirely feasible that you'll soon be preparing complete newspaper ads, including photographs, with your desktop publishing system and laser printer.

MAGAZINE ADVERTISEMENTS

Magazine advertisements typically feature fewer products and require higher production quality.

Fewer products are included, because of the long period of time between when the ad is placed and when it appears in print. The emphasis is usually on the firm's range of products and services rather than specific items and prices.

Magazine ads generally appear in a more dignified editorial atmosphere that dictates careful selection of typefaces, type sizes, type styles and line spacing.

Consider high production quality in designing magazine advertisements.

Magazine ad sizes are limited. Most magazines are created around a three-column grid.

Options usually include the following:

- Full-page
- Two-thirds-page (two out of three columns)
- Half-page horizontal
- Half-page vertical
- One-third-page vertical (one column, full height)
- Third-square (two columns wide, one-third-page high)
- One-third-page horizontal (three columns wide, one-third-page high)

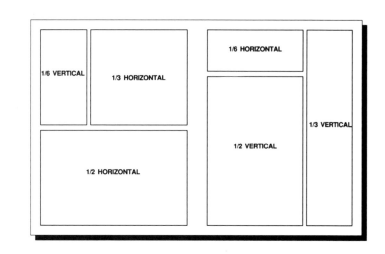

Grids will speed up your ad production.

You should prepare basic formats, or grids, including borders and logo placement, for the two or three sizes you're most likely to use. These will speed up planning and producing your ads.

Because most magazines are printed on high-quality coated paper, advertisements created with desktop publishing programs should be output on a phototypesetter. For this format, 300-dot-per-inch laser printing often doesn't provide the sharpness necessary for the best possible presentation of your ad.

Elements for Success

Borders, headlines and white space are crucial to the success of your magazine advertisements.

Your ad must appear as a self-contained unit, separated from surrounding material. The relatively small size of most magazine ads presents a major challenge. Typically, readers will see your ad in the context of a horizontal 17- by 11-inch spread that includes editorial material as well as other ads.

You generally have no control over where your ad will appear in the magazine and no assurance that it won't be dwarfed by surrounding color ads.

In this busy environment, use contrast provided by white space and type to keep your ad from fading into the background.

Use contrast to keep your ad from fading into the background.

Effective use of asymmetrical column grids and strong head-lines may be essential to the success of your ads.

For example, a strong vertical band of white space on the left can add impact to the headline and focus attention on the text.

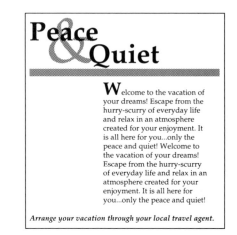

By carefully editing your copy, you can gain enough space to set the headline in larger type, surrounded by more white space or accented by horizontal rules.

One technique that can help your magazine ad emerge from its surroundings is to replace the traditional four-sided box border with horizontal rules, at the top and bottom only. These rules visually reinforce the body copy and emphasize the headline by surrounding it with white space.

NEW HOMES

- carefully selected homesites in the woods overlooking the river
- seasoned architects with solar construction in mind
- your dream house is only a step away

Sunrise Builders
we *always* get an early start

Product photographs are often replaced in magazine ads by strong, bold headlines.

Stock photos can help you stretch your ad budget.

Because of the high costs of custom photography, magazine ads often use stock photographs—previously taken, licensed photographs that can be obtained for a fraction of the cost of a custom photograph. (Check the Yellow Pages of metropolitan phone books or the bibliographies of publications such as *Print* or *Communication Arts*. You can also purchase stock photos on CD-ROM disks.)

Coupons

Magazine ads often include coupons inviting prospective customers to send for further information.

Highest response will occur when the coupons are placed in the lower right corner of a right-hand page. (More time and effort are required for a reader to remove a coupon from a center column or the lower right corner of a left-hand page.)

Make coupons easy to complete and return.

Most desktop publishing programs allow you to create distinctive borders for your coupons. A great deal of attention should be devoted to the design of the coupon. Once created, however, it can be stored as a separate file and used over and over again.

When you submit ads to several publications, you can code the coupons to identify the magazine with the response. Simply add a department designation to your address. (The next time you read a magazine, notice how frequently this is done—and how often the "Department" code matches the magazine's initials!)

Design Usable Coupons

Avoid creating coupons with lines spaced so close together that prospective customers will have difficulty filling them out.

Always make it as easy as possible for readers to respond to your offer.

Spaces should be large enough and long enough to accommodate the responder's name and address, written by hand.

Color

Magazine ads frequently include color.

Color can be used as a background, or spot color can highlight headlines, rules and borders.

Studies have shown that ads using color have up to 80 percent more readership than black and white ads. You might find that fewer, or smaller, color ads will produce more sales than black-and-white ones.

Use spot color to draw attention to your ad.

The addition of a spot color can vastly increase the readership of an ad. Color can be used as a background behind all or part of the ad, or simply used to accent one or more of the rules or other graphic elements.

Four-color reproduction can be used for photographs.

Many desktop publishing programs allow you to create four-color separations. The newest color printers can produce accurate proofs of your ads right in your office.

EVALUATION CHECKLIST

Check your magazine and newspaper ads for effectiveness using the following questions.

Newspaper Ads

1. Are your ads set off from their surroundings by appropriate margins, borders and white space?

2. Is the headline large enough to attract attention without overwhelming other elements of the ad?

3. Are grids or boxes used to organize ads containing multiple products, prices and manufacturer logos?

4. Are captions and prices clearly connected to product photographs or illustrations?

5. Has all buying information—address, hours, credit terms—been clearly spelled out?

6. Is your logo prominent enough to provide a visual signature for your ad?

7. Is the design of your ad appropriate to both its content—the number and importance of products included—and the image you want to project?

8. Have you been consistent in the size and placement of repeating elements such as logos and prices?

9. Do your newspaper ads contain messages that can potentially expand your market?

10. Do you submit your own camera-ready classified ads featuring distinctive headlines and attention-getting borders?

Magazine Ads

1. Is the design of your ad consistent with the long-term image you want to project?

2. Is the appearance of your ad clearly distinctive from ads run by your competitors?

3. Have you used borders, white space, screens and indents to set your ads off from surrounding elements?

4. Are coupons designed to be easily filled out?

5. Have you carefully edited headline and body copy so that only essential words remain, permitting large, easy-to-read type set off by sufficient white space?

6. Have you investigated costs, benefits and alternate ways of adding color to your ads?

11 | SALES MATERIALS: Brochures, Catalogs, Flyers, Menus and Product Sheets

Successful sales materials require careful planning. They can be prepared in a wide variety of shapes and sizes.

Choosing the right format depends on factors such as

- The number, complexity and cost of products and services being advertised. Will the sales piece focus on a single item, or must it accommodate a variety of products and services?

- The targeted point in the purchase cycle. Will materials be designed for a wide range of potential buyers or aimed specifically at prospects who are ready to purchase?

- Whether to appeal to the buyer's emotions. Is the item utilitarian, or will it be perceived as an enhancement to the buyer's lifestyle or self-image?

- Production time and relative longevity of the sales piece. How much time is involved in producing it, and how long will it last?

Consider a product's potential buyers when designing sales materials.

A flyer announcing a neighborhood yard sale requires a totally different approach than an extended warranty program for a luxury automobile.

Likewise, is the brochure intended for casual browsers or is it intended to close a sale? Brochures distributed to a large audience early in the purchase cycle don't need to be as detailed—or expensively printed—as those distributed to qualified buyers who are just about ready to pull out their checkbooks.

BROCHURES

There are several types of brochures: capabilities, line and product-specific brochures.

Capabilities brochures describe a firm or association's goals and products or services.

A health maintenance organization's brochures might describe its preventive medicine and long-term care plans, while a performing arts group's brochures might provide concert and instruction schedules.

Brochures are designed for a long shelf life.

Line brochures feature one category or even one item of a product line. An audio/video manufacturer might have separate brochures for compact disc players, videocassette recorders and car stereo systems.

Product-specific brochures focus on a specific purpose. A college alumni association, for example, might prepare a brochure in conjunction with a fund drive to raise money for a new building.

As for size, brochures run the gamut—from a single 8 1/2- by 11-inch sheet of paper, folded into thirds and printed in one color on both sides, to 16 full pages printed in four colors.

In addition to the various sizes and editorial approaches, brochures can also be categorized by their level of complexity. These consist of "teasers," "tell-alls" and "impressers."

Teasers

"Teasers" are brochures targeted to prospective buyers early in the decision process.

Teasers don't pretend to tell the whole story: their purpose is to direct the reader to the next level of action, such as calling a toll-free telephone number.

Teasers are printed on single sheets of paper, then folded into panels (to fit into a Number Ten business envelope). They're inexpensively produced so that they can be distributed to as many prospective buyers as possible.

Teasers are often displayed conspicuously in free-standing or counter-top racks so that any and all can feel free to take one.

In choosing a format, consider your brochure's level of complexity.

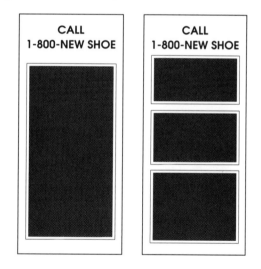

Tell-All Brochures

"Tell-all" brochures target qualified buyers.

They're designed for the next level—serious potential buyers who are closer to the moment of truth. They contain more information and often conclude with detailed specifications of the products or service being offered.

Tell-all brochures are often printed on standard 8 1/2- by 11-inch pages or on larger sheets requiring a 9- by 12-inch envelope. In fact, a great deal of flexibility is possible. The size, shape and quality of paper used for these brochures can help set your presentation of a product or service apart from competing ads. You can even use square or other nonstandard page sizes if they enhance your design.

Tell-all brochures help sway serious potential buyers.

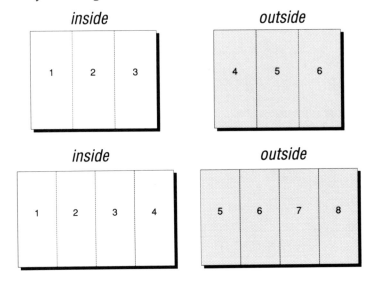

Tell-all brochures tend to be either copy- or illustration-oriented, although they can combine large and small photographs with expanded captions.

Impressers

"Impressers" approach the quality of booklets in design sophistication.

Impressers follow up and reinforce the message at the last crucial phase before purchase. They combine sophisticated graphic design with high-quality printing and paper.

The high quality of impresser brochures reflects the quality of the product.

Impressers are appropriate when the products or services are either emotionally very important to the buyer or in cases where benefits can't be measured until after the purchase is made. Examples include luxury items such as expensive automobiles, complex technical products and services, and intangibles like public relations or financial services. An impresser brochure is designed to be part of the product: the high quality of the sales materials implies high quality in the product or service.

Design Considerations

When several types of brochures are used for one project, they should share a common "look," based on similar typographic and visual elements. Although larger brochures will probably be set on more than one column, there should be as much consistency among the brochures as possible:

- The same typefaces, type sizes and type styles for headlines and body copy.
- The same primary photographs, using additional photos and larger sizes in the more focused brochures.
- Consistent margins, borders and graphic accents.

Other basic requirements for all brochures are

- A front-cover headline that summarizes the primary benefits of the product offered.
- All facts and figures needed to encourage a positive decision.
- Prominently displayed, clear reader-response instructions, including names, addresses and telephone numbers.

One of the pitfalls to avoid is boxing or bordering each page, which can interfere with the reader's natural progression from panel to panel.

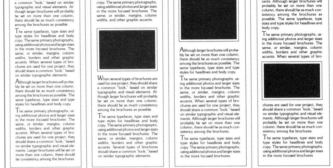

Product sheets can extend the usefulness of a brochure.

Brochures describing a standard line of products or services can be used over an extended period of time. They are typically supported by detailed product sheets (described later in this chapter), which present a more detailed look at a single product. This can save money, because individual product sheets can be revised and reprinted as products are updated, without making the full-line brochures obsolete.

CATALOGS

Catalogs are similar to brochures, except they usually contain more pages and are more product-oriented.

The challenge is to integrate numerous visual elements, captions and prices into an effective and appealing design.

Catalogs are usually produced annually or biannually. Because of their longevity, they're often printed on more expensive paper and include more color.

In many cases, particularly in the retail business, catalogs evolve from newsletters.

The volume of a catalog increases its perceived value.

However, catalogs are often smaller than newsletters. Often, page size is sacrificed for volume, which increases the perceived "reference value" of the catalog and contributes to long life. Many catalogs use a lot of color, which also increases their perceived value and selling power.

Covers

Catalog covers often are printed on a different paper stock than the inside pages.

Often, a heavier, glossy (or smooth, reflective) paper stock is used to provide higher quality photo reproduction and better color saturation.

A single photo of the company's most popular product is often used on the cover to communicate an identity and promote sales.

The cover can also feature a collage, or grouping, of photos or illustrations, calling attention to the diversity of products described inside.

Sometimes, an "atmosphere" photograph is combined with smaller shots of featured products.

Like newsletters, catalog covers often contain a nameplate, or title, that reflects the contents.

Inside Pages

Often a catalog's inside front-cover spread describes the company and its policy. Frequently there's a "Letter From the President" explaining the company's philosophy.

Inside catalog pages are generally more complex than newsletter pages. Often, pages are equally divided into sections for product photos, captions and prices.

You can use varying sizes of artwork.

Artwork can add variety to inside catalog pages.

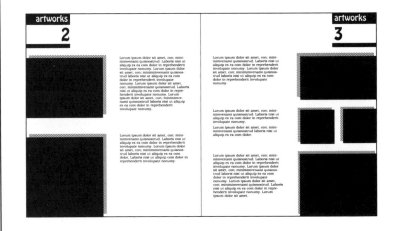

Another useful technique is to place colored or screened backgrounds behind product photos. These provide page-to-page consistency and highlight the photos.

Order Form

Ordering information and forms can be printed as part of the catalog. However, response is encouraged by providing a separate, postage-paid, self-addressed order form inserted into the middle of the catalog.

Inviting readers to respond by offering easy-to-use order forms and placing toll-free telephone numbers in the catalog can greatly increase sales.

FLYERS

Flyers contain time-sensitive information printed on one side of a single sheet of paper.

Flyers are typically used to advertise a special, limited-time promotion of a single product or service. They're ideal when a small budget and immediacy are of paramount importance. They can also be hung on walls, placed on counter-tops or used as shopping bag inserts.

Flyers are ideal for limited-time promotions and small budgets.

Flyers are appropriate vehicles for promoting a drug store's specially priced vitamins, a nightclub's upcoming performance of a popular jazz musician, an office supply dealer's sale on file folders or a music store's sale on a certain label's compact discs.

Flyers must communicate a lot of information at a glance.

For flyers to communicate at a glance, they must include

- Large headlines
- A minimum of body copy
- Attention-getting visuals or graphic accents

Since the primary goal of sending out flyers is to get the message out to as many people as possible, they're usually printed inexpensively in only one or two colors on a cheaper grade of paper.

Printing your flyers on low-cost colored papers can produce attention-getting two-color effects for one-color prices.

Although most flyers are printed on standard 8 1/2- by 11-inch paper, larger sizes are possible.

Tabloid-size 11- by 17-inch flyers approach posters, or miniature billboards, in terms of visual impact and amount of information communicated.

PRODUCT SHEETS

Product sheets are simpler than brochures and more complex than flyers.

Product sheets provide detailed information and specifications about a product or service and are usually printed on high-quality paper stock. The front cover typically contains a large photograph of the product, a paragraph or two of explanatory material (often repeating the information contained in the company's full-line brochure), plus an outline of the product features and benefits.

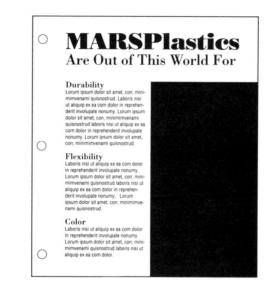

Specifications and details are listed in a product sheet.

The back cover is more detailed. It often includes one or more photos of products being used, followed by specific product information and any related optional or required accessories and supplies.

Product sheets are often three-hole punched, so they can be inserted in binders or added to proposals.

Creating Consistency

Often, a simple graphic can unify single product sheets into a series.

Consistent placement of a graphic can provide the continuity necessary to tie various product sheets together. This graphic symbol is often printed in a different color on each product sheet, to help distinguish it from others.

Consistency can also be provided by using the same sizes, styles and placement for borders, columns, visuals and the logo.

MENUS

A restaurant's menu is its most important advertising medium.

Menus require special care in organizing the material and creating a design that presents an appropriate image.

A menu is an excellent candidate for the application of desktop publishing technology. You can create menu templates that can be easily updated as prices change or new items are added.

A menu's design should reflect a restaurant's character.

Indeed, many fine restaurants print new menus each day—using color printers! This allows each menu to feature the freshest produce and "catch of the day."

Design Considerations

Borders, typefaces and visuals used in the menu's design play a major role in projecting the restaurant's character.

Stylized serif typefaces and ornate borders can communicate an Old World atmosphere.

A contemporary atmosphere is suggested by sparse, angular or geometric sans-serif type.

SOUPS
French Onion Soup
$2.95
Soup Du Jour
$2.85

SALADS
Chef Salad
$4.95
Spinach Salad
$4.50
Chicken Salad
$5.25

BURGERS
Standard Burger
$4.95
Cheese Burger
$5.25
Onion Burger
$4.95

Menus present an ideal opportunity to use clip art in establishing a mood. Clip-art publishers offer a variety of country, urban and other themes.

In creating a layout, remember that patrons must be able to quickly locate food categories. Subheads set in a contrasting typeface, type size and type style are easy to distinguish.

Avoid using dot leaders to connect food descriptions with prices.

Categories can be boxed, or separated by horizontal rules and white space.

One of the clichés of menu design is separate columns with leader dots connecting descriptions to prices. Unfortunately, the result can be a distracting horizontal pattern. Also, isolated prices place undue emphasis on the price rather than on the merits of the cuisine.

As an alternative, try centering descriptions in two or three columns across the page.

Each item can be introduced by a centered, one- or two-word identifier—perhaps in boldface italics—followed by a two- or three-line (mouth-watering) description. The price can then be discreetly tacked on at the end of the description.

This approach also focuses the reader's attention on one item at a time, instead of inviting comparison with other listings.

EVALUATION CHECKLIST

Use these questions to test your brochures, catalogs, flyers, product sheets and menus in terms of the important elements covered in this chapter.

Brochures

1. Have you chosen an appropriate size and format?

2. Does the front cover invite readers inside?

3. Have you maintained page-to-page consistency throughout?

4. Have you supplied all the information prospective buyers need to make favorable buying decisions?

Catalogs

1. Does your catalog begin selling on the front cover?

2. Have you paid as much attention to your catalog's nameplate as you would a newsletter nameplate?

3. Does your catalog contain information describing your company and its credentials?

4. Have you personalized your catalog by including a letter from the owner or employee photographs?

5. Have you made it easy for readers to respond by providing complete ordering information and a large, easy-to-use order form?

Flyers

1. Can readers get your flyer's message at a glance?

2. Have you edited your flyers to provide "who, what, when and how" information in the fewest words possible?

3. Have you avoided unnecessary clutter?

Product Sheets

1. Do your individual product sheets share a common family resemblance through consistent use of typography, photo placement and highlight color?

2. Do your product sheets maintain the "look" established by your brochures and catalogs?

Menus

1. Do type, white space and visual elements on the front cover of your menu provide an appropriate introduction to the restaurant's dining experience?

2. Can patrons quickly locate various food categories?

12 | Books, Documentation and Training Materials

More and more long documents (e.g., books and technical publications such as training materials) are being produced using desktop publishing and word processing software. Designing and producing these multipage documents present big challenges but at the same time more creative opportunities for desktop publishers.

BOOKS

Entire books are being submitted to publishers in camera-ready form.

Book design demands attention to page-to-page consistency.

Desktop publishing gives authors control of the graphic as well as the textual content of their books.

Desktop publishing offers another advantage. Because production costs are reduced, publishers can afford to produce more books and in a timely manner.

Book design requires constant attention to page-to-page consistency and flow.

A great deal of planning is necessary if text and artwork are to be properly balanced and integrated into an overall structure.

Style Considerations

Book design should take into account the writer's style.

If the author frequently uses long paragraphs, one wide column is appropriate.

However, if shorter paragraphs are more common, a two-column format might be better.

Fiction and nonfiction require different page structures. For instance, the use of subheads must be taken into account. Nonfiction books frequently use subheads to introduce new topics.

Fiction requires different design considerations than nonfiction.

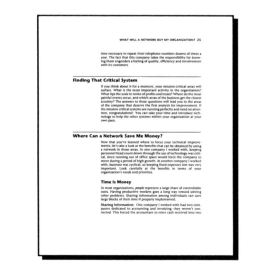

On the other hand, volumes of fiction rarely include subheads and are therefore easier to design. A single wide column often suffices.

Visuals

Visuals play an important role in book design.

A book with numerous illustrations and photographs requires a different layout than a text-oriented book. A book describing the evolution of a painter's style needs a totally different layout than a novel or an economics textbook.

Design books with visuals in mind.

In the case of books devoted to photographs or paintings, the design must accommodate visuals of various shapes and sizes.

One way to organize photographs is to place them in the same location and orientation on each page. They can be placed horizontally or vertically above the first line of text or to the left of the text columns.

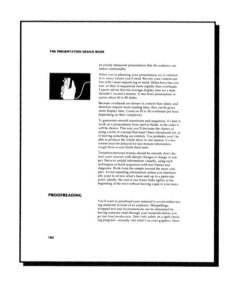

In the example below, photographs "hang" from an invisible "horizon" that spans each two-page spread. Captions are placed in the drop of white space above the photographs. This allows flexibility in using either long or short captions.

Occasionally, photos can bleed to all four sides to add variety.

For variety, an occasional photograph can bleed to all four sides of the page. In this case, its caption is placed above the drop on the facing page.

Captions

A consistent size and placement for captions must be maintained throughout the book.

A caption must be set in a contrasting typeface, type size and type style to distinguish it from the body text.

Annotations

In scholarly texts, placement of footnotes is very important.

Will a citation or reference appear as a footnote at the bottom of the page? Or will all references be listed together at the end of each chapter or grouped together as endnotes at the back of the book?

Organizing Elements

Attention must be paid to headers and footers when designing a book.

Headers let readers locate data quickly.

Readers need certain cues to keep them oriented as they progress. They must be able to see at a glance which chapter they're reading. Headers and footers on each page can provide this location information.

Headers and footers can consist of page number, chapter title and number, section title and number, and book title.

Multiple Page Layouts

Books often require several different master page layouts.

Books are divided into four major categories: front matter, back matter, chapter openings and text. Each section typically requires different page numbering, headers and footers, and column typography and placement. Therefore, layouts must accommodate specific elements yet relate visually to all the other sections of the book.

Front Matter

Front matter often includes separate page layouts for copyright and publisher information, acknowledgments, preface, introduction, author's credentials and a table of contents.

Chapter openings should invite readers to go on.

Usually, these sections are set in larger and smaller sizes of the typefaces used in the main body of the book. Copyright and disclaimer pages are typically set in much smaller type.

Text

Use a consistent style to introduce new chapters and sections.

Chapter breaks should be significant enough to give the reader a chance to pause, reflect and begin reading again with renewed interest. Often, the chapter number is treated as a dominant visual element on the page.

Chapter breaks give readers a chance to pause.

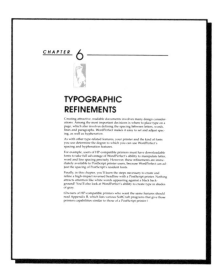

An introductory paragraph set in italics can be used to ease the reader's transition into the text.

Chapters organized around a common theme can be subdivided into sections. These sections should be introduced by their own dividers.

Back Matter

Information at the back of a book typically includes one or more appendices, a bibliography and an index.

DOCUMENTATION

Training materials, such as technical documentation, introduce their own design challenges.

These publications typically include a more complex mix of graphic, textual and typographic elements than do most books.

The ongoing narrative sequence is likely to be interspersed with digressions and related illustrations on specific aspects of a topic.

Training materials must often be produced within a limited time frame and budget allowance. This places extra demands on designers and desktop publishers.

The primary goal is to organize a variety of elements.

These are some of the special concerns in this kind of material:

- Step-by-step sequences must be clearly distinguished.
- Warnings must be highlighted.
- Cross-references must be accurate and easy to follow.

The goal is to enable readers to locate information as quickly as possible.

Technical documentation often includes more header and footer information, such as concise summaries of steps or techniques described on the page. This is especially important when specific instructions continue over several pages.

Hierarchy

The best training materials are based on a design that incorporates multiple levels of heads, subheads and indented text columns.

Take care to organize visuals before you lay out pages.

In addition, technical training materials often include a wide variety of photographs and illustrations. In the case of computer documentation, screen dumps—images from computer screens—must be included.

Confusion is certain to result unless care is taken in organizing text and visuals before page layout begins.

Subheads

Use different sizes of type to distinguish primary subheads from secondary subheads.

The most important subheads—those introducing new topics within a chapter—should be significantly larger than those introducing specific techniques. Subheads within topics should be even smaller.

Hanging indents emphasize first-level subheads. Subheads gain importance when they protrude into the white space to the left of the text column.

Consider type size and white space in setting off primary subheads.

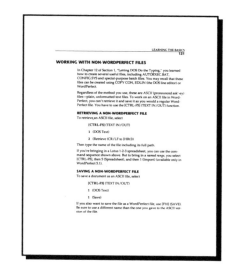

Headers

Headers—chapter and/or section titles, page numbers, etc.—are even more important in documentation than in books.

Readers should quickly be able to locate information by referring to the headers.

EVALUATION CHECKLIST

Check your designs in relation to these questions to be sure you've covered important details.

Books

1. Does your design reflect the author's writing style and the number and type of illustrations or photographs?

2. Are design and typography appropriate to the content?

3. Do two-page spreads harmonize?

4. Do chapter introductions clearly invite readers into the text?

5. Are photographs consistently placed in the same location on all pages?

6. Are captions easy to locate and read?

Training Materials

1. Are the elements organized to make information easy to follow?

2. Do subhead sizes clearly indicate the hierarchy of information?

3. Are warnings and cross-references easy to find?

5. Are illustrations clearly identified and set off by sufficient white space?

13 | PRESENTATION GRAPHICS: PROJECTING THE RIGHT IMAGE

Sooner or later, you'll probably try your hand at designing slides and overhead transparencies on your computer.

It's possible to use your existing desktop publishing program, but specialized presentation software can make the job easier and faster.

For example, you can easily sort or re-arrange the order of slides and overheads. You can also proof your work using various "slide show" features that show your slides on the screen from the audience's point of view.

Presentation software makes it easy and fast to create slides and overheads.

Software programs designed specifically for creating presentation materials let you prepare speaker's notes and audience handouts.

CHOOSING YOUR MEDIUM

Start by choosing the appropriate presentation medium.

Options include 35mm slides, monochrome or color overhead transparencies, or computer-generated on-screen presentations.

- 35mm color slides are best for a short, formal presentation delivered to a large group in a darkened room.

- Black and white or color transparencies are ideal for longer, less formal presentations delivered to smaller groups, in a setting with normal or slightly subdued lighting. Overhead transparencies allow you to maintain eye contact with your audience, invite questions or discussion and eliminate or add transparencies at the last minute. (You can also write on them with a water-based, felt-tip pen.)

- Screen presentations are ideal for small groups in normal room lighting. When the group is very small, everyone can view the presentation on your computer screen. Or, you can use a projector pad on top of your transparency projector. When available, you can use big-screen monitors. Computer-based, on-screen presentations let you add fancy electronic effects—like dissolves or transitions between slides—as well as quickly call up any slide. If your presentation includes charts and diagrams, you can easily update them on the basis of new information.

PRESENTATION DESIGN PRINCIPLES

The same rules for making good-looking pages apply to creating good-looking slides and overheads, particularly in regard to consistency, restraint and contrast.

Concise, straight-forward visuals are essential for effective presentations.

A few simple design tips apply to designing slides and overheads, the two most popular presentation media. Focus slides or overheads around a single point. Simple, concise visuals are essential for effective presentations. Use projected text and visuals as reinforcement, not replacement for your words.

Use plenty of slides, overheads or screens, but limit each one to the development of a single idea. Whenever you find yourself introducing a new concept, create a new frame.

A simple, concise design will get your point across.

Your visuals should serve only as a framework. Carefully edit your text, leaving only the key "action" words. Remember that type size must decrease each time additional words are added. Eliminate adjectives and adverbs; you can add those in your oral presentation in a warm, conversational manner.

Typeface Choices

Many sans-serif typefaces are ideally suited for slides and overheads.

Their straightforward simplicity and lack of decoration can enhance legibility. Although an entire page of sans-serif type can be boring, a slide or overhead set in a single sans-serif typeface, varying only size, placement and color, can be very effective.

Consistency

Apply the same specifications, with as little variation as possible, throughout your presentation.

These include choices for

- Typeface, type size, type style, placement and color for title, subtitle and text.
- Text formatting (e.g., margins and line spacing).
- Background color(s).
- Border size, location and color.
- Repeating elements, such as logo, show title and date.
- Graphic accents, such as shadows and bullets.

Changes that look minimal on your computer screen are likely to be greatly magnified when projected onto a large screen. Your audience will be distracted if your firm's logo or the title jumps to a different place on each slide.

Even the most informal presentation is likely to include several different formats. You're likely to use one format for single-column lists, a second for double-column lists, and a third for charts and diagrams. So be sure to integrate these various formats into a coherent presentation design by using consistent treatments of color, border effects, typographic elements and repeating features.

Adding Contrast

Add visual contrast among the various elements of your slides and overheads to prevent monotony.

The slide title should be significantly larger than the text it introduces. This is especially true if sans-serif type is used for both.

In slides and over-heads, titles should contrast strongly with each other.

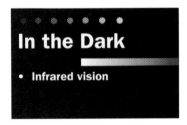

In charts and diagrams, titles should be significantly larger than legends and reference values, such as percentages displayed on pie-chart slices.

In organization charts illustrating chain-of-command relationships, the top levels can be set in larger type than the subordinate levels.

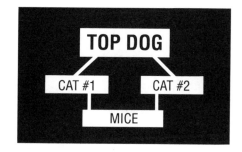

Although background colors for most of your presentation should be the same or similar, long presentations can be broken into "chapters," distinguished by different background colors to indicate different content.

WORKING WITH COLOR

Be careful in choosing colors for backgrounds and text.

Light backgrounds with dark text work best on overhead transparencies. The exact opposite (i.e., dark backgrounds with light text), are preferable for 35mm slides since they're projected in a darkened room.

Colors can have a strong effect on your audience.

Strive for as much contrast between text and background as possible. Light blue text against a dark blue background is extremely difficult to read. Yellow text against a blue background is preferable.

You can add impact to boxed titles by choosing a background color for the box that contrasts with the background in the rest of your slide.

Reactions to color appear to be biologically and emotionally based. A case in point is red, which can arouse feelings of excitement, aggression and stress. Some studies show that red increases blood pressure and pulse rate. Accountants and bankers are apt to reject proposals presented with conclusions drenched in red ink!

Blues and greens can be relaxing, while grays are often somber and depressing.

Other color properties should be considered as well. For instance, some colors "wash out" when projected. A strong yellow accent on the screen of your computer often looks too pale or actually gets lost when projected from an overhead transparency.

Black and White Are Colors!

Use black and white as text colors.

Against a color background, black or white text really stands out.

Black or white text can form a strong contrast for many background colors. The text stands out against the background yet doesn't "fight" with it as many other colors do. Bullets set in a stronger color can add visual interest.

HORIZONTAL OR VERTICAL?

Choose landscape (horizontal) instead of portrait (vertical) orientation.

Although printed pages are usually formatted vertically, slides and overheads are typically prepared and projected horizontally. (Aspect ratios are 3:2 for slides and 4:3 for overhead transparencies.)

Using a vertical orientation requires small type sizes and packs too much information on each slide. You end up with frames that resemble printed outlines.

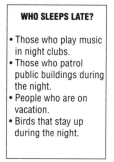

Because fewer lines are available, horizontal orientation forces you to be more selective in the words you use on slides and overheads. So, exercise restraint in the number of points you include and in how you elaborate them.

Vertical slides can end up looking like printed outlines.

USING BUILDS

Builds are an effective way to pace your presentation.

Builds allow for progressive introduction of new information. Instead of revealing an entire list or chart at once, letting the audience read ahead, you can present the material in steps:

- Lists: Introduce one item or one subhead level at a time.
- Pie charts: Show one pie-chart slice at a time.
- Bar charts: Present sales information one quarter or one department contribution at a time.
- Organization charts: Introduce management levels one by one.
- Illustrations: When showing how the various parts of an item fit together, add each successive part on a separate slide or overhead.

Another technique for keeping your audience interested—especially with text-heavy slides and overheads—is to pace your presentation, using an oversized number for each frame.

Use builds to present complex material one step at a time.

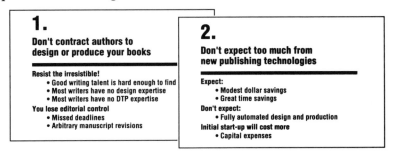

Icons can be used for the same purpose. Examples include adding bricks to a building, leaves to a tree or parts to a car.

CHOOSING THE RIGHT INFORMATION GRAPHIC

Charts and diagrams interpret and display information differently.

Pie charts illustrate part-to-whole relationships, translating percentages into proportional sections.

Different types of charts can show the same data in varied ways.

Bar and column charts compare information categories side by side.

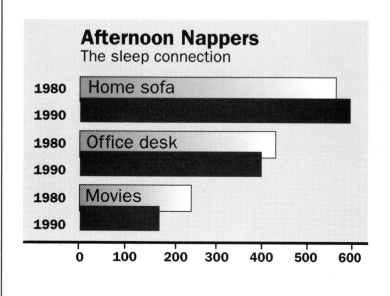

Line charts illustrate trends.

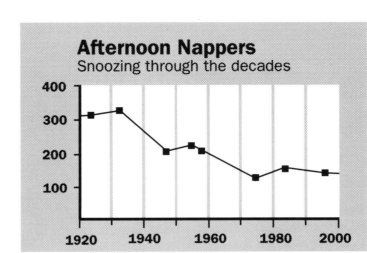

Area diagrams show trends using special comparisons.

Stacked bar or column charts display the parts that contribute to the totals.

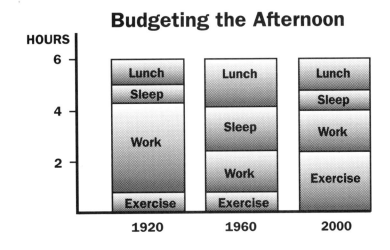

Combination charts compare two different categories of information, using a different data symbol for each category.

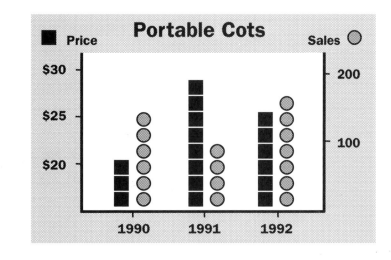

Avoid Complex Charts and Diagrams

Group small subdivisions together or use separate charts and diagrams.

Avoid pie charts with more than six sections. If your pie chart has a few large slices and numerous small ones, combine the smaller slices into a "miscellaneous" or "other" classification. If necessary, create a second pie chart.

A clear, simple design is important for black and white overheads.

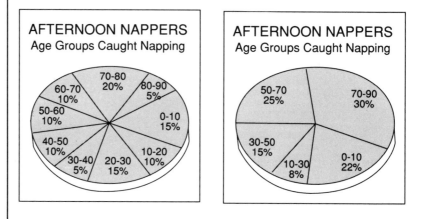

Also, avoid bar or column charts with so many segments that it's difficult to isolate the most important information and make comparisons.

Simplicity is especially important when working with black and white overhead transparencies. Too many dot patterns and angled lines can quickly become distracting.

Enhancing Charts and Diagrams

You can improve a visual's communicating power by modifying the type specifications.

Often, typeface, type size and color defaults are inappropriate for a particular slide or overhead. Here are some of the ways you can selectively enhance the typography in your diagram.

- Choose a different typeface and increase the type size of pie or bar chart or diagram value labels.
- Reset X and Y axis annotation in a larger type size to improve legibility.
- Make the legend more noticeable by using a larger type size and adding white space around it.

Visual Formatting

Add grid lines and tick marks as needed.

Horizontal and vertical grid lines provide a frame of reference and help the viewer's eye connect the data symbol with the reference value.

Most charts need grid lines or tick marks as a frame of reference.

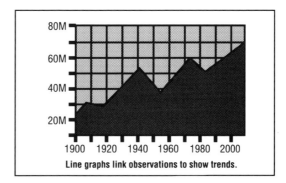

Line graphs link observations to show trends.

Too many marks produce unnecessary clutter. Be sure you use the minimum necessary to provide visual landmarks.

Charts and diagrams can be emphasized by setting them on a background color that contrasts with the color used for the slide background.

SPEAKER'S NOTES

Speaker's notes help you rehearse your presentation and focus your attention on the audience, instead of the screen behind you.

A note page can contain a miniature reproduction of a single slide or overhead, plus enough space for you to list the points you want to emphasize during your presentation.

In speaker's notes, include data not given in your projected image.

Use a large type size for your speaker's notes: 36 points is ideal—you can see them at a glance without squinting. Use only as many words as you need to provide detail while maintaining the momentum of your presentation.

In your speaker's notes, you can include details not given in your projected image, such as information sources. This data will come in handy if someone asks for it.

Audience Handouts

Most presentation software programs can produce audience handouts with reduced representations of your visuals.

These contain two, three, four or six images per page.

You can redesign these handouts by repositioning the image and adding the presentation title in large type at the top of each page, followed by the date in smaller type. You can set off the title and date with rules or boxes, if desired. You can also add page numbers at the bottom of each page.

EVALUATION CHECKLIST

Check your work against these criteria to see if you've added the right ingredients for effective visuals.

1. Did you choose the presentation format most appropriate for your message, audience and environment?

2. Are all slides, overheads and screens in your presentation assembled with the same background color, typography, borders and repeating elements?

3. Have you created visual interest by adding contrast between slide titles and supporting information?

4. Have you used builds to introduce information on a step-by-step basis?

5. Have you chosen the type of chart or diagram most appropriate for displaying your data?

6. Have you modified type specifications for chart and diagram annotation so that all information is legible?

7. Have you used grid lines and tick marks to provide visual frames of reference?

8. Can you read your speaker's notes from a comfortable distance, grasping key words and important ideas at a glance?

9. Have you designed audience handouts to include presentation title, date, logo and appropriate rules or graphic accents?

14 | BUSINESS COMMUNICATIONS

As you develop your design sense and become more familiar with the capabilities of desktop publishing, you'll continue to discover new applications. For in-house projects, you'll probably come to rely more and more on your desktop system rather than on professional service bureaus for design and production.

LETTERHEAD

A good letterhead must communicate subliminal as well as practical information at a glance.

Letterhead design is not as simple as it might seem. It's important to express something of the nature or character of your firm or association in your letterhead design, in addition to providing its name, address and phone number as response information. For instance, a district attorney requires a very different letterhead style than a tanning salon.

Letterheads must include basic response information.

Basic components of all letterheads are

- Firm or organization name
- Logo
- Motto or statement of business philosophy
- Street address and mailing address (if different)

- Telephone number(s)
- Telex and/or facsimile number

Corporate and nonprofit letterheads often list officers or board members as well. All too often, however, that leaves little space for the actual message area and presents a real design challenge!

Logo Size and Placement

The size of your logo must be proportional to the amount of supporting information.

Logos must be large enough to be noticed, yet not so large they visually overwhelm the letterhead. In the example below, the logo detracts from the message area.

A logo shouldn't be so large that it overwhelms the message area.

Placement can be flexible. Although logos are frequently centered above the letterhead, there is no reason why they can't be placed differently, as long as basic rules of good design are observed.

For example, logos can be set flush-left or flush-right at the top of the page.

The House Specialists   244 Emerson Boulevard   Wilson, NC 27846

The House Specialists
244 Emerson Boulevard
Wilson, NC 27846

The letterhead can be designed on an asymmetrical grid. This will leave a vertical band of white space along the left-hand side of the letterhead.

Designing letterhead on an asymmetrical grid increases the white space.

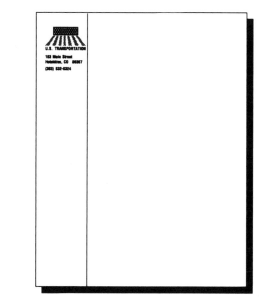

Addresses and Phone Numbers

Be sure to include all information the letter's recipient needs in order to respond.

Insufficient address and phone information can cause problems for your correspondents.

Letterhead design becomes a bit more complicated when both telephone and facsimile numbers (and/or both street address and post office box number—sometimes with different ZIP Codes) must be included.

One common mistake is to print a telephone number without the area code. That's all right for local callers, but it puts long-distance callers at a distinct disadvantage!

Don't forget to add the area code to your phone number.

Placement of telephone and address information usually depends on logo placement. When the logo is centered at the top of the letterhead, telephone and address information is often centered in a smaller type size along the bottom of the page.

When both telephone and fax numbers are included, as well as separate street address and post office box number, the information is often divided into thirds and placed across the bottom of the letterhead. For example, the street address can be aligned flush-left on two lines, telephone and fax numbers centered on two lines in the middle, and post office box number placed flush-right.

| 1845 United Terrace | PHONE 987/765-5432 | P.O. Box 1659 |
| Salem, Oregon 12345 | FAX 987/765-2345 | Salem, Oregon 12345 |

When fewer items are included, they can be placed on one line and separated by white space and oversized bullets.

P.O. Box 146 ✦ Kittering, PA 15401 ✦ 900/735-8976

Another option is to indent logo and address information from the left-hand edge of the letterhead. The logo is placed at the top of the page, while address and telephone information are placed at the bottom.

The logo and address should complement each other.

Motto

Mottos are often run along the bottom of a letterhead, forming an umbrella over address and phone information.

In these cases, the motto is typically set slightly larger, and the italic version of the typeface is used for the address and the telephone number.

"Your Professional Insurance Agency"
P.O. Box 146 ✦ *Kittering, PA 15401* ✦ *900/735-8976*

Message Area

The final challenge is to effectively set off the letterhead elements so they don't interfere with the contents of the document.

One way to do this is to box the message area.

Or, a single rule can separate the two areas from each other.

A screened column or panel or a second color can also be used to isolate supplementary information. This technique works well for listing board members or officers of an organization.

Screens can separate the message area from the rest of the letterhead.

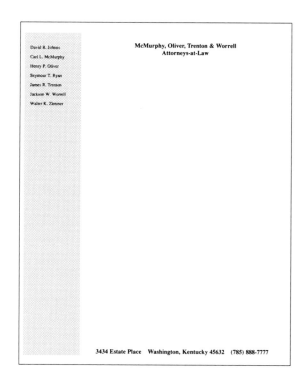

Envelope Design

The letterhead design should be scaled down and repeated on the envelope.

All sizes of an en-
velope family should
repeat the same
design.

More and more businesses are using "window" envelopes, which eliminate the need for addressing separate envelopes or labels. Care should be taken with the design of the letterhead to allow for properly positioning the inside address. The recipient's name and address must be placed on the page so they can be seen through the window when the letter or form is folded and inserted into the envelope.

Often a "family" of envelopes is created: a small, inexpensive envelope for sending invoices and paying bills; a Number 10 envelope, printed on the same paper stock as the letterhead, for standard correspondence; and a 9- by 12-inch envelope for formal proposals or oversize documents.

Sometimes logo and address information are rotated 90 degrees and placed vertically along the side of the envelope.

BUSINESS CARDS

Business card design is even more challenging than letterhead design.

On a business card, a lot of information must be presented in a relatively small amount of space—typically 3 1/2 by 2 inches. Not only must address, phone and fax numbers, and a logo be included, but an individual's name and title must also be prominently displayed.

This format is an ideal candidate for the application of desktop publishing technology. Once the basic card has been designed and stored as a template, it takes just a few seconds to replace one name and/or position with another.

Establishing Priorities

Which should be larger—the individual's name or the firm's logo?

Often, the logo is so large it dwarfs all other items on the page—including the individual's name.

A "quadrant" layout can provide a framework for designing business cards.

The "quadrant" technique is one solution to this problem. The firm's logo is placed flush-left in the upper left quadrant of the card. The logo is balanced by the phone number set flush-right in the upper right quadrant. The street address is flush-left along the bottom of the card in the lower left quadrant; post office box information is flush-right in the lower right quadrant. These four elements form a framework around the individual's name and title located in the center of the card.

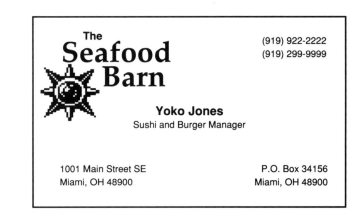

Another solution is to indent logo, address and phone information from the left, as is often done on business letterhead.

FAX COVER SHEETS

Fax transmissions are an important part of today's business world.

Cover sheets help ensure safe, efficient facsimile communications that are delivered quickly to the right people.

Fax cover sheets ensure quick, complete transmissions.

It's important for the facsimile cover sheet to indicate the total number of pages sent. This helps the recipient know that the entire transmission has been received and nothing is missing. Other important items are

- Recipient's name
- Sender's name

- Date of transmission
- Subject matter or summary of contents

FAX
Date: _____

TECO U.S.
Chapel Hill, NC 27515-2496
Telephone (939) 732-9449
Telefax 939 142-3898

Attention: _____

Company: _____

From: _____

Number of pages_____including this page

Comments:
_____
_____
_____
_____
_____
_____
_____

In choosing type, remember that fax transmission quality varies.

Some fax cover sheets include space or lines for a brief handwritten message. Or, a message can be set in a significantly smaller type size to distinguish it from the items listed above.

Be careful when choosing typefaces for facsimile messages. Since the quality of reproduction varies, it's important to choose a typeface that remains legible regardless of circumstances.

Typefaces with thin strokes or detailed serifs tend to reproduce poorly and are not the safest choices for fax transmissions.

RÉSUMÉS

A résumé is direct-response advertising in its purest form.

With the skillful use of typographic elements, résumés can take full advantage of desktop publishing's power to set a tone or project an aura. Also, they're an ideal format for utilizing desktop publishing's ability to organize data and establish hierarchies of importance.

Changing Trends

Today, the trend is toward less formal, more goal-oriented résumés.

Design résumés so that employers don't have to hunt for your qualifications.

Contemporary résumés focus more on what an individual has to offer a company. In past years, résumés tended to be organized chronologically, focusing on a progression through a person's education, career and extracurricular activities.

In any case, white space, subheads and graphic accents should be used to separate categories of information. A prospective employer should be able to quickly locate relevant qualifications without playing detective.

Design a résumé as you would an ad.

Although many desktop-published documents use a combination of sans-serif type for subheads and serif type for body copy, many résumés use the italic version of the serif type in a larger type size for subheads. This softens the contrast between subheads and body copy.

Résumés should be designed like advertisements: "selling" information should precede "supporting" or "qualifying" information. Thus, address, phone number, health and marital status should be subordinate to statements that relate to benefits the hiring firm will gain by hiring the individual.

Perhaps the best beginning for a résumé is a quoted personal recommendation from an individual noted in the field, a description of a significant accomplishment or a statement of goals and objectives.

Since your résumé is actually an advertisement for yourself, pay careful attention to the smallest details of letter and line spacing. At all costs, avoid errors in grammar, spelling and punctuation.

EVALUATION CHECKLIST

Check your work against these criteria to see if you've added the right ingredients for effective business communications.

Letterheads

1. Does the design of your letterhead accurately reflect your firm's philosophy and way of doing business?

2. Are your firm's logo, motto and address/phone number sized in correct proportion to the size of the message area?

3. Is the message area clearly set apart from the information area?

4. Has all necessary information been included, such as area codes, fax numbers, post office box numbers and street addresses?

5. Do envelopes repeat important information, including telephone and fax numbers? (Often, envelopes get separated from letters.)

Business Cards

1. Do business cards contain all necessary response information, as well as the individual's name and title?

2. Is background information visually distinct from the name and title?

3. Does the design of your business card reflect the design of your letterhead?

Fax Cover Sheets

1. Do your fax sheets clearly document sender, recipient, transmission date, the total number of pages sent, and subject matter details?

2. Do your cover sheets include the phone number and extension of the person sending the fax, in case a transmission error is detected and the machine operator needs to be contacted?

3. Is space for a short message added directly to the fax cover sheet?

Résumés

1. Have you presented information in your résumé in its order of importance to the reader?

2. Do the typeface, type size and type style send the right message about the type of person you are and the type of job you're applying for?

3. Have you used white space, subheads and graphic accents, such as rules, to organize the information in your résumé?

15 | RESPONSE DEVICES— FORMS, COUPONS AND SURVEYS

The preceding chapters dealt primarily with "passive" communications—advertisements and publications designed to attract the reader's attention and communicate information.

This chapter looks at "active" communications: reader-response formats such as coupons, order forms, contracts and surveys.

Coupons are valuable for providing names and addresses of prospective customers for later follow-up. *Employment application forms* help find the right person for the job. *Price quotations* and *order forms* make it possible to sell things to people across town or around the world. *Surveys* let customers and employees express their opinions and make suggestions.

The success criteria for passive communications apply equally to active formats. Just as effective newsletters and ads can be easily read, successful response devices can be easily understood and used.

Regardless of specific function, coupons, forms and surveys are composed of the same basic parts. Appropriate design of these parts is essential.

Reader-response formats follow the same design principles that "passive" communications do.

TITLE

Titles should clearly identify the form's purpose. The title should be set in a typeface, type size and type style that contrasts with the other type elements on the form.

Like the headline of an ad or newsletter article, the title should be significantly larger than the words that follow.

In most cases, the title should be the dominant visual element on the form.

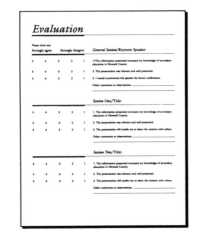

The title should contrast with other type elements.

INSTRUCTIONS

A successful response device gives clear directions for filling out and sending in the form.

Coupon instructions should include payment options—prepayment, C.O.D. shipment and credit cards accepted—and to

Surveys should carefully explain the rating scheme used.

whom the check should be made out, if that payment method is used. If items are to be shipped via United Parcel Service, customers should be reminded that a post office address does not provide enough information for delivery.

Employment applications should indicate how and where the applicant can fill in education and previous employment information and references.

Surveys should carefully explain the rating scheme used—whether high numbers indicate agreement or disagreement with the statement, for instance.

Instructions are typically set in a small type size (6, 7 or 8 points) compared to other type on the page.

RESPONSE AREA

Response areas can be designed with lines to be filled in or ballot boxes or pairs of parentheses to be checked.

Forms with ballot boxes and parentheses are quick and easy to fill out. They're typically used for simple "yes" or "no" entries.

Lines accommodate names, addresses and other detailed textual information that may be required.

Category Identifiers

Categories should be clearly labeled and distinguished typographically.

Column headers identify quantity, item number, description, unit price and total price listings.

Column headers are typically centered over their listings. Other column headers might include Years, Firm or Institution, Highest Degree Earned, etc.

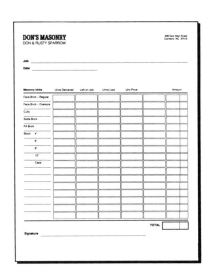

There should be no question in the respondent's mind as to whether the title relates to the line above or the space below. Yet, numerous response devices resemble the example shown here:

Name
Address
City, State, ZIP
Phone

Labels should be carefully placed to identify the column they accompany.

Graphic Accents

Rules organize information by acting as horizontal and vertical dividers between items and sections.

Vertical rules, in partnership with column headers, provide directional cues and guidance to the respondent to ensure that all necessary information is entered in the proper locations.

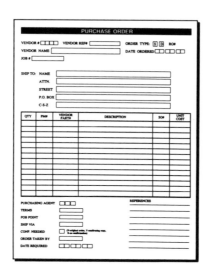

Screens and rules are effective devices to set off prices.

You can also use screens for organization and emphasis. For example, you can add a light screen behind the "total price" column to draw attention to it.

Coupons are typically bordered with a dashed line. Government or institution forms are often enclosed in boxed borders.

More formal response devices, such as surveys, often use borders along with the firm or association's letterhead or logo.

FUNCTIONAL ISSUES

A well-designed response device is easy to fill out.

Ballot boxes are close enough to each other so that a minimum of hand and eye movement is needed from one item to the next.

Designs that leave too much space between the ballot boxes create unattractive pools of white. This effect discourages the respondent from taking the time or effort to complete the form.

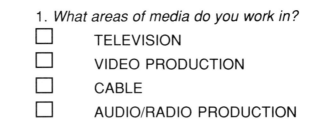

Always provide sufficient line length and space between lines. If you've ever tried to write in a long name or address on a tiny coupon, you know how frustrating it is, particularly if you must include rank, serial number and mail stop.

Always provide enough space for respondents to fill in a complete address.

It's in the best interest of everyone involved to provide adequate horizontal and vertical space to permit a comfortable, readable handwriting size.

Forms that have line spacing based on standard typewriter line spacing are always appreciated. The user can fill out the form without manually adjusting the spacing for each line.

Always provide enough address lines. Include space for five-line addresses. In addition to firm name, street and city, etc., the extra lines accommodate department or division names or numbers and suite, floor or building numbers.

Addresses for many large firms now include mail-stop information—their own internal ZIP Codes. Unless you make it easy for users to include complete delivery information, order fulfillment or return communications can be seriously delayed or may never arrive at all!

CHANGING WORLD...

As the world's economies become more interdependent, addresses become longer and more complex.

The ZIP Code portion of the address area should allow for the additional four-digit ZIP Code for carrier-route sorting. Having this information can expedite mail delivery and save your organization postage costs in the years to come.

It's also important to allow space to specify the country as well as the state.

It's always a good idea to include telephone extension numbers to avoid delays in case a follow-up call is necessary.

EVALUATION CHECKLIST

Check your work against these criteria to see if you've added the right ingredients for effective response devices.

Coupons

1. Is it clear to the respondent where he or she should send the coupon?

2. Does the coupon provide enough lines for itemizing information?

3. Is the coupon large enough to be easily filled out, yet not so large it dominates the advertisement?

Order Forms

1. Is there space to list quantity, item number, item description and total price?

2. Does the pricing area provide space for adding shipping charges and taxes?

3. Do order forms spell out the customer's payment and shipping options?

4. Does the order form include space for the respondent's telephone number, in case of problems?

5. Does the order form have sufficient space for full delivery information, including department, division, mail stop and suite number?

Employment Applications

1. Does the employment application direct the applicant through the form with typographic cues and graphic accents?

2. Does line spacing allow applicants to use a typewriter to fill out their education and employment history?

3. Have you subdivided the application form into logical, clearly defined categories?

Surveys

1. Are rating values for yes/no or agree/disagree questions clear? Are the entries closely spaced?

2. Have long surveys been subdivided into categories, avoiding the appearance of essay questions or final exams?

3. Is the appearance of the survey consistent with the organization's other print communications?

Appendix A | COLOR AND PREPRESS TECHNIQUES

Looking good on your computer screen isn't enough. The proof of the pudding is the quality of the printed product, which depends on a number of processes that combine to create your publication's final appearance.

Let's take a brief look at these processes:

SCREENS

Screens are used to break up continuous-tone photographs into tiny discrete units of black and white in preparation for the printing process.

A continuous-tone black-and-white photograph needs to be screened so that the printing ink can't smear and alter the composition and clarity of the photograph.

Black areas are created by placing black "cells" very close together. Grays are formed by mixing black and white cells. The human eye blends the black and white together, creating the illusion of gray. These screens can consist of dot patterns or very fine parallel lines.

Screening has been done traditionally by commercial printers, but now many scanning and desktop publishing programs let you handle this process yourself. Therefore, you can place scanned images and screened photographs directly into your desktop-published documents. You can also modify your photographs by lightening or brightening some areas. This allows you to anticipate distortions due to laser printing, phototypesetting or the paper your document will be printed on.

You can modify photos by brightening some areas.

Although conventional black-and-white photographs are often scanned and used for desktop publishing, there's a growing trend toward all-digital solutions. Several companies produce digital cameras that dispense with film entirely. These cameras record visual images on magnetic floppy diskettes that can be played back on special players added to your computer.

You can also use frame grabbers, special hardware and software that let you capture images with a video camera or anything previously recorded on your video cassette recorder.

PRINTED COLOR QUALITY

Printed colors don't look the same as computer-screen colors.

If you're using a new-generation color printer, you've probably noticed that colors on the screen rarely match the colors of the printed document.

One reason is that screen colors are generated from additive colors (red, green and blue) inside your computer and shine through the coating of the computer screen. These colors tend to be bright and fully saturated, even in small areas.

Printed colors, however, are derived from subtractive color—the intermediate colors cyan, yellow and magenta. They lack the saturation of on-screen colors and are often deeper, or darker, than their screen counterparts.

Because of this fundamental difference, small areas of printed color—yellow rules against a green background, for instance—are often "lost" in their environment when printed.

Paper Quality

Paper quality also has a great deal to do with color quality.

Paper quality affects color quality.

Reflective, or coated, paper reproduces brighter color than paper with a flat, or matte, finish, which tends to absorb rather than reflect the color.

Calibrating Colors

Progress is also being made in precisely correlating screen colors with printed colors. As already mentioned, screen colors and printed colors are not created through the same process. Screen colors are produced by wavelengths of light while printed colors are derived from pigments.

However, many software programs let you specify colors by entering their exact Pantone Matching System (PMS) numbers, rather than trying to match them across two different systems. You simply choose the desired colors from a sample book that lists the corresponding PMS numbers, and disregard any discrepancies in the screen display colors.

In addition, there are hardware solutions that let you calibrate screen colors to printed colors.

Such features will likely improve and proliferate as four-color prepress continues to migrate from large commercial printers to individual users.

COLOR PRINTING

There are two ways to add color to printed pages: spot-color printing and four-color printing.

Spot Color

Spot color can en-liven graphic accents.

Spot colors can be used for graphic accents, such as rules, name-plate backgrounds and borders around illustrations and photos. Also, oversize initial caps can be set in a second (or third) color. Spot colors are added from a second negative that picks up only the ink required for the spot color. All other page elements are printed from the original negative, which reproduces the remaining words, visuals and graphic accents.

Spot color is applied in a single ink—either a process (primary) color or a custom-mixed shade.

PMS is used to identify exact color shades, numerically identifying major colors and listing proportions for mixing others.

Four-Color Printing

Four-color printing is used to reproduce complex color photographs and sophisticated illustrations using four separate negatives, or layers.

You can accomplish these sophisticated prepress techniques with desktop publishing software. For each page, a separate negative is prepared for each primary color—cyan, magenta, yellow and black. Each negative contains precisely the amount of cyan, magenta, yellow or black needed to produce all other colors.

Because of the high-resolution reproduction required for very small areas, laser printers are not suitable for preparing color separations. These must be prepared using high-resolution phototypesetters, ideally at 2,470 dots per inch.

Color separations can be either positives or negatives. When positives are submitted, the commercial printer must convert them to the negative state required by the printing press.

Increasingly, however, prepress preparation is being handled by phototypesetting service bureaus and in-house photo-typesetters, providing direct film negative separations ready for the printing press.

Trapping

Trapping is a method of overlapping adjacent ink colors so they blend smoothly at the "seams." As the four-color negatives go through the printing press, the layers may become slightly misaligned with each other, or the printing paper may slip. As a result, white "outlines" may appear between colors.

Trapping prevents this unsightly effect by slightly overlapping the colors to avoid the "telltale white."

Trapping and retouching can assure precise, even color.

Although some advanced desktop publishing programs allow you to specify the amount of trapping, this feature hasn't yet been universally adopted.

The order in which ink colors are placed on the page also affects the appearance of the finished product. Bottom-layer colors often benefit from increased density.

Color Scanning and Retouching

Color scanners are used for importing color photographs. Today's color scanners can work from photographs or 35mm slides. The process divides the color image into the red, green and blue colors that can be reproduced on your computer screen. Once the photograph is saved as a file, image-retouching software is available that can airbrush or clean it up.

The previous generation of image-manipulation programs could work only with black-and-white images. These programs could remove distracting background elements, as well as selectively brighten or darken portions of an image.

The newest image manipulation programs work in color as well. You can simplify or manipulate the image and also adjust the color balance, adding the orange tint of a sunset or the brightness of a sky at high noon.

PROJECTED COLOR QUALITY

Projected colors, too, often differ from screen colors. Just as the type and quality of paper affect printed colors, room lighting plays a role in the quality of 35mm color slides and overheads used in presentations.

A darkened room provides the best setting for showing color slides. The best-looking slides combine dark backgrounds with light lettering and graphic accents.

Room lighting is a factor in choosing colors for your overheads.

The exact opposite is true for overhead color transparencies, which are typically projected in normal or slightly reduced lighting. Light backgrounds with dark type work best for overheads; this combination provides the contrast needed to make the slide easily readable under normal lighting conditions.

PREPRESS IS THE FRONTIER

Four-color prepress, although rapidly progressing, is still in its infancy. Automation of prepress techniques has been slow, mainly because software-based processes can't replicate the intuitiveness of human intervention in making subtle aesthetic and conditional adjustments.

Prepress technology still can't replace human intuition.

For example, in preparing color separations, commercial printers take into account such factors as the paper stock, temperature and humidity. Commercial printers are also intimately familiar with the idiosyncracies of their printing presses; they know how to compensate for slight variations in order to achieve the best possible alignment of the four color negatives.

File compression is an important area of advancing prepress technology. Computer files of scanned images can become extremely large—too large for most computer hard disks to accommodate. For this reason, hardware and software solutions are being developed to compress graphics files to more manageable sizes for storage and transmission to service bureaus.

Increased speed is another important issue. Because of the complexity of color images, image manipulation programs can be frustratingly slow. Video monitor accelerator boards are being developed to increase screen redraw speed—the speed at which the monitor updates the changing screen image. These video accelerator boards are self-contained systems dedicated to serving your video monitor, thus relieving your computer of the additional drain on its resources.

THE FUTURE

As technologies develop, more activities once confined to commercial printing will take place on computer screens.

The benefit will be faster transfer of a creative idea to the printed page. Once the initial hardware, software and training investments have been amortised, this will not only save time and money, but will move desktop publishing closer to its ultimate goal—placing control of publication quality in the hands of people who originate the ideas they share with others.

THE TECHNOLOGY CONNECTION

Use the technology to the fullest to express your creative ideas.

It's impossible to do high-quality design if you're working ineffi-ciently. So take full advantage of the power built into your desk-top publishing or word processing hardware and software. The time you save translates into better-looking projects by provid-ing more time for you to refine your initial designs and fine-tune their execution.

The following examples show how creativity and technology can overlap.

FORMATS AND TEMPLATES

Formats define document structure (i.e., the placement of margins, borders, columns, rules, headlines, titles, page numbers and other ele-ments common to every page).

Many desktop publishing programs let you establish master page layouts, usually referred to as "master" or "default" pages.

Templates let you spend more time on creative design.

A *template* defines a specific framework for a format that will be used from project to project. When you've formatted the first issue of your newsletter, for example, subsequent issues can simply be built on the framework established in the original issue.

And once you've established a "look" for your newspaper advertisements, week-to-week product and price changes can be easily inserted each time without having to start from scratch.

Templates create a family resemblance between documents.

Thus, templates speed up the production cycle and help maintain consistency. In addition, they add a highly desirable "family resemblance" to your issues.

Templates are easy to create. When a previously saved desktop publishing file is opened, most desktop publishing programs prompt you to choose "Open Original" or "Open Copy." When you select "Open Copy," you're presented with a duplicate copy to work in while the original file stays intact. You then fill the empty template with current copy for your advertisement, brochure or newsletter.

When saving a file, you can choose to save it under its original name or create a different name. For example, when starting work on your February newsletter, begin by opening a copy of the "NEWSTEMP" file, but save it under "FEBNEWS."

Style Sheets

Use style sheets, or "styles," to save even more time.

Style sheets are computer files containing formatting specifications (e.g., typeface, type size, type weight, alignment scheme, line spacing and color).

It's important to prepare and print out a style sheet for each project. Style sheet printouts can be stored in three-ring binders along with copies of the finished project. (Oversized projects can be reduced to binder size on a photocopier.)

A backup copy of your style-sheet file should be kept at a second location, in case the original is lost or damaged.

Formatting While Writing

The formatting abilities of your word processing program save time.

That's particularly important when creating documents, such as books, that have many blocks of identically formatted copy.

Many *word processing* programs let you do a lot of formatting as you write the file, before it's used by your *desktop publishing* program. Many word processing programs let you store "electronic style sheets" as separate files that can be shared and referred to as you prepare different projects.

Although style sheets usually are associated with word processing, some desktop publishing programs also have them.

MACROS

Use macros to simplify repetitive tasks.

Macros can do those repetitive typing tasks for you.

Word processing programs let you create self-executing sequences of keystrokes that can modify the number, size and placement of columns, add rules and borders and vary other repeating page layout features.

For example, you might create a "2space" macro that automatically searches for every occurrence of two consecutive spaces throughout your document and replaces it with one space. This will help if you haven't broken the "two spaces after every period" habit you were taught in your high-school typing class.

DESIGN-ENHANCING SOFTWARE COMMANDS

Familiarize yourself with the various software commands that can contribute to better-looking pages.

Almost all desktop publishing and word processing programs incorporate features that let you customize indents, tabs and paragraph spacing, although different programs have different names for those features.

Commands used less frequently include "Block" or "Keep lines together" commands to prevent related elements from being separated from each other. For example, you can add a command to your style definitions to avoid having a two-line subhead split between the bottom of one column and the top of the next.

Most desktop publishing programs let you lock subheads with text.

Almost all desktop publishing and word processing programs incorporate features that allow you to customize indents, tabs and paragraph spacing, although their nomenclature may differ from one program to another.

Commands used less frequently include "Block" or "Keep lines together" commands to prevent related elements from being separated from each other. For example, you can add a command to your style definitions to avoid having a two-line subhead split between the bottom of one column and the top of the next.

Almost all desktop publishing and word processing programs incorporate features that allow you to customize indents, tabs and paragraph spacing, although their nomenclature may differ from one program to another.

Commands used less frequently include "Block" or "Keep lines together" commands to prevent related elements from being separated from each other. For example, you can add a command to your style definitions to avoid having a two-line subhead split between the bottom of one column and the top of the next.

Almost all desktop publishing and word processing programs incorporate features that allow you to customize indents, tabs and paragraph spacing, although their nomenclature may differ from one program to another.

Commands used less frequently include "Block" or "Keep lines together" commands to prevent related elements from being separated from each other. For example, you can add a command to your style definitions to avoid having a two-line subhead split between the bottom of one column and the top of the next.

Almost all desktop publishing and word processing programs incorporate features that allow you to customize indents, tabs and paragraph spacing, although their nomenclature may differ from one program to another.

NEW HOPE FOR

SPLITTING SUBHEADS

Almost all desktop publishing and word processing programs incorporate features that allow you to customize indents, tabs and paragraph spacing, although their nomenclature may differ from one program to another.

Commands used less frequently include "Block" or "Keep lines together" commands to prevent related elements from being separated from each other. For example, you can add a command to your style definitions to avoid having a two-line subhead split between the bottom of one column and the top of the next.

Almost all desktop publishing and word processing programs incorporate features that allow you to customize indents, tabs and paragraph spacing, although their nomenclature may differ from one program to another.

Commands used less frequently include "Block" or "Keep lines together" commands to prevent related elements from being separated from each other. For example, you can add a command to your style definitions to avoid having a two-line subhead split between the bottom of one column and the top of the next.

Almost all desktop publishing and word processing programs incorporate features that allow you to customize indents, tabs and paragraph spacing, although their nomenclature may differ from one program to another.

Commands used less frequently include "Block" or "Keep lines together" commands to prevent related elements from being separated from each other. For example, you can add a command to your style definitions to avoid having a two-line subhead split between the bottom of one column and the top of the next.

Almost all desktop publishing and word processing programs incorporate features that allow you to customize indents, tabs and paragraph spacing, although their nomenclature may differ from one program to another.

The "Keep with next paragraph" command locks a subhead to the text it introduces, so the subhead doesn't appear by itself at the bottom of a column.

Graphics and text can "float" together as copy is added or deleted elsewhere.

Use the "Block" or "Keep lines together" command to avoid having a one- or two-sentence paragraph isolated at the bottom or top of a column.

Many programs now allow you to lock visuals and graphic accents (e.g., horizontal rules) to adjacent text, so they will "float" as text is added or deleted. Learning how to implement these commands will save you hours of work.

Learning how to adjust hyphenation in your program—for instance, using the "Limit number of hyphenated lines" command—can also save time. You should also learn how to avoid hyphenating proper nouns and how to place hyphens at desired locations.

The more "fine-tuning" you build into your styles and macros, the faster you'll be able to work.

COPYFITTING

Let layout precede writing.

Good typography can be compromised by "shoehorning" previously written text into existing space. Numerous design sins are committed in the name of necessity: smaller type sizes are chosen, line spacing and line length decreased, and white space surrounding headlines reduced.

All these problems can be solved by copyfitting, or preparing the amount of copy that will fit comfortably into the available space. Successful copyfitting is a two-step process:

Don't compromise design by squeezing too much text into available space.

1) Before you sit down to write or assign an article, ad copy, etc., decide how much space you want to devote to that item. By planning your layouts, you can determine how much space to allocate to each piece.

2) Quantify the space available before writing copy. Translate the allocated space into numbers that mean something to you, whether they're character or word counts or column inches.

Copyfitting lets the writer think in terms of a specific document length during the writing process. It thus contributes to tighter, more focused writing, better-looking documents and faster document preparation.

Tips on Copyfitting

The easiest approach to copyfitting involves reshaping the text pre-pared with your word processor to the parameters of your desktop publishing format.

Start by adjusting the margins of your word processor so that each line of word-processed copy equals a line of type set in the typeface and type size used for body copy.

Copyfitting helps you write articles that are neither too long nor too short.

For example, if your desktop-published document will be set in 10-point Times Roman type and placed in columns 18 picas wide, set up an 18-pica column in your desktop publishing program, and type out a typical line of text set in 10-point Times Roman.

If you count the number of characters that fit on the line, you'll find that a typical line holds 49 characters.

Set the margins of your word processor to accommodate the number of characters on each typeset line. In this example, you will probably find that the side margins will be 2 1/4 inches wide.

You've now created roughly a one-to-one relationship between lines of word-processed copy and lines of desktop-published copy—although hyphenation and alignment still may need to be modified.

Next, compute the number of lines per vertical column inch. This involves determining how many lines of word-processed copy are needed to fill the space reserved for each article. Simply count the number of lines per column inch set in the type size and leading you've chosen.

Let's assume you're using 10-point type with 11-point leading, and each column inch contains eight lines of text. By simply multiplying lines-per-inch by the number of column inches allocated to each article, you can obtain an approximate line count for word-processed copy.

Knowing how many lines of word-processed copy to write for each article will help you and your staff write no more or less than the amount needed for the space. (Many word processing programs have an automatic line-count feature that helps you keep track of the number of lines in your manuscript.)

You can also "reverse-engineer" previously written copy to calculate the amount of space required. Using the ideas described above, you can develop your own method of translating pages of word-processed copy into column inches, taking into consideration the typeface, type size, line spacing and column width used in your publication.

For example, you may find that each page of word-processed copy requires eight column inches of type. You then can find the approximate number of column inches a manuscript will occupy in a layout.

Copyfitting is never 100 percent accurate.

The reason copyfitting provides you with an approximate, rather than exact, measure is that typewritten copy is monospaced, while typeset copy is proportionally spaced.

If you prepare copy on a standard office typewriter, you can see that every letter is of equal width; lowercase i's occupy the same amount of space as uppercase W's. This is characteristic of monospaced type.

Most word processing programs display monospaced type because it's easier to read on the computer screen.

When you set type with your desktop publishing program, however, most typeface characters are proportionally spaced. This means that in the printed copy thin letters occupy significantly less space than thick letters.

```
Wishing you were here.
```
Wishing you were here.

The relative number of thick and thin letters in your document will influence your copyfitting. In most cases, however, discrepancies will reduce rather than increase the number of column inches needed when your word-processed text is set in type. This works in your favor, since it typically means more white space will be available to surround headlines and subheads.

CONCLUSION

These are only a few examples of the intimate relationship between creativity and your particular hardware and software. The list could go on and on.

As you become more involved in desktop design, your hardware and software demands will probably increase. Resist the temptation to view hardware options such as large-screen monitors and fast laser printers as "luxuries."

Just as carpenters do better work when they have the right tools for the job, you'll produce better documents if you take advantage of the electronic tools that help you work more efficiently and creatively.

BIBLIOGRAPHY

BOOKS

American Press Institute. *Newspaper Design: 2000 and beyond.*
Reston, VA: American Press Institute, 1989.
Contains "before" and "after" versions of some of the country's
most famous newspapers, showing how they are adapting to
changing reader tastes in the television age. The use of full color
throughout this publication adds to its impact.

Bauermeister, Benjamin. *A Manual of Comparative Typography: The
PANOSE System.* New York: Van Nostrand Reinhold, 1987.
A valuable guide to evaluating and selecting typefaces, using letters
of the alphabet (uppercase P, A, N, O, S and E) that are numerically
categorized on the basis of serifs, strokes and other architectural elements. Contains full uppercase and lowercase alphabet sets.

Beach, Mark, and Russon, Ken. *Papers for Printing: How to Choose the
Right Paper at the Right Price for Any Printing Job.* Portland, OR:
Coast to Coast Books, 1989.
Takes the mystery out of choosing paper; contains numerous
samples showing how paper choice affects the appearance of text
and illustrations.

Beach, Mark, with Silberfeld, Heath, and Wollman, Elizabeth. *Content Ideas That Work: Hundreds of proven topics for editors and writers of newsletters, magazines and tabloids.* Portland, OR: Coast to Coast Books, 1990.
Help for the stranded newsletter editor with a deadline two days away and three pages to fill.

Beach, Mark, Shepro, Steve, and Russon, Ken. *Getting It Printed: How to Work with Printers and Graphic Arts Services to Assure Quality, Stay on Schedule, and Control Costs.* Portland, OR: Coast to Coast Books, 1986.
Invaluable advice about what to do after the laser printer or phototypesetter has churned out the last page of your brochure, newsletter or book.

Beale, Stephen, and Cavuoto, James. *The Scanner Book: A Complete Guide to the Use and Applications of Desktop Scanners.* Torrance, CA: Micro Publishing Press, 1989.
Describes what to look for in choosing a scanner and how to make the most of it when you get it home. Reviews hardware and software options and shows how to manipulate scanned images on your computer screen.

Binns, Betty. *Better Type: Learn to see subtle distinctions in the faces and spaces of text type.* New York: Watson-Guptill, 1989.
Concise text with numerous illustrations showing how the slightest changes in letter, line and word spacing can have a major effect on a publication's appearance and readability.

Bly, Robert W. *Ads That Sell.* Brentwood, NY: Asher-Gallant, 1988.
An "advertising agency in a box," *Ads That Sell* teaches advertising design by example, by analyzing numerous examples of ads large and small.

Bly, Robert W. *The Copywriter's Handbook.* New York: Henry Holt & Co., 1990.
An entertaining but thorough review of the tools of effective copywriting that can restore vigor to tired copy.

Bly, Robert W. *Secrets of a Freelance Writer*. New York: Henry Holt & Co., 1990.
Although focused on surviving as a freelance writer, many of the ideas in this book can be used by freelance graphic designers and desktop publishers.

Bly, Robert W. *Create the Perfect Sales Piece: How to Produce Brochures, Catalogs, Fliers and Pamphlets*. New York: John Wiley & Sons, 1985.
Bly stresses the importance of project planning before beginning work and lists numerous sources of outside help.

Brady, Philip. *Using Type Right: 121 Basic No-Nonsense Rules for Working With Type*. Cincinnati, OH: North Light Books, 1988.
An entertaining book of tips and techniques to help you make better use of your desktop publishing or page layout program. Combines concise descriptions of design principles with graphic examples in an oversized format that's a joy to read.

Brown, Alex. *In Print: Text and Type in the Age of Desktop Publishing*. New York: Watson-Guptill, 1989.
Combines concise, highly readable descriptions of the aesthetic qualities of different typefaces and techniques to make effective use of any typeface.

Burke, Clifford. *Type from the Desktop: Designing with Type and Your Computer*. Chapel Hill, NC: Ventana Press, 1990.
A thought-provoking exploration into the world of typography and design. Filled with type examples, this book explores the functions and aesthetics of type.

Cavuoto, James, and Berst, Jesse. *Inside Ventura Publisher*. 3rd ed. Chapel Hill, NC: Ventana Press, 1990.
The all-time best-selling Ventura book, now revised and updated for DOS Version 3.0. Offers dozens of tips and techniques not found in the manufacturer's reference manual. Clear, no-nonsense instructions help you improve the look of your documents with strategies the pros use.

Cook, Alton, ed. *Type and Color: A Handbook of Creative Combinations.* Rockport, MA: Rockport Publications, 1989.
Previews more than 800,000 possible type/background combinations. Contains more than 100 pages of color samples and removable acetate overlays to let you experiment with black, colored or reversed type on a variety of background colors.

Dair, Carl. *Design with Type.* Toronto, Canada: University of Toronto Press, 1982.
A welcome reprint of the 1960 original, this slim, unpretentious volume contains unforgettable lessons that extend far beyond page design and typography into writer/designer/reader relationships.

Finberg, Howard I., and Itule, Bruce D. *Visual Editing: A graphic guide for journalists.* Belmont, CA: Wadsworth, 1990.
More than just guidelines for the effective use of photographs, charts and information graphics, *Visual Editing* thoroughly investigates how computerized publishing is revolutionizing newspaper production.

Holmes, Nigel. *Designer's Guide to Creating Charts and Diagrams.* New York: Watson-Guptill, 1984.
Well illustrated and written by an innovator in the field of visual information journalism, this book shows you how to convert numbers and comparisons into eye-catching graphics.

Hudson, Howard Penn. *Publishing Newsletters.* rev. ed. New York: Charles Scribner's Sons, 1988.
Comprehensive coverage of all aspects of newsletter publishing, by one of the industry's most respected observers, the founder and publisher of the influential *Newsletter on Newsletters.*

Kaatz, Ron. *The NTC Book of Advertising and Marketing Checklists.* Lincolnwood, IL: NTC Business Books, 1988.
A unique, interactive approach to planning advertising design—you learn by answering questions about the desired goals of your advertising.

Kieper, Michael L. *Illustrated Handbook of Desktop Publishing and Typesetting*. Blue Ridge Summit, PA: TAB Books, 1987.
Combines a historical perspective with a carefully annotated overview of just about every desktop publishing hardware and software program available.

Lubow, Martha, and Pattison, Polly. *Style Sheets for Newsletters: A Guide to Advanced Designs for Xerox Ventura Publisher*. Thousand Oaks, CA: New Riders Publishing, 1988.
"First aid" for newsletter editors at deadline time who use Xerox Ventura Publisher. Contains many alternative ways of handling the elements of newsletter design.

Moen, Daryl R. *Newspaper Layout and Design*. 2nd ed. Ames, IA: Iowa State University Press, 1989.
Detailed analysis of the component parts of a modern newspaper, including observations on current trends.

Naiman, Arthur, ed. *The Macintosh Bible: Thousands of tips, tricks & shortcuts, logically organized and fully indexed*. 2nd ed. Berkeley, CA: Goldstein & Blair, 1989.
An invaluable aid for both experienced and first-time Macintosh users. Contains capsule reviews of hardware and software plus software-specific practical tips on the most popular programs.

Nelson, Roy Paul. *The Design of Advertising*. 6th ed. Dubuque, IA: William C. Brown, 1989.
A no-nonsense favorite, focusing on effective use of color, space and typography when designing magazine and newspaper ads.

Nelson, Roy Paul. *Publication Design*. 4th ed. Dubuque, IA: William C. Brown, 1989.
This large-format volume focuses on the challenges presented by the various types of publications.

One Club for Art and Copy, Inc. *The One Show: Judged to Be Advertising's Best in Print, Radio and TV.* Vol. 11. New York: One Club for Art & Copy, 1990.
The annually published *The One Show* is a lavishly illustrated, large-format book containing full-color reproductions of award-winning advertisements of all types. *The One Show* often provides fresh insight into solving your current design problem.

Parker, Roger C. *Desktop Publishing With WordPerfect for 5.0 and 5.1.* 2nd ed. Chapel Hill, NC: Ventana Press, 1990.
Now updated to include Release 5.1, *Desktop Publishing With Word-Perfect* includes invaluable information on organizing your documents into attractive layouts, working with graphics and creating style sheets for consistency and speed.

Parker, Roger C. *The Makeover Book: 101 Design Solutions for Desktop Publishing.* Chapel Hill, NC: Ventana Press, 1989.
Hundreds of actual examples, tips and techniques that let you compare original documents with their makeovers.

Parker, Roger C., and Kramer, Douglas. *Using Aldus PageMaker.* 3rd ed. New York: Bantam Books, 1990.
The latest edition of one of the earliest PageMaker books to appear. Shows how to use the latest 4.0 features.

Pattison, Polly, Pretzer, Mary, and Beach, Mark. *Outstanding Newsletter Designs.* Available from: Polly Pattison, 5092 Kingscross Rd., Westminster, CA 92683.
A potpourri of inspirational ideas for newspaper publishers. Any one of its ideas is well worth the cost of this fully illustrated, large-format book.

Quark, Inc. *Quark XPress Tips.* Denver, CO: Quark, Inc. (300 S. Jackson St., Denver, CO 80210), 1989.
This should be required reading for Quark XPress users who want to make the most of the many features built into their software.

Rabb, Margaret Y., ed. *The Presentation Design Book: Projecting a Good Image with Your Desktop Computer*. Chapel Hill, NC: Ventana Press, 1990.
This generic design guide reviews the essentials of creating good-looking slides, overheads, charts, diagrams and handouts. Alerts you to basic pitfalls of producing presentation graphics, and provides examples of how to choose the best medium and tailor it for your audience.

Romano, Frank J. *Desktop Typography with Quark XPress*. Blue Ridge Summit, PA: Windcrest Books (TAB Books), 1988.
An indispensable guide for newsletter editors using Quark XPress, relating the tools of typographic manipulation to the specific Quark commands used to implement them. Users of other software programs will also benefit from this book, because many other programs offer similar commands.

Shushan, Ronnie, and Wright, Don. *Desktop Publishing by Design: Blueprints for Page Layout Using Aldus Pagemaker on IBM PC and Apple Macintosh Computers*. Redmond, WA: Microsoft Press, 1989.
This large-format volume contains hundreds of samples and annotated comments describing a wide variety of desktop-published projects produced with Aldus PageMaker.

Sitarz, Daniel. *The Desktop Publisher's Legal Handbook: A Comprehensive Guide to Computer Publishing Law*. Carbondale, IL: Nova Publishing, 1989.
A new set of challenges faces writers who become publishers. This concise volume provides copyright information essential to today's computer-based publishers.

Solomon, Martin. *The Art of Typography: An Introduction to Typo.icon.ography*. New York: Watson-Guptill, 1986.
An excellent starting point for those who want a historical perspective on typographic design as well as suggestions for effectively integrating type with page design.

Strunk, William, Jr., and White, E.B. *Elements of Style*. 3rd ed. New York: Macmillan, 1979.
Required reading for any publisher, providing an entertaining review of the basics of effective writing, as well as a quick reference for grammar and usage issues.

Swann, Alan. *How to Understand and Use Design and Layout*. Cincinnati, OH: North Light Books, 1987.
This handsomely illustrated volume does an excellent job of balancing theory and practical example. Numerous rough layouts illustrate various formats and ways of placing type on a page.

Tufte, Edward R. *The Visual Display of Quantitative Information*. Cheshire, CT: Graphics Press, 1983.
One of the classics, this book describes various charting and graphing tools, and helps you choose the right type of graphic to get your message across. Describes possible pitfalls and ways of maintaining data integrity.

White, Alex. *How to Spec Type*. New York: Watson-Guptill, 1987.
Reviews the basics of typography in a straightforward and entertaining fashion.

White, Alex. *Type in Use*. New York: Design Press, 1990.
Further explores the seemingly infinite number of ways type can be placed and manipulated on a page. Contains hundreds of thought-provoking examples.

White, Jan. *Color for the Electronic Age*. New York: Watson-Guptill, 1990.
Demonstrates, in dozens of examples, many shown in three stages (no color/badly used color/cleverly used color), how color can be used to enhance text, charts and graphs.

White, Jan. *Using Charts and Graphs: 1000 ideas for getting attention*. New York: R. R. Bowker, 1984.
Reviews the advantages and disadvantages of the various types of charts and graphs, with an emphasis on presenting data as accurately as possible.

Xerox Press. *Xerox Publishing Standards: A manual of style and design*. New York: Watson-Guptill, 1988.
A comprehensive survey of the many design and editorial components involved in establishing a consistent corporate identity throughout a wide range of publications.

Zinsser, William. *On Writing Well: An Informal Guide to Writing Nonfiction*. 3rd ed. New York: Harper & Row, 1988.
This is a book you'll want to use over and over again, long after you've read it the first time. Emphasizes the importance of clarity and simplicity.

PERIODICALS

Aldus Magazine, Aldus Corp., 411 First Ave. South, Ste. 200, Seattle, WA 98104. Bimonthly.
Helpful hints and general information for users of Aldus PageMaker, Freehand and Persuasion. One idea can save you dozens of hours of work.

Before & After: How to Design Cool Stuff on Your Computer, PageLab, 331 J. Street, Ste. 150, Sacramento, CA. 95814-9671. Bimonthly.
This exciting, full-color, monthly publication is full of tips and techniques for advanced desktop publishers—and those who want to become advanced desktop publishers. Concisely written and profusely illustrated—not an inch of wasted space.

Communication Arts, Coyne & Blanchard, 410 Sherman Oaks, Palo Alto, CA 94303. Eight issues/year.
Traditional "required reading" for art directors and graphic designers, now devoting increased space to desktop publishing concerns. Special focus issues showcase samples of the year's best designs in advertising, illustration and photography.

Desktop Communications, 2 Hammarskjold Plaza, New York, NY 10017. Bimonthly.
This design-oriented publication features articles written by some of the most famous names in typography.

Font & Function: The Adobe Type Catalog, Adobe Systems, P.O. Box 7900, Mountain View, CA 94039-7900. Thrice yearly.
This free publication includes articles on new typeface designs, gives samples of Adobe typefaces in use, and shows specimens of all available Adobe fonts.

In-House Graphics, United Communications, 4500 Montgomery Ave., Ste. 700N, Bethesda, MD 20814. Monthly.
Practical advice for results-oriented graphic designers. Recent articles have ranged from the use of metallic inks and software-specific design techniques to compensation trends for designers and desktop publishers.

MacWeek, Coastal Associates Publishing, One Park Ave., New York, NY 10016. Weekly (with few exceptions).
Every Macintosh desktop publisher should receive *MacWeek*. This free tabloid contains authoritative reviews and previews of the latest Macintosh hardware and software.

Newsletter Design, Newsletter Clearinghouse, 44 West Market St., P.O. Box 311, Rhinebeck, NY 12572. Monthly.
A visual treat, each month's issue contains illustrations of the front cover and inside spread of over 20 newsletters, along with detailed commentary on their strengths and weaknesses. Provides numerous ideas that can be incorporated in your newsletter.

Newsletter on Newsletters, Newsletter Clearinghouse, 44 West Market St., P.O. Box 311, Rhinebeck, NY 12572. Biweekly.
Want to know what's going on in the newsletter business? This concise publication contains a capsule look, along with features focusing on graphic, economic, postal and promotional issues.

The Page, P.O. Box 14493, Chicago, IL 60614. Monthly.
A delightful publication written for Macintosh desktop publishers. *The Page* is an impartial, informed and reader-friendly look at Macintosh desktop publishing from a hands-on perspective.

PC Publishing, Hunter Publishing, 950 Lee St., Des Plaines, IL 60016. Monthly.
Hardware and software solutions for desktop publishers operating in the MS-DOS environment, along with a monthly "before and after" makeover feature.

Personal Publishing, Hitchcock Publishing, 25W550 Geneva Rd., Wheaton, IL 60188. Monthly.
Balanced treatment of both Macintosh and MS-DOS desktop publishing issues, along with a monthly "update" feature that keeps you informed about the latest revisions of your favorite software.

Print: America's Graphic Design Magazine, RC Publications, 6400 Goldsboro Rd., Bethesda, MD 20817. Bimonthly.
The techniques and economics of professional graphic design, with an eye on advances in desktop publishing. Its yearly regional design and advertising design issues by themselves justify its subscription price.

Publish! PCW Communications, 501 Second St., San Francisco, CA 94107. Monthly.
In-depth critiques of the latest hardware and software, along with design- and technique-oriented articles. Of special interest is its monthly typography column.

Step-By-Step Electronic Design: The How-To Newsletter for Desktop Designers, Dynamic Graphics, 6000 North Forest Park Dr., P.O. Box 1901, Peoria, IL 61656. Monthly.
Advertising-free, technique-oriented advice for advanced desktop publishers and others who aspire to greater expertise in layout and design.

TypeWorld, PennWell Publishing Co., P.O. Box 2709, Tulsa, OK 74101. Biweekly.
Its motto says it all: "No other publication on earth reports as much news about typography and professional publishing." Approaches desktop publishing issues from a typographer's point of view.

U&lc, International Typographic Corp., 2 Hammarskjold Plaza, New York, NY 10017. Bimonthly.
This free large-format tabloid contains features written by many of the world's leading typeface designers. It balances a historical perspective with down-to-earth treatment of contemporary publishing issues.

Ventura Professional, Ventura Publisher Users Group, 8011D South Wheeling Ave., Tulsa, OK 74136. Monthly.
Unbiased, hands-on tips and techniques for users of Ventura Publisher. Written by many of the best-known authorities in the field.

Weigand Report: The Working Newsletter for Desktop Publishers. Rae Productions Int'l., P.O. Box 647, Gales Ferry, CT 06335. Eight issues/year.
Unbiased reporting and analysis of current hardware/software issues, along with analyses of the marketing plans of the major desktop publishers.

WordPerfect: The Magazine, WordPerfect Publishing, 1555 North Technology Way, Orem, UT 84057. Monthly.
An easy way to keep up-to-date on WordPerfect's growing range of page layout commands and features.

ORGANIZATIONS

Dynamic Graphics & Education Foundation
6000 North Forest Park Dr.
P.O. Box 1901
Peoria, IL 61656-1901
Sponsors both generic and software-specific workshops around the world focusing on desktop publishing design issues.

Electronic Directions
21 East Fourth St.
New York, NY 10003
Software-specific courses and seminars for desktop publishers.

Folio/Magazine Publishing Congress
Six River Bend Center
Stamford, CT 06907-0949
Each year, *Folio: The Magazine for Magazine Management* presents a
series of two- and three-day conferences around the country, featur-
ing presentations by leading designers and other professionals.

National Association of Desktop Publishers
Computer Museum, Computer Wharf
Boston, MA 02115
Publishes a newsletter and quarterly magazine, sponsors seminars,
and works toward establishing standards for desktop publishers.

Newsletter Association
1401 Wilson Blvd., Ste. 403
Arlington, VA 22209
Sponsors seminars and publishes periodicals for newsletter editors.

Newsletter Clearinghouse
44 West Market St.
Rhinebeck, NY 12572
Publishes books and newsletters, membership listings and special
reports. Sponsors conferences, seminars and design competitions.

Performance Seminar Group
204 Strawberry Hill Ave.
Norwalk, CT 06851
One of the world's largest seminar firms; offers seminars on newsletter publishing and desktop design.

Popular Communication
Box 21008 S-400-71
Goteborg, Sweden
Sponsors desktop publishing design conferences and seminars
throughout Europe.

Promotional Perspectives
1955 Pauline Blvd., Ste. 100A
Ann Arbor, MI 48103
Offers seminars on design issues for desktop publishers, newsletter design and more.

Ragan Communication Workshops
407 S. Dearborn Ave.
Chicago, IL 60605-1173
Presents seminars and publishes a variety of newsletters specializing in communications skills and newsletter production.

Serendal Research Institute
3003 Arapahoe St., Ste. 109
Denver, CO 80205
Presents seminars throughout the U.S. and the Far East on desktop publishing design and newsletter publishing.

INDEX

CREDITS

Pages 13, 14 and 79
Mark Sparshott
PhotoResolutions
Denver, CO

Pages 156, 157, 159, 160, 170, 171
Originals and makeovers provided by
Promotion Perspectives
Ann Arbor, MI

Pages 80-84
Photographs by
Seth Tice-Lewis
Chapel Hill, NC

Page 84
Photograph by Mark Adams
Mountain Photo

Page 85
Photograph by
Southern Media Design and Production, Inc.
Chapel Hill, NC

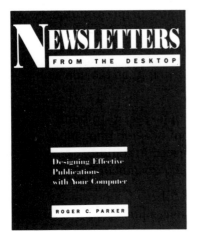

the Ventana Press Desktop Design Series

Available from bookstores or Ventana Press. Immediate shipment guaranteed. Your money returned if not satisfied. To order or for more information contact:

Ventana Press, P.O. Box 2468, Chapel Hill, NC 27515
919/942-0220   FAX 919/942-1140

Harvard Graphics Design Companion
$23.95
300 pages, Illustrated
ISBN: 0-940087-78-2

This book explores Harvard Graphics's many useful features, and will help users add pizzazz to their slides, overheads, screen shows and other presentation forms. Filled with helpful examples, this book includes how-to instructions for creating persuasive presentation visuals.

PageMaker Design Companion
$23.95
300 pages, Illustrated
ISBN: 0-940087-79-0

A complete, fact-filled guide which illustrates PageMaker's powerful graphics capabilities and teaches users to create a wide range of appealing documents.

Inside Xerox Ventura Publisher: The Complete Learning and Reference Guide, Third Edition
$24.95
692 pages, Illustrated
ISBN: 0-940087-61-8

The all-time best-selling Ventura book is now revised and updated to give desktop publishers access to the full power of Ventura 3.0 and help them produce better-looking documents with strategies the pros use.

Newsletters from the Desktop
$23.95
306 pages, Illustrated
ISBN: 0-940087-40-5

Now the millions of desktop publishers who produce newsletters can learn how to improve the design of their publications.

The Makeover Book: 101 Design Solutions for Desktop Publishing
$17.95
282 pages, Illustrated
ISBN: 0-940087-20-0

"Before-and-after" desktop publishing examples demonstrate how basic design revisions can dramatically improve a document.

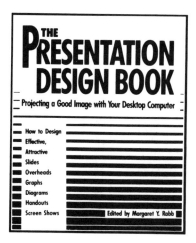

Type from the Desktop
$23.95
226 pages, Illustrated
ISBN: 0-940087-45-6

Learn the basics of designing with type from a desktop publisher's perspective.

The Gray Book: Designing in Black and White on Your Computer
$22.95
210 pages, Illustrated
ISBN: 0-940087-50-2

This "idea gallery" for desktop publishers offers a lavish variety of the most interesting black, white and gray graphic effects that can be achieved with laser printers, scanners and high-resolution output devices.

The Presentation Design Book
$24.95
280 pages, Illustrated
ISBN: 0-940087-37-5

How to design effective, attractive slides, overheads, graphs, diagrams, handouts and screen shows with your desktop computer.

Desktop Publishing with WordPerfect, Second Edition (For 5.0 and 5.1)
$21.95
325 pages, Illustrated
ISBN: 0-940087-47-2

WordPerfect offers graphics capabilities that can save users thousands of dollars in design and typesetting costs. Includes invaluable information on creating style sheets for consistency and speed.

TO ORDER additional copies of *Looking Good in Print* or any of the other books in our desktop design series, please fill out this order form and return it to us for quick shipment.

	Quantity		Price		Total
Looking Good in Print	_____	×	$23.95	=	$_____
Desktop Publishing w/ WordPerfect	_____	×	$21.95	=	$_____
Type from the Desktop	_____	×	$23.95	=	$_____
The Presentation Design Book	_____	×	$24.95	=	$_____
Newsletters from the Desktop	_____	×	$23.95	=	$_____
The Makeover Book	_____	×	$17.95	=	$_____
PageMaker Design Companion	_____	×	$23.95	=	$_____
The Gray Book	_____	×	$22.95	=	$_____
Harvard Graphics Design Companion	_____	×	$23.95	=	$_____

Shipping: Please add $4.10/first book for standard UPS, $1.35/book thereafter; $7.50/book UPS "two-day air," $2.25/book thereafter. For Canada, add $8.10/book.   = $_____

Send C.O.D. (add $3.75 to shipping charges)   = $_____

North Carolina residents add 6% sales tax   = $_____

Total   = $_____

Name _____

Company _____

Address (No P.O. Box) _____

City_____ State _____ Zip_____

Daytime Phone_____

_____ Payment enclosed (check or money order; no cash please)

_____VISA _____ MC   Acc't # _____ - _____ - _____ - _____

Expiration date_____   Signature _____

Please mail or fax to:

Ventana Press, P.O. Box 2468, Chapel Hill, NC 27515

919/942-0220, FAX: 919/942-1140

MORE ABOUT VENTANA PRESS BOOKS . . .

If you would like to be added to our mailing list, please complete the card below and indicate your areas of interest. We will keep you up-to-date on new books as they're published.

_____Yes! I'd like to receive more information about Ventana Press books. Please add me to your mailing list.

Name _____

Company _____

Street address (no P.O. box) _____

City _____ State _____ Zip_____

Please check areas of interest below: _____ Operating systems

_____AutoCAD   _____ Newsletter publishing

_____Desktop publishing   _____ Networking

_____Desktop design   _____ Facsimile

_____Presentation graphics   _____ Business software

**Return to: Ventana Press, P.O. Box 2468, Chapel Hill, NC 27515, 919/942-0220, FAX 919/942-1140.
(Please don't duplicate your fax requests by mail.)**

NO POSTAGE
NECESSARY
IF MAILED
IN THE
UNITED STATES

BUSINESS REPLY MAIL

FIRST CLASS MAIL   PERMIT #495   CHAPEL HILL, NC

POSTAGE WILL BE PAID BY ADDRESSEE

Ventana Press

P.O. Box 2468

Chapel Hill, NC 27515